THE HISTORICAL ARCHAEOLOGY OF MASSACHUSETTS

The American Experience in Archaeological Perspective

UNIVERSITY PRESS OF FLORIDA

Florida A&M University, Tallahassee
Florida Atlantic University, Boca Raton
Florida Gulf Coast University, Ft. Myers
Florida International University, Miami
Florida State University, Tallahassee
New College of Florida, Sarasota
University of Central Florida, Orlando
University of Florida, Gainesville
University of North Florida, Jacksonville
University of South Florida, Tampa
University of West Florida, Pensacola

The Historical Archaeology of Massachusetts

Joseph Bagley and Holly Herbster

Foreword by Michael S. Nassaney and Krysta Ryzewski

UNIVERSITY PRESS OF FLORIDA

Gainesville/Tallahassee/Tampa/Boca Raton
Pensacola/Orlando/Miami/Jacksonville/Ft. Myers/Sarasota

Cover: Map courtesy of the Library of Congress Geography and Map Division. Ivory fid courtesy of The Public Archaeology Laboratory, Inc. Ceramics and projectile point courtesy of Joe Bagley, City of Boston Archaeology Program.

Publication is made possible in part by a grant from the estate of Mary C. Beaudry.

31 30 29 28 27 26   6 5 4 3 2 1

DOI: http://doi.org/10.5744/9780813079530

Library of Congress Cataloging-in-Publication Data
Names: Bagley, Joseph M., 1985– author | Herbster, Holly author | Ryzewski,
Krysta author of foreword | Nassaney, Michael S. author of foreword
Title: The historical archaeology of Massachusetts / Joseph Bagley and
Holly Herbster ; foreword by Michael S. Nassaney and Krysta Ryzewski.
Other titles: American experience in archaeological perspective
Description: Gainesville : University Press of Florida, [2026] | Series:
The American experience in archaeological perspective | Includes
bibliographical references and index
Identifiers: LCCN 2025027425 (print) | LCCN 2025027426 (ebook) | ISBN
9780813079530 hardback | ISBN 9780813081298 paperback | ISBN
9780813075150 ebook | ISBN 9780813074191 pdf
Subjects: LCSH: Archaeology and history—Massachusetts | Historic
sites—Massachusetts | Massachusetts—Antiquities
Classification: LCC F66 .B34 2026 (print) | LCC F66 (ebook) | DDC
974.4—dc23/eng/20250925
LC record available at https://lccn.loc.gov/2025027425
LC ebook record available at https://lccn.loc.gov/2025027426

The University Press of Florida is the scholarly publishing agency for the State University System of Florida, comprising Florida A&M University, Florida Atlantic University, Florida Gulf Coast University, Florida International University, Florida State University, New College of Florida, University of Central Florida, University of Florida, University of North Florida, University of South Florida, and University of West Florida.

University Press of Florida
2046 NE Waldo Road
Suite 2100
Gainesville, FL 32609
floridapress.org

GPSR EU Authorized Representative: Mare Nostrum Group B.V., Mauritskade 21D, 1091 GC Amsterdam, The Netherlands, gpsr@mare-nostrum.co.uk

CONTENTS

FIGURES

MAPS

FOREWORD

Both of us are native New Englanders with archaeological connections to Massachusetts. I (Michael) cut my archaeological teeth in 1974 on a site in Swansea, Massachusetts, some fifteen miles from the Providence College campus where I was enrolled in my first archaeology class ("Early Man and Race") taught by a sociocultural anthropologist, Tom Lux, who was an active member of the Massachusetts Archaeological Society. Once I exhibited a proclivity for fieldwork, Mr. Lux (as I called him), invited me to dig with Maurice "Doc" Robbins on another southeastern Massachusetts site. Though neither site dated to the recent past (both were Archaic in age), I formed an early bond with the materiality of ancient Massachusetts. I would go on to participate in the I-495 Mitigation Project (1978) with The Public Archaeology Laboratory at Brown University. On the way to earning my doctorate at the University of Massachusetts Amherst, I served as a teaching assistant for Bob Paynter's field school at Historic Deerfield (1985–6) and as a Project Archaeologist for UMASS Archaeological Services (UMAS). UMAS provided me with the opportunity to investigate the site of the John Russell Cutlery Company (1989). Though a short-term project, the enormity of the site—purported to have been the largest culture factory in the world—and the wide implications of the work for understanding the American system of manufacture left a lasting impression.

I (Krysta) owe my career to the training in history and archaeology I received in Massachusetts. At the same time as Michael was in graduate school at UMass Amherst, I was a child from Connecticut enjoying annual summer vacations to Old Sturbridge Village, an early nineteenth-century living history museum in south-central Massachusetts. From a young age, I was fascinated by how Old Sturbridge Village brought to life the everyday experiences of early New Englanders and the worlds they inhabited. Other trips to historic sites in Plymouth, Boston, Salem, and Cape Cod deepened my fascination. My formal training came from the archaeology and history programs at Boston University, from which I received my BA degree in 2001. As soon as I learned from Mary Beaudry, my undergraduate adviser, that

I could channel my eclectic passions for history, geology, and archaeology into a focus on historical archaeology, I never turned back. My first hands-on encounter with Massachusetts archaeology was as a student assistant in Beaudry's lab, where she assigned me to wash and label artifacts excavated from the Spencer-Peirce-Little Farm (SPL) in Newburyport. Later, my senior honor's thesis charted the transition from homemade medicinal remedies to patent medicine usage at the SPL Farm based on data and interpretations I derived from botanical remains, medicine bottles, and archival sources. Midway in between my artifact washing days and my senior thesis, I landed my first professional job in 1999 as a student intern for the Massachusetts Historical Commission. For two years, I assisted in Section 106 review and compliance under the supervision of State Archaeologist Brona Simon and the venerable archaeology staff, including Ed Bell, Eric Johnson, and Ann-Eliza Lewis. This era coincided with the Big Dig/Central Artery Tunnel Project, which involved the movement of interstate highway I-93 underground across the most historic sections of downtown Boston. The Massachusetts Historical Commission (MHC) archaeology staff were inundated with administrative work and collections intake from the Big Dig alone, not to mention activities across the remainder of the state, yet they remained focused on the tasks at hand and were generous with their mentorship. It was an exciting time to experience the inner workings of cultural resource management and urban archaeology. Shortly before I graduated from Boston University, I was hired by the National Park Service Northeast Regional Headquarters as an archaeological technician under the supervision of archaeologist William Griswold. I spent several months in 2001 excavating at what historical archaeologists might consider to be among the most well-known sites in the US: the Boott Mills in Lowell. Our excavations were conducted in the backlot of the Kirk Street Agents' House, where the managers of the Boott Mills and Massachusetts Mills lived between 1847 and 1920. The findings produced additional insights into the experiences of Lowell's managerial class and provided comparisons with the assemblages Mrozowski and Beaudry's team excavated during the 1980s from the workers' boardinghouses just a block away. A couple of years later, I began the PhD program down the road at Brown University in Providence, Rhode Island. During my time as a graduate student, I continued to maintain ties with the archaeological community in Massachusetts, especially through Boston University and UMass Boston, where I had the opportunity to participate in excavations in Boston at the African Meeting House, Robert Roberts House in Beacon Hill, and other projects elsewhere in the state. My own fieldwork in Warwick, Rhode Island, at the seventeenth- and eighteenth-century plantation of Green Farm produced constant reminders in the archives and archaeological record of the inseparable personal, economic, and political ties between the colonies of Massachusetts and Rhode Island. Indeed, from the time of its establishment as a colony in the early seventeenth century, Massachusetts played a leading role in shaping social, political, and economic life New England. It might also be said that Massachusetts's historical sites and educational institutions have shaped the professional development of historical archaeology throughout the region.

In *The Historical Archaeology of Massachusetts,* Joseph Bagley and Holly Herbster provide an overview of historical archaeological scholarship across the state and introduce readers to the history of the region's archaeological practice in the process. They discuss the archaeologists associated with work in the Commonwealth, the sites they examined, the collaborations they formed, and the stories they revealed. As the Boston City Archaeologist (Bagley) and Principal Investigator and Senior Archaeologist at New England's leading cultural resource management firm, The Public Archaeology Laboratory Inc. (Herbster), the authors are well-positioned to present this broad overview, given their experiences working across the state and their comprehensive grasp of the literature from academic, governmental, and cultural resource management studies. In foregrounding the archaeological history of Massachusetts, they recognize that the narrative history of the Commonwealth is far too important to leave to historians whose perspectives derive predominantly from the written record. By weaving together documentary sources with material evidence, Bagley and Herbster provide a far richer—indeed, more interesting—story about Massachusetts and its inhabitants over the past four hundred years. Their case studies demonstrate how the people of Massachusetts participated in the formative trends of the American experience and how historical archaeologists have been at the forefront of efforts to reveal local populations who were written out of the dominant narratives.

The extant literature about Massachusetts's archaeological record, as it exists in scholarly publications and unpublished gray literature (CRM reports), is vast. There has been a plethora of archaeological studies conducted in the state, driven by not only federal mandates but also the creation of Massachusetts General Law (MGL) Chapter 9, sections 26–27C which requires review of state-licensed, permitted, and funded projects. The result is comprehensive coverage of the state's cultural resources and opportunities to relate the history of the Bay State with developments at the regional, national, and global scales.

Historical archaeologists in Massachusetts have used the detritus of everyday life to develop methodologies to assess significant social variation expressed in material remains. For example, house sites can be differentiated from taverns based on the relative percentages of food preparation vessels, glass containers, and pipestems. These analytical results demonstrate that statistical data can be used to interpret the function of historical sites in the absence of written records. Similarly, rural and urban taverns can also be distinguished; rural taverns have greater percentages of ceramics and lesser percentages of tobacco pipes than urban taverns, reflecting their predominant function as places for food and sleeping accommodations of travelers. In contrast, urban taverns were principally places of community gathering. Archaeological evidence of consumerism and commercialism exhibit interesting rural and urban distinctions but also patterns that rural elite often sought to emulate their urban counterparts.

Owing to its coastal location and the international mercantile networks maintained by its inhabitants, Massachusetts was an active participant in a global economy from the initial decades of its English settlement. For example, Massachusetts's role in the global market is manifest in the largest Portuguese tin-glazed earthenware assemblage documented in North America from the eighteenth-century Garrett site, a merchant household in Charlestown. Archaeological remains from urban and rural sites in Massachusetts link daily life to broader patterns of global exchange, industrialization, capitalist production, and domesticity. For example, animal remains from Boston's Nanny Naylor privy index a shift from anadromous fish-like herring to near-shore species such as cod and later deeper water fish represented by haddock. Differences are apparent between consumption in the urban cores of Boston, Salem, and Newburyport, and other smaller eastern and more rural towns. However, material evidence supports the idea that elite practices and customs diffused to the lower classes and rural spaces as merchants and ministers migrated inland. For instance, the accoutrements of the tea ceremony became widely available by the mid-eighteenth century much as it was enjoyed in England.

Massachusetts farmers were also at the forefront of progressive agricultural techniques as evidenced by new practices that Ebenezer Williams and his elite associates introduced in the Connecticut River Valley in the early nineteenth century. Among those documented archaeologically were several large, cobbled platforms that were designed to process animal waste into fertilizer and to store it as needed, thereby increasing agricultural productivity. The wealth of Williams and other elites throughout the Commonwealth reflected in an ostentatious home, imported goods, and landscape modifications demonstrates the ability for white men to achieve upward mobility, a widespread feature of the American experience.

Landscape modifications were rampant throughout the colony demonstrating a significant investment in time and resources on land and along the waterfront. Much of the labor to build the Commonwealth was performed by indentured, enslaved, and under-remunerated segments of the populations whose activities went under recorded and under analyzed. For instance, archaeological work conducted for the Big Dig/Central Artery Tunnel project produced massive quantities of locally produced redware that remain relatively understudied at the City of Boston Archaeology Lab. They have the potential to provide an entry point into the study of enslaved labor and the influences of West African and Caribbean styles on design motifs. Archaeology provides ample evidence for the ways in which the economy of Massachusetts and the lives of its residents were deeply entangled in the unpaid labor of enslaved and working-class men, women, and children.

Archaeological studies at early and mid-nineteenth-century Black homesites show how individuals and families defined themselves and negotiated their identity and freedom in a state that was becoming increasingly ethnically and culturally diverse. Bagley and Herbster discuss various patterns of nineteenth-century material culture, structural features, and yard spaces associated with Black households that reveal how individuals and families reinforced their own individual, family, and community identities. Likewise, archaeologies of African American spaces are among the most effective examples of community-based archaeology in Massachusetts. Studies at the African Meeting House were designed at the outset by Black community leaders to educate and inform Bostonians and others about the rich heritage of African Americans in the Beacon Hill area. Massachusetts archaeologists are using material analysis to illuminate many places that document African American and Black history to bring their silenced and under-celebrated histories to the fore.

The contributions of the class were similarly significant, even though they were often ignored. From its earliest colonial settlement, Massachusetts was poised for industrial prowess. Endowed with abundant natural waterpower along hundreds of rivers and streams, ample English capital for investment, and experienced artisans who planned and built mills and the machinery within them, it is no wonder that Massachusetts is seen as the birthplace of the Industrial Revolution in the United States. Most histories credit the investors with the success of this enterprise and pay less attention to those who spent sixteen-hour days toiling in the mills. Archaeological study aims to illuminate the lives of this often-overlooked population and their role in the success of American industry.

Perhaps this is best illustrated through the multidisciplinary studies of the Lowell textile factories, and specifically the Boot Mills, along with smaller projects like the Russell Cutlery Company that demonstrate the potential for industrial sites to animate human stories of dominance, resistance, innovation, and perseverance that are common to the American experience. Factories and their associated infrastructure provide clear evidence of the adjustments and hardships that industrial lifestyles thrust onto immigrant and native-born populations alike. Examinations of industrial life have focused on technological developments in the workplace to animal butchering patterns in managers' yard spaces, highlighting the structural constraints owners sought to impose on workers, as well as the agency of operatives in the face of repressive conditions. The diversity of material culture in various contexts of production, use, and discard point to a complex and expanding American mosaic marked by sharp social divisions along lines of ethnicity, race, gender, status, and religion that served to demarcate groups. As Bagley and Herbster note, archaeological study of the places where groups of people lived, worked, worshipped, were confined, and died provides an opportunity to investigate individual and collective identity and expressions of power, control, and resistance which characterize the American experience everywhere.

Disparate social groups have long been in conflict in Massachusetts and archaeological studies of warfare have left tangible markers on the landscape from ditches and embankments to musket balls and shipwrecks. Studies of the Battle of Great Falls/Wissatinnewag-Peskeompskut utilized the KOCOA military terrain analysis system which examines aspects of terrain, sight lines, fields of fire, and other military tactics. Similar work at Revolutionary War sites combined patterns of British and militia musket balls with detailed landscape study and historic research to reconstruct critical events surrounding Parker's Revenge at the Minute Man National Historical Park in Lexington. Historical archaeology adds nuance to these stories of military activities by integrating detailed material and personal accounts of action that illustrate a more holistic experience that amplifies our understanding of the experiences of historical conflicts.

While patriotic and military histories in Massachusetts often foreground the episodes and sites associated with the Revolutionary era, including Paul Revere's midnight ride, the Battle of Bunker Hill, the Boston Tea Party, the USS Constitution, and other sites one might encounter along Boston's Freedom Trail, the histories of Massachusetts residents as revealed by archaeological investigations span far beyond these sites. For example, archaeological studies have exposed how Native American inhabitants experienced some of the most severe effects of European incursions. The homelands of the Wampanoag near Plymouth were decimated by disease as early as 1619 and tensions remained high throughout the seventeenth century, culminating in King Philip's War (1675–1676), a conflict spanning the colonies of Massachusetts and Rhode Island that resulted in scattering Native populations and dispossessing them of their lands. Massachusetts's colonists made repeated attempts to control and constrain Native American lives, including through the establishment of over a dozen Praying Indian Villages across the colony, such as the village within Hassanamesit Woods in Grafton. Archaeological sites in Hassanamesit Woods examined by Stephen Mrozowski, Heather Law Pezzarossi, D. Rae Gould, and the Nipmuc Nation demonstrate how Native Americans responded to colonialization and continued to play significant roles in events that shaped the history of the Bay State. Indigenous communities across the state continue to do so in the present.

For such as small state, Massachusetts has indeed played an outsized role in much of American history and the profession of historical archaeology in the US. Massachusetts historical archaeologists have advanced the field by creating new historical narratives that incorporate the experiences of children, women, the working-class, BIPOC, and other marginalized groups. Often this work is conducted with collaborators, and such practice has become more common in many communities in Massachusetts, including between Native Americans and archaeologists. Under constraints dictated by cultural resource management where time is money, costs associated with developing an authentic collaborative archaeology can be challenging, but not impossible. Yet, if the arc of archaeology bends toward social justice as the authors contend, then the future is bright and archaeologists in Massachusetts will move to the forefront of efforts to illuminate the American experience as they embrace more inclusive and emancipatory practices.

Michael S. Nassaney, *Founding Series Editor*

Krysta Ryzewski, Series *Co-Editor*

ACKNOWLEDGMENTS

The authors wish to thank The Public Archaeology Laboratory, Inc. for providing access to unpublished reports, research files, and staff expertise. We are also grateful to the late Mary C. Beaudry, whose legacy and extensive archaeological library greatly enhanced the writing and production of this book.

Thank you to our colleagues who reviewed our work plan and provided information and suggestions to improve the manuscript including Edward Bell, Christa Beranek, Suzanne Cherau, Dianna Doucette, Rae Gould, Eric Johnson, John Kelly, David Landon, Diana Loren, Jane Miller, Stephen Mrozowski, Jonathan Patton, Duncan Ritchie, and David Robinson.

The authors are grateful for the careful review and suggested edits to the draft manuscript provided by the series editors Michael Nassaney and Krysta Ryzewski. Acquisitions Editor Mary Puckett provided excellent guidance and support throughout the entire process.

Very special thanks to Jennifer Macpherson for preparing the maps and graphics included in this volume.

Finally, we are grateful to the many archaeologists who have worked in Massachusetts for over a century and continue to rediscover important places that represent the diverse histories of all Massachusetts residents past and present. This book would not be possible without their efforts.

1

Introduction

Like the early colonists, historical archaeologists have been drawn to Massachusetts for its resources and opportunity. As an early British colony in North America, instigator of the American Revolution, industrial juggernaut, abolitionist leader, immigration destination, and educational powerhouse, Massachusetts has played an outsized role in much of American history. Massachusetts's people, places, and historical events have provided fertile ground for decades of historical archaeological excavations. This work now represents the growth and evolution of historical archaeology method and theory. Because historical archaeology can provide insights beyond written history, it uncovers a more complete and inclusive historical narrative. The historical archaeology of Massachusetts therefore provides both an opportunity to explore the evolution of historical archaeology and the diversity of the American experience.

This book is about the historical archaeology of the Commonwealth of Massachusetts, our colleagues who have and continue to work here, the places they have investigated, the stakeholders they have engaged with, and the stories they have uncovered. We will explore how the goals and interests of historical archaeologists have changed over time with legal, political, and social changes. We will also focus on the significant and unique contributions historical archaeology has made toward the story of Massachusetts and the broader nation.

Map 1.1. Map of eastern United States showing the location of Massachusetts.

Massachusetts Defined

Massachusetts is located in the northeast area of the United States (US) along the Atlantic coast. It functions as the capital of its sub-region, New England, and borders New Hampshire, Vermont, New York, Connecticut, and Rhode Island. The scope of this book is the current state boundary of Massachusetts, although its borders extended across most of present-day Maine in the late seventeenth century, and the Indigenous people whose homelands include Massachusetts did not recognize these artificial geographic markers (see Chapter 2).

Today, Massachusetts is bounded by arbitrarily and naturally defined borders. The boxy western portion of the state is demarcated by borders settled following seventeenth- through nineteenth-century land claim disputes between neighboring colonies of New Hampshire and Vermont to the north, New York to the west, and Connecticut and Rhode Island to the south. The more naturalistic borders of the eastern part of the state are defined primarily by the Atlantic Ocean, original colony borders defined as distances from rivers and bays, and through land claim disputes with New Hampshire and Rhode Island.

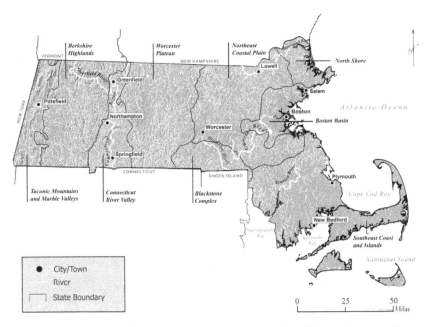

Map 1.2. Map of Massachusetts showing ecoregions, major cities, and geographic features.

Massachusetts is divided into nine ecoregions (US EPA 1994). The Southeast Coast and Islands Region includes Plymouth and Bristol counties and the cities of Plymouth and New Bedford; Barnstable County within includes all of Cape Cod; and the islands of Martha's Vineyard and Nantucket. This region contains the Taunton River and coastal lowlands of pine and oak forests, dunes, and sandy soils. North along the coast is the Boston Basin Region, today's "Metro Boston" in Suffolk County, which is a low-lying area defined by volcanic ridges to the north and south, the Boston Harbor Islands to the east, and the Charles and Neponset River drainages. The Merrimack River is the boundary between New Hampshire and the North Shore Region, which includes level areas of glacial outwash with extensive mudflats, salt marshes, and tributary river systems. The city of Salem in Essex County is within this ecoregion.

The Northeast Coastal Plain Region extends into the state from New Hampshire and Maine and covers the rest of interior eastern Massachusetts and is generally higher in elevation than the coast but lower than the hilly and mountainous areas to the west. This region includes Middlesex and Norfolk counties and the city of Lowell. Large, well developed wetland drainages including the Concord River characterize this area, as do somewhat poor acidic soils. At the southern end of the coastal plain is the Blackstone Complex, a geographically small low-lying area around the Blackstone River that extends south into Connecticut and Rhode Island. The Worcester Plateau Region includes the city of Worcester and covers what is commonly referred to as central Massachusetts. This region consists of hilly, upland terrain and historically forested areas that extend north into New Hampshire and south to Connecticut. This region includes the thirty-nine-square-mile Quabbin Reservoir, one of the largest unfiltered water supplies in the United States.

Massachusetts's three remaining ecoregions collectively comprise what is known as western Massachusetts. The Connecticut River Valley Region extends north–south separating the mountainous western third of the state from the uplands and lowlands to the east. This "failed" rift valley formed during the Jurassic Period break-up of the Gondwana mega-continent, creating the Atlantic Ocean and nearly resulting in eastern Massachusetts remaining part of western Africa. The Connecticut River that formed along this valley extends more than 400 miles from the Canadian border with Vermont and New Hampshire to Connecticut's southern shoreline in Long Island Sound. This region is characterized by verdant agricultural land and a mild climate. The river cuts through Franklin, Hampshire, and Hampden counties and includes the cities of Greenfield, Northampton and Springfield. The western end of Massachusetts consists of two parallel highlands that together comprise Berkshire County. The Berkshires Highlands Region is west of the Connecticut River Valley and includes the Berkshire Mountains at the southern range of the Green Mountains of Vermont. This region does not contain any large metropolitan areas but many small rural towns. Just west along the Massachusetts-New York border is the Taconic Mountains and Marble Valleys Region, a geologically diverse ecological zone that extends from Vermont through Pennsylvania and contains the highest mountains and mountain ranges in Massachusetts. The city of Pittsfield is located in this region.

Despite being one of the smallest states in the United States, Massachusetts's coastal areas on the east, central plains and agricultural river valleys, and western mountains reflect the ecological zones found across much of the US. This ecological diversity has contributed significantly to Massachusetts's historical development and parallels broader historical settlement and land use patterns seen in America as a whole.

Framework of Massachusetts History

The history of Massachusetts is complex, and while this book covers significant periods, the following provides a general overview that helps to contextualize the archaeological examples that follow. There are few comprehensive general histories of Massachusetts (Tager and Brown 2000) but dozens of county, regional, and local histories, most written in the late nineteenth and early twentieth centuries, provide details on the people and events that shaped Massachusetts (e.g., Banks 1911; Carpenter and Morehouse 1896; Green 1886; Hurd 1883; Parmenter 1898; Smith and Cushing 1885; Waters 1905, 1917). Massachusetts histories written by Indigenous scholars and from Indigenous perspectives provide a critical counternarrative to those written from a colonizer viewpoint (e.g., Brooks 2006, 2018; Bruchac and Hart 2012; Coombs 2002; Delicia 2019, 2020; Gould 2013).

Massachusetts is and has been the homeland of multiple Native tribes for millennia prior to the arrival of the first European colonists. Tribal borders were fluid, and historically trade, ceremony, and alliance connected most of New England Indigenous communities to one another. In the first centuries of European colonization, these Indigenous peoples were decimated by disease, warfare, enslavement, and genocide. Some were forcibly taken from New England in bondage, some were confined to "praying Indian" towns at the end of the seventeenth century, and some formed geographically distinct communities in as-yet uncolonized areas. The descendants of the survivors of these events make up Massachusetts's present-day tribal communities.

Today, many members of distinct Massachusetts tribal communities share ancestry and kin with neighboring tribes. Using self-defined tribal names at the time of this publication, historical tribal areas included the Massachusett in the northeastern and east central portions of Massachusetts; the Wampanoag in the southeast, Cape, and islands; the Nipmuc in the central portion of the state; the Pocumtuck in the Connecticut River Valley; and the Mohican in the west (see Chapter 2), although these historical homeland claims remain actively disputed between individual tribal groups.

An 1861 survey of Massachusetts's Native people known as the Earle Report (1861) identified ten tribal groups with living descendants listed here with their contemporary tribal affiliation in parentheses: Chappaquiddick (Chappaquiddick Wampanoag), Christiantown (Aquinnah and Chappaquiddick Wampanoag), Gay Head (Aquinnah Wampanoag), Marshpee [*sic*] (Mashpee Wampanoag), Herring Pond (Herring Pond Wampanoag), Natick

(Natick Nipmuc), Punkapoag (Massachusett Tribe at Ponkapoag), Troy/Fall River (Pokanoket Wampanoag), Hassanamisco (Hassanamesit Nipmuc and Nipmuc Nation), and Dudley (Chaubunagungamaug Nipmuc). Among these tribal groups, only two have received federal recognition: the Wampanoag Tribe of Gay Head (Aquinnah) in 1987 and the Mashpee Wampanoag Tribe in 2007. The Stockbridge-Munsee Community Band of Mohican Indians left western Massachusetts in the 1780s, eventually settling in Wisconsin where they received federal recognition in the 1970s. Tribal members remain active in documenting the Indigenous history of the Stockbridge area (see Chapter 7). The Nipmuc were federally recognized from 2001 to 2004 but are not currently though they remain "state-recognized," and the Herring Pond Wampanoag received state recognition in 2024. None of the other tribal groups have formally been recognized by the state or federal governments despite the fact that Massachusetts includes many organized and active tribes whose ancestors are included in the Earle Report (see Chapter 7). All descendants of Native people in the Earle Report are eligible for the Native American Tuition Credit for state colleges and universities in Massachusetts, a measure of the state's support of Indigenous identity among non-federally recognized tribes.

Although there were multiple early European explorers and small temporary settlements in Massachusetts during the first decades of the seventeenth century, the first official chartered colony settled in Plymouth in 1620. This was soon followed by the Massachusetts Bay Colony in 1630. Following these, there was rapid growth of European settlements in eastern Massachusetts as thousands of English settlers arrived prompting westward expansion into central and western Massachusetts. With King Philip's War of the 1670s, conflicts with the Native populations resulted in the abandonment of many central and western English towns (Brooks 2018). In the late seventeenth century, the original charter for Massachusetts Bay was recalled by the Crown due to increasing financial independence of the colonies (Steele 1989). This resulted in a new charter in 1691 combining the two original colonies into the Province of Massachusetts Bay.

In the eighteenth century, Massachusetts became an economic powerhouse due to the Commonwealth's natural resources, busy ports, and growing population (Tager and Brown 2000). The ongoing rebellious nature of the Massachusetts colony came to a head in the 1770s over increasing tensions between the colonists and the Crown, which led to the American Revolution. Though Massachusetts played a significant role in beginning the war, its role decreased toward the end of the war (Nash 1979). Following independence, the colony of Massachusetts was added to the United States in 1788. Massachusetts adopted the legal name of the Commonwealth of Massachusetts in its constitution, then a popular term for an independent body politic. Three other states are also legally "Commonwealths," though the term does not represent any political or legal difference from a state. The two terms can be used interchangeably and will be in this book.

In the early Federal Period, the Massachusetts economy continued to grow as its merchant class expanded into markets beyond the prior English restrictions. Favoring their strong and newly established financial relationship with England in the early nineteenth century, Massachusetts opposed the War of 1812 (Ellis 2009). The resulting disunity between Massachusetts and the other states as well as the blockade on maritime trade imposed upon Massachusetts by the British, despite their early support, resulted in a significant economic depression. Forced to look toward inland resources for economic opportunity, Massachusetts became a leader in the early Industrial Revolution taking place in America as rivers were harnessed to power factories and mills at a scale never attempted before.

As Massachusetts's fishing, whaling, and trading industries declined, its interior textile milling industries boomed during the mid-nineteenth through early twentieth centuries resulting in the rapid development of new cities, the expansion of railroads and canals westward, and the rise of new towns in rural parts of the state (Malone 1983). Toward the end of the nineteenth century, Massachusetts played a leading role in the abolitionist movement and contributed significantly to the Union army during the Civil War, including the first Black regiment with white officers (Hardesty 2019). After the Civil War, Massachusetts's industries attracted massive waves of immigrant labor, greatly expanding populations in cities and leading to large-scale building projects to produce multifamily housing (Handlin 1974). These industries began to leave Massachusetts during the early twentieth century following the Great Depression and the expansion of industrial areas in the southern and midwestern regions of the United States (Gordon and Malone 1994).

Many mill towns in central and western Massachusetts experienced large population losses that continue to the present. The economy of Massachusetts pivoted away from product industries toward service industries resulting in the simultaneous growth of its cities, especially around Boston, and decline in its rural and industrial towns. Highways, universities, and tech industries transformed Massachusetts's economy and resulted in the development of suburbs and redevelopment of some industrial areas located closest to universities and cities. The population centers around universities and cities in the twenty-first century also have largely liberal populations, resulting in the enaction of progressive policies such as Massachusetts becoming the first state in the US to legalize same-sex marriage (Bonauto 2005). Today, Massachusetts remains characterized by its liberal populations, academic opportunities, and tech-oriented industry as well as a strong tourism industry focused on history, the urban hub of Boston, nostalgic "New England charm," outdoor recreation, and coastal and island beaches.

The history of Massachusetts is a microcosm of the American experience as it spans most of the significant aspects of the growth and change of the US. So too, the changes of Massachusetts's people and populations reflect the American experience as it has evolved over centuries. These experiences are somewhat captured in historical documentation and records, but these records were relatively exclusive regarding who recorded them, who they discussed, and who their audiences were. Archaeology can play a significant role in uncovering stories that were otherwise under recorded, underrepresented, erased, avoided, or lost. The historical archaeology of Massachusetts is an ideal way to explore the broader history of America.

Uncovering the American Experience in Massachusetts

Historical archaeology is built upon a few fundamental assumptions, which may even be considered proven facts: the written record is incomplete, material culture can provide information about the past, and that material culture in combination with archaeological analysis of written records provides a more complete and nuanced story of the past than either of the two sources of data can alone (Beaudry 1988; Deetz 1977). This field allows for the revisiting of the past—even in places that have been thoroughly studied, debated, and analyzed by historians—and uncovering new and significant information that can add to or even redefine our understanding of the past (Deetz 1977). Or, as one historical archaeologist has quipped: "History is far too important to leave to the historians."

A subdiscipline of the broader field of archaeology, historical archaeology is temporarily defined here as the archaeological study of the modern world (Deetz 1977; Hume 1968; Orser 1996). This uses the European definition of "modern" as the period immediately following the end of the medieval period in Europe, circa 1500, and marked by European expansionism across the world and the resulting entanglement of cultures at a global scale. In Massachusetts, it more specifically refers to the archaeology of the time during and after the earliest arrival of European colonists. Although this is inclusive of any and all cultures present and interacting together in the state, this is an inherently Eurocentric and colonial view of history (Atalay 2010), a critique that informs this book. This viewpoint also reflects the broader reality that archaeology has been for much of its existence a colonial endeavor; a practice that assumes that archaeologists have the rights and authority to dig up, study, and interpret "other" people's stuff (Atalay 2006). While uncovering the foreign, lost, or forgotten has been part of the public attraction of archaeology, our field as a whole has recognized this inherently problematic, damaging, and even violent (Nicholas and Smith 2020) reality and is actively working toward restorative social justice (Apaydin 2020). As will be discussed in this book, this includes not only expanding the field to be more diverse and inclusive of the histories in Massachusetts that archaeologists work to uncover, but also working to engage and become more responsible to communities impacted by archaeology, and to combat "othering" by making archaeology viable, accessible, and safe for people of diverse backgrounds to pursue as a career (Mullins 2012).

Historical archaeology as a career and discipline arose in a nonlinear fashion during the nineteenth century from a combination of political, social, and academic movements. In Massachusetts, many of these early efforts developed out of a desire to preserve places of significant historical events related to European settlement and the American Revolution (Lindgren 1991). The 1850s saw some of the first excavations of historical sites in Massachusetts. In 1852, physician John Batchelder began his search in Bourne for the Aptucxet Trading Post established by Myles Standish in 1627 for trade with the Dutch and Native Americans (NPS 2021). James Hall began excavating the 1620s home site of Myles and Barbara Standish in Duxbury using field methods including point-plotted artifact locations and site datums (Cotter 1993) (see Chapter 2). The interest in excavations at early Massachusetts colonial sites were minor aspects of a broader "Colonial Revival" American cultural trend of the late nineteenth and early twentieth centuries when there was a noted interest in colonial architecture, styles, history, and places (Lindgren 1995).

A function of historical archaeology that developed in the early twentieth century included the use of archaeological data in the accurate reconstruction of colonial architecture and living spaces known as "restoration archaeology" (Jameson 2004). This was most notable at places like Colonial Williamsburg (Brown and Chappell 2004) but happened also in Massachusetts with the archaeologically informed reconstructions of the Aptucxet Trading Post in the 1920s (Lombard 1953) and Saugus Iron Works in the 1940s (Griswold and Linebaugh 2010), the latter led by Roland Wells Robbins. Robbins was a self-taught archaeologist who pioneered many of the techniques that are common practice for professional archaeologists today, though during his lifetime he was never considered by academics to be an equal (Linebaugh 1996). Between 1940 and 1980, Robbins excavated more than sixty sites (most in Massachusetts), gave more than 700 lectures and presentations, and published four books including *Hidden America* (1959), which presented his archaeological work at sites in Massachusetts and the Northeast (Linebaugh 1996).

The Massachusetts Archaeological Society (MAS) was founded in 1939 at a meeting held at the Robert S. Peabody Foundation at Phillips Academy in Andover, and it has continued uninterrupted to the present day. One of the main reasons the MAS was formed was to ensure "cooperation between professional and non-professionals to increase their knowledge and to raise the quality of their work" (Robbins 1949, 50), and this is emphasized in the Society's *Bulletin of the Massachusetts Archaeological Society*, a quarterly journal that publishes the work of avocational and professional members. While the MAS and its members were primarily interested in pre-European Native American archaeology, the Society's members documented some of the earliest historical archaeology in the state. These included reports on work at three seventeenth-century sites in Plymouth County (Hornblower 1943) and a report on the homesite of a free Black woman (Bullen and Bullen 1945).

Academic archaeology in Massachusetts had its roots in early Harvard excavations of the Marietta Earthworks site in Ohio during the 1780s (Browman and Williams 2013) and later with the opening of the Peabody Museum of American Archaeology and Ethnology at Harvard in 1866. With the development of graduate studies programs and a growth in academic interest in the humanities, anthropology, and archaeology both became viable academic and career pursuits. At Clark University in Worcester, Franz Boas was offered the first lecture position in anthropology in 1888 (Browman and Williams 2013). In 1890, Harvard added a Department of American Archaeology and Ethnology, led by Frederic Putnam, with undergraduate and graduate courses including a three-year PhD program (Browman and Williams 2013). Although the earliest historical archaeologists evolved from other fields in archaeology, these academic institutions provided formal training in historical archaeological methods and theory, and they produced many of the archaeologists who transitioned from academic pursuit of archaeology to the growing world of professional archaeology.

At Harvard, Professor J. O. Brew connected James Deetz with Harry Hornblower in the late 1950s (Gomes 1985). As described in Chapter 2, the work of Hornblower and Deetz were the foundations of the Plimoth Patuxet Museums (formerly Plimoth Plantation) (Gomes 1985). James Deetz, then a graduate student at Harvard, was hired to design a Wampanoag wetu structure within the village (Deetz and Deetz 2000, Beaudry 2003). A uniquely American tourism experience, the goals of the attraction were to recreate as accurately as possible the daily lives of the Pilgrims in full scale. After joining the staff in 1967, Deetz used reconstruction archaeological methods and data from period sites in Plymouth to more accurately inform the museum's structures, displays, and interpretive materials (Baker 1997).

At this same time, the 1966 National Historic Preservation Act (NHPA) radically shifted the work of professional archaeologists. Section 106 of this act created the requirement for archaeological review as part of most federal projects. In addition to creating funding to establish State Historic Preservation Officers (SHPOs) who would oversee archaeological review, the legislation set out National Park Service standards requiring minimum academic credentials for archaeologists working on projects subject to federal funding or permitting. In Massachusetts, the first State Archaeologist was Maurice "Doc" Robbins (no relation to Roland) who had been a founding member and first president of MAS as well as first director of the Society's Bronson Museum (Lux 1991). Maurice Robbins, like Roland, had not studied archaeology and began his career as an electrical engineer (Lux 1991). His interest in archaeology led him to work at ancient Native American sites in Massachusetts with renowned Harvard pre-contact archaeologists Warren K. Moorehead and Charles Willoughby, to take courses in archaeology and geology at Brown, and to eventually receive a doctorate degree from the McKinley-Roosevelt Institute in Chicago (Lux 1991). Robbins, through his MAS association, was a major supporter of the legislation that created the Massachusetts Historical Commission in 1969, was a commissioner from 1969 to 1972, and State Archaeologist from 1972–1979 (Lux 1991).

The NHPA required archaeological review as part of federally licensed, funded, and permitted projects, but in Massachusetts, the creation of Massachusetts General Law (MGL) Chapter 9, sections 26–27C expanded the review to include state-licensed, permitted, or funded projects. The federal regulations created an entire industry for archaeology across the United States, requiring professionals to document the historic significance of resources and make recommendations to the SHPOs. In Massachusetts, it led to the completion of thousands of archaeological projects, and the identification of many of the sites covered in this text. With these regulations, the new field of cultural resource management (CRM) created a need for professional archaeologists, and it turned to the place where most archaeologists were located that met the NHPA academic standards: universities.

In the mid-1970s, colleges and universities began to create their own private non-profit contracting organizations to bid on massive CRM projects. These organizations and later CRM companies are responsible for the majority of historical archaeological data recovered in Massachusetts. These included Brown University's Public Archaeology Laboratory (PAL) in 1976, Harvard's Institute for Conservation Archaeology (ICA) in 1977, UMass Amherst's Archaeological Services (UMAS) in 1983, and Boston University's Office of Public Archaeology (OPA) in 1981 (Rahn 1983; Wiseman 2002). Of these, Harvard's ICA was the first to shut its doors in 1983, followed by BU's OPA in 1995. Archaeological Services remained open for considerably longer but closed in 2018. After Brown decided to close PAL in 1982, a group of archaeologists who had stayed at Brown to run the program transformed PAL into the private not-for-profit, full-service historic preservation firm that is still in operation today. A new model for academy-house contract archaeology in Massachusetts arose in 1999 with the creation of the Fiske Center for Archaeological Research at UMass Boston by founding director and former Boston City Archaeologist, Stephen Mrozowski. Unlike previous academic CRM firms, the Fiske Center's model was based around a large endowment from Alice Fiske, in memory of her husband, Andrew Fiske. The Fiske Center conducts selective collaborative CRM projects in and around Massachusetts that mesh with faculty and student research. With an academic-leaning set of multidisciplinary approaches to their surveys including in-house expertise in floral, faunal, and micromorphological analyses; artifact conservation; geophysical and remote sensing technologies; and other specialized laboratory and analysis offerings, the Fiske Center is a model for public/private CRM organizations (Fiske Center for Archaeological Research 2010) that has rarely been replicated elsewhere in the US.

The rise of CRM and expansive projects in Boston created new opportunities for municipal archaeology. The office of the Boston City Archaeologist was created in 1983 largely through the efforts of James Bradley, who was directing a statewide historic and archaeological survey at the MHC. Boston was in the midst of a multiyear, multisite archaeological survey ahead of the proposed Central Artery Project, or "Big Dig" which was designed to move the main highway running the city underground. This massive federal project resulted in some of the earliest large-scale urban archaeological surveys in the region. Through Bradley's efforts, the Commonwealth of Massachusetts requested that the City of Boston create a position to manage current and future archaeological review and engagement. Using federal funds, the City of Boston created the City Archaeologist position within Boston's Department of the Environment and was modeled after similar Dutch and English programs (Bagley 2017).

Today, the bulk of archaeological research in Massachusetts is completed as part of CRM studies required as part of new development projects, with significant contributions from academic projects and field schools. Since 1977 more than 3,800 archaeological reports have been filed with the MHC covering projects across the Commonwealth (Galvin 2024). As of January 2021, there are more than 4,700 recorded historical archaeological sites in 293 of the 351 cities and towns (MHC 2024) in Massachusetts. These sites span the seventeenth through twentieth centuries and document the diverse domestic, military, institutional, maritime, industrial, educational, agrarian, and social history of Massachusetts and its people.

Scope of This Book

As the site of some of the first US colonies, Massachusetts has been a continual presence in the historic narrative of the nation. Through its Indigenous occupants, waves of colonial and immigrant settlement, expansion west, and economic evolution, the history of Massachusetts reflects many of the broad trends in American history spanning more than four centuries. With a diverse and ever-changing population, its people represent the spectrum of the American experience spanning the full range of economic, social, political, and cultural identities. The people of Massachusetts have left their mark not only in the written records but also in the material culture of their lives. In this text, we will explore how the historical archaeology of Massachusetts can provide a unique and comprehensive opportunity to explore the American experience.

Given the sheer number of archaeological sites in Massachusetts, it is not possible to discuss in one volume the complete breadth of research that has been conducted across the Commonwealth. The sites highlighted in the following chapters have been selected to represent the broadest range of Massachusetts historical archaeology, include examples from every time period and every part of the state, and document the overall themes that are covered in each chapter and that are representative of the American Experience in Archaeology theme of this book series. The examples have been drawn from avocational, academic, professional CRM, and public archaeologists and include some sites that will be well-known to practicing archaeologists and others that have not been detailed in published documents before. Inevitably, many significant contributions to Massachusetts archaeology and many archaeologists who work in Massachusetts have not been included. While a truly comprehensive accounting of Massachusetts archaeology is beyond the scope of this volume, the bibliography is extensive and includes many important studies and reports that contributed to the research for this book. Readers are encouraged to explore these resources and to see, as the authors have, how much incredible archaeological data has been generated in Massachusetts.

The book will move roughly chronologically through the history of Massachusetts briefly introduced above but will be organized thematically. Chapter 2 focuses on expressions of identity. Whether this be self-identity, the identity of "the other" or the identity of place, this chapter focuses mostly on the interactions between Indigenous and European groups across Massachusetts in the seventeenth century. Having established the natural landscape of Massachusetts in Chapter 1, this chapter will revisit this landscape through the lens of the period just before European colonialism with examples of Indigenous spaces and places along the coast, Connecticut River Valley, and western Massachusetts. We will discuss the earliest English colonization of Massachusetts showing how archaeological data combined with documented history reveals a more complete picture of how English and Indigenous people represented themselves, were seen by others, and how material goods and ideas were exchanged. We will also cover the arrival of the first permanent settlers at Plymouth and then westward European colonization in the context of bounding and placemaking. This chapter will include a discussion of the historical veneration and memorialization of the Pilgrims and other "founding fathers" contrasted with the erasure of Native peoples in local histories, and how these histories are being reframed in the modern period through collaborative descendant community archaeology and social movements. The discussion will highlight the ways in which Massachusetts's written, remembered, and archaeological history served as a model for other parts of the United States, and how recent research is helping to decolonize the field.

Themes of globalism, commercialism, and gentility appear in Chapter 3, where we explore the cultural events and changes that resulted in their rise. These include the fall of Puritanical rule, the rise of mercantilism, and the increased role of gentility in all aspects of daily and public life. This will be accomplished through sites representing diverse time periods, functions, and locations within Massachusetts such as taverns, farms, and shadow economies, focusing on what the archaeological results have revealed that go beyond historical documentation and how these revelations embody the American experience.

Slavery and its aftermath in Massachusetts are the dominant topic in Chapter 4, spanning the period from the first European arrivals through the modern period to the present. We discuss Massachusetts's role in enslaving Native Americans and African Americans from the earliest period of the colonies, including archaeological evidence of Native indenture or bondage at seventeenth-century colonial sites, archaeological research at the Royall House, and Massachusetts-Caribbean plantation connections between both groups. It will also explore group and individual Black identity in the context of a developing American identity. We examine the domestic and professional sphere through the lens of matriarchal households of African American and Black home sites and the materiality of eighteenth- and early to mid-nineteenth-century communal action. Finally, we look at how Black activism in the twentieth century has shaped community archaeology projects.

Chapter 5 will focus on war and revolution including sites associated with conflict and defense across all time periods including the Pequot War, King Philip's War, the French and Indian Wars, The Revolutionary War, War of 1812, Civil War, and World War I and II. This will include examples of newly developed survey techniques and analysis including key terrain, observation and fields of fire, cover and concealment, obstacles, and avenues of approach/withdrawal (KOCOA) analyses; metallic and geophysical survey; and landscape analyses. We will also explore associated military sites including maritime and underwater sites and the Springfield Armory and discuss the roles of commemoration, veneration, and remembrance as they relate to the American experience.

Industry and labor are the key themes of Chapter 6, which covers the seventeenth through twentieth centuries to explore the connection between the natural environment, technological developments, demographic evolution, and economic change over time. We will discuss archaeological aspects of production spanning locally distributed small-scale artisan operations to large-scale factories with international export. We use domestic sites associated with laborers to show how individual and group identity was expressed and suppressed over time.

Chapter 7 will explore the archaeology of communities. This chapter will focus primarily on nineteenth-century archaeological sites and historical themes that document social, cultural, and religious collective activity in life and in death. The case studies will include utopian communities, Native spaces, sites of voluntary and involuntary communal activity (for example, schools, poor farms, hospitals, prisons) and forgotten and/or unmarked cemeteries and the groups interred there. The chapter will compare and contrast differences in material cultural, spatial organization, and health and hygiene. We will explore broader national trends in the development of rigid social and cultural class divisions in the nineteenth century as they are expressed in Massachusetts with a focus on how archaeology can provide a critique of and alternative to popularized ideals and historical norms of the period. The development of more rigid social and cultural class divisions in the nineteenth century will be explored in the context of Massachusetts history and broadened to include similar trends across the country. Discussion will include how the archaeological record supports or refutes the stated ideals and historical narratives about these groups and organizations.

We explore contemporary historical archaeology and the bending of archaeology toward justice in Chapter 8. Social justice movements of the twenty-first century have greatly impacted historical archaeology in Massachusetts, expanding the topics and time periods investigated in historical archaeology and emphasizing the role of contemporary communities in the acts of archaeological investigations. We conclude in Chapter 9 with a reflection on how the historical archaeology in Massachusetts described in this book reflects the American experience, and we suggest future avenues for historical archaeology in Massachusetts.

This book explores the historical archaeology of Massachusetts to reveal insights into the history of our nation that cannot be found through written documents alone. We will show how the people of Massachusetts have been revealed and celebrated through thousands of archaeological sites and surveys across the Commonwealth; how the focus of historical archaeology has shifted over time following national cultural trends; how historical archaeology has revealed and created space for the voices that have been silenced, erased, or ignored; and how the future historical archaeology of Massachusetts has and will continue to remain relevant to the ongoing discussion of the American promise.

2

Cultural Entanglement

Any discussion of a historical archaeology of Massachusetts must begin with the Indigenous people within whose homelands present-day Massachusetts is located. The 1620 arrival of the Mayflower and the establishment of Massachusetts's first permanent English colony is a foundational event in the history of the United States, but like many other American historical moments it has been venerated and mythologized. For over four hundred years, this narrative has privileged Eurocentric documentary and archaeological narratives over others. In recent decades, archaeological study of seventeenth-century Massachusetts has attempted to challenge some of these institutionalized histories through the reexamination of sites and material collections, a more nuanced reading of period texts, the incorporation and prioritization of Indigenous knowledge, and collaborative study with Indigenous knowledge keepers and descendant communities. These efforts are helping to bring multiple histories forward that break down the narratives of a Native American "prehistory" and the arbitrary beginning of an American "history" at the start of European exploration and settlement (Schmidt and Mrozowski 2014). This important work of decolonization is being done by Indigenous scholars and knowledge keepers, archaeologists, anthropologists, and historians across the country (e.g., Bragdon 1999; Brooks 2018; Bruchac et al. 2010; Coombs 2002; Delucia 2019, 2020; Fermino 2001; Gallivan 2021; Gould 2013; Gould et al. 2020; Nassaney 1994, 2000; Schmidt and Mrozowski 2014; Silliman 2020). The case studies presented in this chapter highlight the evolution of historical archaeology at some of Massachusetts earliest sites of cultural entanglement.

Massachusetts's Indigenous History

Europeans arrived in Indigenous homelands in Massachusetts that had been settled for time immemorial (Bruchac 2005; Senier 2014). Archaeologists have reconstructed the deep human history of southern New England through fragmentary material objects and features that provide an incomplete picture of more than 12,000 years of continuous occupation and movement across the land (Boisvert 2007; Bradley and Boudreau 2006; Chandler 2001; Chilton et al. 2005; Curran and Dincauze 2006; Goodby 2021; Snow 1980; Speiss et al. 1998; Zoto 2023). Interpretations are still largely based on empirical data and western science, but collaborative work between archaeologists and Indigenous scholars and knowledge keepers in Massachusetts and southern New England is broadening understandings of Native pasts, and Massachusetts (e.g., Bendremer and Thomas 2008; Cipolla et al. 2019; Gould et al. 2020; Hart 2004; Kerber 2006; Sebastian Dring et al. 2019; Stockbridge-Munsee Mohican Tribal Historic Preservation Office 2024; Stubbs et al. 2010).

Native American homelands covered all of present-day Massachusetts and extended beyond its present-day borders. The Massachusett, Mohican, Nipmuc, Pennacook, Pocumtuck, and Wampanoag were the largest Indigenous tribes in Massachusetts, but many Native Americans identify themselves by other distinctive tribal group names. While Indigenous peoples had distinct cultural, linguistic, and geographic identities, they did not consider land to be territorially "bounded" in the same ways that Europeans did (Brooks 2008; Kupperman 2000). Native people across Massachusetts and the wider New England region moved with purpose across the landscape and came together for social and spiritual gatherings, to share and exchange food and natural resources, and to form alliances and extend kin networks that stretched across southern New England and beyond (Bragdon 1996; Bruchac and Hart 2012, Johnson 2000).

Archaeological sites dating from approximately AD 1500 to 1600 have been identified across Massachusetts. Still, the state's archaeological database of these sites appears more concentrated near the coast and along inland rivers and waterways, especially the Connecticut River Valley. This may be at least partly a reflection of bias based on material culture identification because these are the general areas where sites containing maize and evidence of horticulture have been identified (Chilton 2002). These are also the locations in Massachusetts where Europeans had the earliest and most consistent contact with Native Americans, and which were described in

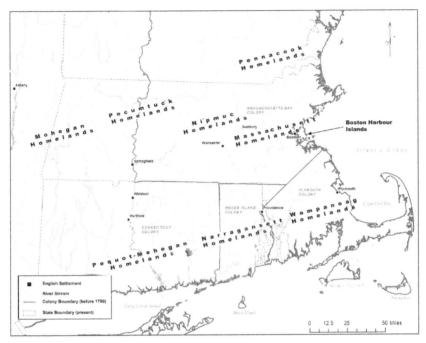

Map 2.1. Overview map of Massachusetts Indigenous homelands.

detail by seventeenth-century European visitors as agricultural villages (see discussion below) (Hasenstab 1999; Thomas 1984).

Maize was adopted by at least some southern New England Indigenous populations beginning sometime in the last one thousand years, although its importance and effect on lifeways, including sedentism, has been debated by archaeologists for decades (Chilton 2002, 2010; George and Bendremer 1995; Kerber 1988; see below). Most archaeologists now agree that horticulture was one part of a diverse subsistence base that included the harvest of terrestrial and marine species collected through hunting, gathering, and fresh and saltwater fishing and shellfish collection, an interpretation that is supported by Indigenous knowledge. Foodways revolved around seasonal availability and utilized the abundance and variety in the fertile river valley. Soils at these sites that are rich in calcium from discarded fish bones near a fall line at Peskeompskut just north of Deerfield are material manifestation of seasonal intertribal fishing events that are known from oral traditions (Brooks 2008; Bruchac and Hart 2012; Thomas 1985).

Archaeologists from the University of Massachusetts Boston worked at the Sandy's Point site in Yarmouth, on Cape Cod, as part of a field school in environmental archaeology in the summers of 1991 and 1992. They determined that the best methodologies to investigate the possible cornfields there were to expose a large horizontal area and use ground-penetrating radar (Mrozowski 1994). Two six-square-meter areas were initially excavated revealing forty low-mounded hills that ranged from seventy to ninety centimeters in diameter and were spaced about one meter apart. After adding several exploratory trenches, the size of the field was estimated to be twelve by twelve meters (1,600 square feet). Twenty-one of the hills were excavated through bisection in five-centimeter levels, and soil flotation and micromorphological analysis were conducted on approximately half of the collected samples. Despite the interpretation of the features as corn mounds, only two kernels (identified as Northern 8 Row Flint) were collected, and both were found outside the field (Mrozowski 1994, 57). Soil flotation did reveal the bones and scales of whiting (Merluccius bilinearis), cod (Gadidae species), and a member of the herring family (Clupeidae) that resembles alewife, which may support accounts by William Bradford and Edward Winslow that Native people used fish as fertilizer to enhance growing in poor soils (Mrozowski 1994, 58; see also discussion below regarding Champlain's observations on Cape Cod). The thin-section analysis of epoxy-coated column samples from the corn hills revealed details that were not visible during excavation, including evidence of hoe marks around the bases of the hills that showed subsoils were pulled in as the hills were periodically re-mounded with organics (see above) (Currie 1994).

Massachusetts Indigenous maritime resource utilization focuses on inland freshwater rivers, lakes and ponds, estuaries, and the ocean that surrounds its shorelines. It also includes the watercraft (skin and wooden boats), tools (for example, fishing hooks and weights, netting), and features (weirs and dams) which can be considered part of Native "wet homelands" (Patton 2013). The archaeological study of wet homelands depends largely on preservation in salt versus freshwater and aerobic versus anaerobic conditions, but one documented submerged watercraft site in Massachusetts indicates the potential for more to be present (Patton 2013, 15–18; Orcutt 2014; Plane 1991; Robinson 2002). Nipmuc and Wampanoag oral histories document the use of *mishoon* or *mishoonash*, wooden dug-out vessels that were created by burning and scraping out the interior of a large, heavy log and shaping the bow and stern for maneuverability.

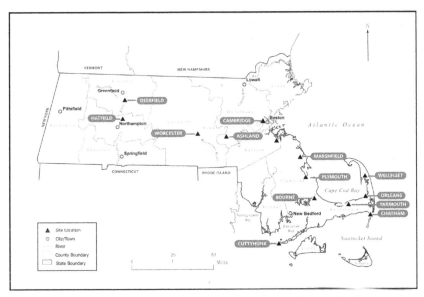

Map 2.2. Map of Massachusetts showing locations of sites discussed in Chapter 2.

In 2000, a recreational diver discovered what appeared to be an intact log boat on the bottom of Lake Quinsigamond in Worcester. A second vessel was identified on the opposite side of the lake in 2001. That same year, members of the Hassanamisco Nipmuc Band founded Project Mishoon, directed by tribal member Cheryl Stedtler (http://projectmishoon.homestead.com). The project team includes tribal members, volunteers, recreational divers, and professional archaeologists who have spent the last two decades studying these submerged objects within the Nipmuc wet homelands. After the initial rediscovery of the two craft, side-scan sonar was used to map the entire lake bottom. Two more mishoonash were identified and subsequently mapped and photographed in place. The boats are similar in size, ranging in length from fourteen feet, seven inches to at least fifteen feet, nine inches long (the bow of this vessel is still buried in sediment) with a flattened bottom and pointed bow (Robinson and Stedtler 2011; Orcutt 2014).

All of the boats are filled with large rocks that were intentionally placed in each boat so that they would completely sink below the water line. Patton (2013, 16), basing his interpretation on Indigenous history, notes that, "Functionally, this practice preserves the canoe by keeping the wooden structure moist and serves as a kind of storage during winter ice or as camouflage. After multiple cycles of 'burial' and recovery, the canoe becomes waterlogged and does not float again after the stones are removed." Tribal history indicates that mishoonash were typically made of white pine or chestnut and primarily used in lakes and large ponds. They were too heavy to be moved over long distances and would have been filled with rocks and sunk before the lake froze over for the winter. Keeping the mishoonash in a cold, wet environment prevented them from going through freeze and thaw cycles in the cold months which would likely have cracked the wood or otherwise damaged the vessels (Robinson and Stedtler 2011; Orcutt 2014). A wood sample from one canoe was removed and radiocarbon dated to AD 1640–1680 (Orcutt 2014, 64). As of 2024, the project team is considering options for future investigation that may include preservation in place or excavation and conservation (http://projectmishoon.homestead.com).

Project Mishoon maintains an active social media presence and regularly reports on its activities (https://www.facebook.com/projectmishoon/). Since 2001, Project Director Stedtler has delivered public lectures and presentations about the mishoonash and their significance to Nipmuc tribal members in local communities across Massachusetts. There have been several Mishoon burns at nearby lakes where tribal members and volunteers spend several days creating a mishoonash using traditional techniques and tools to pass the cultural knowledge from one Nipmuc generation to the next and to educate local residents about Nipmuc history and culture. Like other studies referenced throughout this book, Project Mishoon serves as a model for a decolonized Massachusetts archaeology that is guided by Indigenous research interests and supported by professional archaeologists and technical specialists. Project Mishoon's broad public outreach work and inclusivity ensures that the history of this Massachusetts site will not be forgotten.

European Encounters

Archaeologists studying sixteenth- and seventeenth-century Native American lifeways in southern New England have utilized the detailed written observations of European visitors as a resource to both locate and interpret Indigenous sites. Recorded encounters between Europeans and Native Americans in the region date as early as 1524 when Italian explorer Giovanni da Verrazzano sailed from the Cape Fear area in North Carolina to Cape Breton in Nova Scotia, stopping near present-day Newport, Rhode

Island, and somewhere in Maine (McManis 1975). Other Europeans visited with increasing frequency in the early seventeenth century: Bartholomew Gosnold in 1602, Martin Pring in 1603, Samuel de Champlain in 1604 and 1606, George Weymouth in 1605, and John Smith in 1614 (Archer 1843; Brereton 1968; Champlain 1922; Pring 1930; Levermore 1912; Quinn 1975; Rosier 1930; Smith 1614; Winship 1905).

Several of these explorers left written accounts of where they landed and their observations about the Indigenous people they encountered (Carpenter 1994; Karr 1999; Levermore 1912). Archaeologists have used these accounts to try to locate temporary camps and trading sites from the sixteenth and seventeenth centuries, but the lack of accurate geographic details coupled with development and shoreline erosion make it a difficult task, if sites even survive. These short-term, temporary sites likely left few archaeological signatures, another factor that hampers their documentation.

Englishman Bartholomew Gosnold's 1602 exploratory voyage included stops on Cape Cod, Martha's Vineyard, and the Elizabeth Islands and, like Champlain's account, includes detailed descriptions of coastal Massachusetts's geography and Indigenous people. Gabriel Archer and John Brereton, both sailors on Gosnold's Concord, each recorded their impressions (Levermore 1912). Brereton's *A Briefe and True Relation of the Discoverie of the North Part of Virginia* was published soon after his return in 1602 and was the first published English account of New England. The narratives provide some of the earliest written descriptions of Wampanoag people in what is today Massachusetts. While the descriptions must be viewed through the lens of seventeenth-century European perspectives and biases, they still provide useful information about the physical environment and Indigenous people at that time.

Arriving on one of Massachusetts's islands which was uninhabited "saving a little old house made of boughs, covered in barke, an olde piece of a weare ... to catch fish, and one or two places where they had made fires" the men decided to make a temporary settlement (Levermore 1912, 34). On the nearby islands they "found no townes, nor many of their houses, although we saw manie Indians ... they gave us of their fish readie boiled, (which they carried in a basket made of twigges) ... they gave us also of their Tabacco, which they [smoke] greene, but dried into powder ... the necks of their pipes are made of clay hard dried ... the other part is a piece of hollow copper, very finely closed and cemented together. We gave unto them certaine trifles, as knives, points, and such like, which they much esteemed" (Brereton in Levermore 1912, 33–34).

While Gosnold and some of his men were off exploring other areas, part of the crew was left on Cuttyhunk Island and over three weeks constructed what Archer described as "our Fort and place of abode" on a small upland in the center of a pond on the western end of the island (today known as Westend Pond) (Archer in Levermore 1912, 49). The English structure was likely not built as a long-term defensive work because Brereton described it as "an house, and covered it with sedge" and noted that when a group of fifty Native men approached the island in watercraft, the sailors "being loth they should discover our fortification . . . went out on the sea side to meet them" (Brereton in Levermore 1912, 37). They reportedly planted some European grains and vegetables to test the suitability of the soil. Although Gosnold had envisioned leaving a small contingent behind to establish a more permanent trading post, too few of the men wanted to stay and after spending six weeks touring the New England coast, they sailed back to England.

Like many early European "first encounter" sites in New England, the Gosnold encampment on Cuttyhunk was venerated in written histories that repeated the sailor's accounts as highly accurate. Harvard historian Jeremy Belknap visited the Elizabeth Islands in 1797 and reported that the remains of the "Gosnold fort" were still visible (Bosworth 1993). At the tercentenary of the landing in 1902, a commemorative stone tower was proposed for the site of the ruins which was described at that time as "an excavation overgrown with grass and briars" (Boston Post 1902). A committee of men formed to oversee the memorial's construction traveled to Cuttyhunk and selected stones reportedly from the original "fort" to form the base of the tower on the actual site, but nowhere in the documents is there any discussion about actually investigating or preserving the original seventeenth-century site (Ricketson 1903). The planning, financing, and construction of the tower was extensively reported and the tower's dedication attended by "eminent historians, scholars, lecturers and divines, [and] men representing millions won in the business world" but the participants did not include any Native Americans nor were the Indigenous people Gosnold encountered or their descendants mentioned once in the many speeches delivered that day (Old Dartmouth Historical Society 1903). The Gosnold memorial is just one of many in Massachusetts and across New England that were designed to permanently enshrine the "founding" of America as a white colonial space without an earlier history, to visibly and physically mark the site as hallowed ground (DeLucia and Howey 2022; O'Brien 2019).

Today the seventy-foot-tall stone Gosnold Monument stands on the spot reported to have been the 1602 encampment. No archaeological investigations have been conducted at the site, nor have any European materials been reported from the small interior island, which is protected from development or disturbance. Future noninvasive geophysical study at this location may be able to identify any remnant structural remains or artifact deposits and provide more information to support or refute this location as Gosnold's camp. Archaeological studies of the monument itself, now more than 120 years old, could be used to interrogate the creation of historical narrative and remembrance at the site.

Archaeologists often date late sixteenth-century and early seventeenth-century Native American sites to the period before or after Europeans arrived on the presence or absence of European trade goods including iron, brass, or metal objects; glass beads; and white clay pipes described in many of the European encounter narratives (see below) as trade objects. These materials have also been identified at burial sites dating to this period (Gibson 1980; Robinson et al. 1985; Simmons 1970). However, dating sites from this period solely on the basis of mixed Native and European material culture likely excludes (or misidentifies) a large number of late sixteenth-century and early seventeenth-century Native American sites. A recent study at the Smith/Great Island Tavern site in Wellfleet on Cape Cod used radiocarbon-dated features to document a significant Native American presence between AD 1500 and 1650 in activity areas that did not contain European goods (Steinberg et al. 2021). These sites contained the chipped and ground stone tools, lithic flakes, and pit and shell-bearing features that (in the absence of radiocarbon dating) would have typically been assumed to date to the period before Europeans began to interact with Indigenous people. This assumption may represent an unconscious (or conscious) bias that Native peoples unilaterally incorporated European goods into their material culture as soon as they had the opportunity to do so, and that the later seventeenth-century written accounts upon which so much archaeological interpretation has relied accurately depict Native habitation areas.

When used critically, the accounts of seventeenth-century European travelers provide useful details about the appearance, dress, food, structures, language, material culture, and social order of Native peoples as well as the geography, flora, and fauna of the region that have been used to locate, identify, and interpret Indigenous sites from the period (e.g., Carpenter 1994; Kerr 1999; Loren 2008). Researchers assumed that the people and places described (usually with similar language) by these men were somewhat representative of Indigenous lifeways prior to European contact, and that their accounts could be used to locate and interpret Late Woodland Period archaeological sites.

At the two-acre Area D site on the Connecticut River in Pocumtuck (present-day Deerfield), archaeologists have been able to study a possibly fortified Native American village dating from the late sixteenth to mid-seventeenth century that provides clues about interactions among Native and non-Native individuals at the local and regional level (Bruchac and Hart 2012; Hart and Dillon 2019). Pocumtuck was situated at an active riverine and overland transportation nexus that had been traveled by Native people for thousands of years but also brought the Native community into contact with Europeans. These Europeans used the same routes as part of the fur trade, to explore and extract natural resources, and to barter with the Indigenous residents. As settlers poured into the coastal region, Native people faced increasing pressure for resources and to practice their traditional lifeways, and some migrated west into the homelands of neighboring Indigenous groups. Pocumtuck was a place where, increasingly, people from overlapping communities and kin networks came together. These interactions and entanglements are represented in the archaeological record by a wide variety of materials (lithic tools and waste flakes, metal Native-made pottery, European ceramics, glass and shell beads, mammal and fish bones, copper kettle fragments, soapstone pipes) and feature types (storage and trash pits, posts, burning and baking areas) (Hart and Dillon 2019).

Between 1604 and 1606, French explorer and cartographer Samuel de Champlain traveled the Eastern Seaboard from Nova Scotia to Nantucket, paying particular attention to protected bays and harbors that might be suitable for settlement. In addition to detailed observations about the people, floral and fauna, and geography of the region, his maps of harbors in the present-day Massachusetts towns of Gloucester and Plymouth and on Cape Cod (which he named "Cap Blanc") depict "the dwellings of the savages and where they plow their land," and the locations of "great quantities of oysters" (Levermore 1912). While in Nauset Harbor on Cape Cod, Champlain wrote, "we found the place very spacious, being perhaps three or four leagues in circuit, entirely surrounded by little houses, around each of which there was as much land as the occupant needed for his support" (Levermore 1912, 124). Going ashore with a small party, he wrote that: "Before reaching their cabins, we entered a field planted with Indian corn . . . We saw many Brazilian beans, and many squashes of various sizes, very good for eating; some tobacco, and roots which they cultivate, the latter having the taste of an artichoke . . . There were also several fields entirely uncultivated, the land being allowed to remain fallow. When they wish to plant it they set fire to the weeds, and then work it over with their wooden spades" (Levermore 1912, 124).

Champlain's and other seventeenth-century accounts of Native fields and maize horticulture have been considered markers of sites dating to that period; however it has proven difficult for archaeologists to document whether this practice (and the use of fish as fertilizer) was adopted before or after European contact in southern New England (e.g., Bendremer et al. 1991; Ceci 1975, 1990; Nanepashemet 1993; Trigger 1990;). While the Sandy's Point site described above provides clear documentation of an Indigenous planting field, there has been little archaeological documentation of the expansive Native agricultural landscape described in seventeenth-century texts. Rather features containing rich organic soils, plant remains, and in some cases fish bone suggest that smaller garden-like planting areas may have been located within coastal habitation areas (Herbster and Cherau 2001; Herbster et al. 2014; Oswold et al. 2020).

These few recorded interactions (often written years or decades after the voyages were complete) document what were likely many short-term encounters between Native Americans and European fishermen and explorers over more than a century (Bragdon 1996). By the time the Pilgrims landed in 1620, several generations of Native Americans living in Massachusetts's coastal communities and along its major riverways were conversant in English and familiar with European trade goods (Bragdon 1996; Harrington 1994).

European interaction and cultural exchange did not dramatically alter Native lifeways in the early seventeenth century, but waves of devastating epidemics did. The first swept through Massachusetts between 1616 and 1619 (possibly lasting until 1622) killing between 75 and 90 percent of the Native people living at and near the coast (Cook 1976; Dobyns 1983; Salisbury 1982; Speiss and Speiss 1987). When Martin Pring and John Smith visited the New England coast in 1603 and 1614 (respectively), they reported encountering many Native Americans who they described as robust and healthy. Only a few years later in 1619, Thomas Dermer traveled from Maine to Patuxet (present-day Plymouth) and described what he interpreted as abandoned villages where only a "remnant remains, but not free of sicknesse. Their disease the Plague, for wee might perceiue the sores of some that had escaped, who described the spots of such as usually die" (Dermer 1905, 251). Over the next decades, English settlers described abandoned homesites and fields that were being reclaimed by the woods and skeletal remains lying on the ground surface, noting that there were not enough living to bury the dead (Bradford 1952). This period is remembered by Wampanoag descendants as "The Great Dying" in Massachusetts Bay (Plymouth 400 Inc.). Various pathogens have been identified as possible sources, including bubonic plaque, chicken pox, viral hepatitis, or some combination for which Indigenous New Englanders had no immunity (Baker 1994, 35–36). Researchers have relied on seventeenth-century European accounts, ethnohistorical sources, and archaeological investigations at burial sites to hypothesize that between 75 and 90 percent of Massachusetts coastal population died during this period, while interior portions of New England and Narragansett homelands to the southwest were not affected (Cook 1976; Dobyns 1983; Salisbury 1982; Speiss and Speiss 1987).

From 1633–1634, a possible smallpox epidemic affected a much larger portion of New England's Native population, which further decimated the Massachusetts coastal settlements and took the lives of large numbers of Narragansett in Rhode Island and Pocumtuck in the Connecticut River Valley (Baker 1994; Snow and Lanphear 1988). Native deaths due to disease continued to be documented throughout the seventeenth and early eighteenth century as Native people and English settlers and missionaries came increasingly into physical contact with one another (Salisbury 1982). Many English settlers saw the widespread loss of life across Massachusetts as a divine sign that the land was being cleared for them to inhabit, and early missionaries told potential converts that a merciful God would spare them if they renounced their spiritual beliefs and accepted Christianity (Bowden and Ronda 1980; Cogley 1999; Karr 1999; Salisbury 1982).

Immigrants Arrive

European diseases for which Indigenous residents had little or no immunity were likely introduced during early encounters along the coast but rapidly spread into the Massachusetts interior through tribal kin, social, and trade networks. Early settlers described deserted Native villages and used the perceived absence of Indigenous people to justify their colonization. While Native communities did suffer great population loss due to foreign disease in the seventeenth century, they did not abandon their homelands nor disappear. Settlements may have become smaller and more mobile as family members were lost, and kin groups may have reorganized or temporarily relocated away from growing European populations. This pattern would be repeated across America as white settlement expanded westward and Native people were pushed into more concentrated areas, or eventually forcibly relocated.

Native villages located along the Massachusetts shoreline and its coastal bays were targeted by the first permanent European colonists because they were located on level dry ground near sources of freshwater and other natural resources, had already been cleared or partially cleared of vegetation, and were often along well-maintained trails. The earliest colonial settlements were in turn improved, expanded, and developed over succeeding centuries. This reutilization of the same areas over generations and into the modern period resulted in the complete or partial destruction of many early historic sites, both Native and European. Near coastal sites that may have escaped urban development were affected by nineteenth-century summer resort and recreational construction and continue to be threatened by sprawling residential vacation homes. Finally, the effects of climate change and rapidly intensifying coastal erosion pose perhaps the most large-scale threat to the earliest sites that remain.

Permanent European settlers began to arrive in Massachusetts in the 1620s and while the 1620 Pilgrim village at Plymouth is best known, during this decade they also established small communities on Cape Ann and in Salem north of Boston. Plymouth Colony was chartered by a group of English investors who wanted to establish settlements in North America for the export of timber, fish, furs, and other commodities back to England for sale. The initial group of Puritan separatists who sailed on the Mayflower seeking religious freedom from England were joined by "strangers," non-Puritan tradesmen, military leaders, and indentured servants who were sent by the Company to assist with the establishment of the settlement and to ensure that the new colony would succeed (Deetz and Deetz 2000; Demos 1970).

The Massachusetts Bay Company was established in 1628 and received its royal charter in 1629. John Endicott arrived during this period with a small group and started a settlement in present-day Boston at the mouth of the Charles River. John Winthrop was appointed governor but did not take the position until he arrived in 1630. Between 1620 and 1640, a period known as the Great Migration, more than 20,000 primarily English families and individuals emigrated to Massachusetts Bay, which became the largest and most rapidly expanding colonial area in New England (Anderson 1991). The majority of those who left England did so for religious rather than economic reasons, making Massachusetts's seventeenth-century history different from that of the Chesapeake Bay and Virginia colonies, which were set up primarily as economic plantations where many of the first immigrants were men who arrived alone as tradesmen and laborers (Anderson 1991).

Most Great Migration immigrants spent at least a few weeks and sometimes their entire first winter in their Massachusetts port town of arrival or joined a small community that had already become established while they searched for a permanent location where the head of the household could become a proprietor and receive a land grant. The early arrivals often moved several times over only a few years' time, constructing semipermanent homes for their families and few possessions (Anderson 1991). This pattern of impermanence is one reason so few seventeenth-century sites have been identified in Massachusetts, and why early American settlement sites from later time periods may also be lacking at entry points where immigrant groups first arrived.

Seventeenth-century towns were generally founded by a colony grant which dictated how many proprietors could be named and then given shares in the land grant, often hundreds or even thousands of acres. Once that limit was reached, the town was considered "closed" and later residents needed to purchase land from one of the proprietors. Twenty-three Massachusetts towns were founded in the 1630s, primarily along the coast north and south of Boston. As these communities filled, settlement began to radiate westward away from the coast and into Native American homelands that had initially been free of colonists (Anderson 1991; Innes 1983, 1995; McManis 1972).

History and Archaeology at Plymouth

As one of America's most well-known historical sites, Plymouth, Massachusetts, has been the focus of archaeological investigation and interpretation for more than 150 years. The historical trajectory of its interpretation and representation provides a useful case study to understand how American mythology is created and how it can be decolonized and made relevant today.

In the late nineteenth and early twentieth centuries, avocational and self-taught archaeologists like James Hall and Roland Robbins excavated sites associated with the original Pilgrim colony including the Myles Standish House, Alden House, and Aptucxet Trading Post. In 1856, James Hall began excavating at the 1620s home site of Myles and Barbara Standish in Duxbury, MA, which had already been casually looted for relics for several decades. Hall's excavations were remarkably systematic for the period in that he recorded the foundations of the house using two datum points and piece-plotted the exact location of individual artifacts he recovered on a map. James Deetz credits Hall's excavations as the earliest example of historical archaeology (Deetz 1968).

In 1852, physician John Batchelder had begun his search for the Aptucxet Trading Post established by Myles Standish in 1627 for trade with the Dutch and Native Americans. The structure was destroyed by a hurricane in 1635 and never rebuilt. Batchelder researched seventeenth-century deeds to find its probable location south of the original Plymouth Colony on the Monument River in Bourne. He identified two small depressions that he assumed were its cellar holes and excavated one of them, recovering several "notable relics" including a knife and a hoe that were provided to the Pilgrim Society. The only record of Batchelder's work is a letter he wrote to the Massachusetts Historical Society summarizing his excavation and deed research (NPS 2021).

Percival Hall Lombard, president of the newly created Bourne Historical Society (BHS), returned to the site in 1926 and completed more extension excavation in the two depressions, documenting two remnant fieldstone foundations and a chimney fall between them. Lombard was not trained in archaeology but kept detailed field notes, plan drawings of the excavations and exposed structural elements, and an artifact inventory with general provenience information. His work, combined with Batchelder's earlier research, was considered confirmation that this was indeed the site of the Pilgrim structure and led the BHS to purchase the property in 1926.

A fundraising effort that included most of Massachusetts's wealthy preservation advocates led to the reconstruction of the building on top of one of the exposed foundations in 1929 and the site was opened to the public the following year. Since the 1929 reconstruction, the site has been investigated periodically during a CRM survey of the Cape Cod Canal, as part of a University of Massachusetts Boston archaeological field school, and by professional archaeology conducted for the Aptucxet Trading Post Museum (NPS 2021).

Descendants of the original Pilgrim settlers founded the Pilgrim Society in 1820 for the purpose of buying land and creating a monument to their ancestors from two centuries prior. While their intended monument was not built for nearly fifty years, in 1824, the Pilgrim Society created the Pilgrim Hall Museum in 1854, which is now the oldest public museum in the country and dedicated to the material culture of the seventeenth-century colony (Hosmer 1965).

Archaeologists returned to Plymouth and its individual homesites sporadically over the twentieth century, most notably by James Deetz who joined the Plymouth Plantation staff in 1967 and the results of his excavations at Pilgrim-era sites to more accurately inform the museum's structures, displays, and interpretive materials (Baker 1997).

A major research effort was launched with Project 400 (http://www.fiskecenter.umb.edu/Projects/Project400.html), a decade-long collaborative project between the Andrew Fiske Memorial Center for Archaeological Research, the Institute for New England Native American Studies at the University of Massachusetts Boston (UMB), and Plimoth Patuxet Museums (formerly Plimoth Plantation). Planned to coincide with the 400-year anniversary of the Pilgrims first settlement, this multidisciplinary project incorporated Indigenous and community participation and encompassed extensive historical research, geophysical survey and investigation, the reexamination and reanalysis of existing archaeological collections, archaeological fieldwork conducted as part of field schools, conservation and artifact analyses, and a strong public outreach and education component (Landon and Beranek 2014; Beranek and Landon 2023). Members of the Mashpee Wampanoag Tribe have been involved in the ongoing identification and interpretation of sites and materials, and in student and public education about how the Wampanoag interacted with the Europeans who settled in their homelands. The work is providing an opportunity to critically examine the legacy of colonialism, challenging narratives about the Pilgrim settlement that have become ingrained in early American history, and which were supported by the foundational work of Massachusetts historical archaeologists in the first half of the twentieth century (see Chapter 1).

The study focused on the present-day downtown Plymouth area, which was the Wampanoag village of Patuxet in 1620 when the Mayflower arrived. The early work utilized historic map and land ownership research, remote sensing, and archaeological soil coring and hand excavation to identify potential seventeenth-century sites and features below a landscape that has been dramatically altered over the past four hundred years. The original enclosed settlement was known to have extended from what is now a large town cemetery known as Burial Hill down to the waterfront. The site was adjacent to a tidal estuary that was altered three times: for waterpower in the eighteenth century, heavily industrialized to support a commercial waterfront in the nineteenth century, and during twentieth-century urban renewal and the creation of a public commemorative landscape. One of the main goals of the project was to understand how the geography of Plymouth had changed over time and to determine if and where seventeenth-century sites might still be present (Beranek et al. 2014).

The fieldwork within the town-owned cemetery was restricted by nineteenth-century burial vaults (which had also cut through a section of the seventeenth-century site) and disturbance from a row of nineteenth-century buildings. The intact area included the remains of a house and multipurpose structure dating from approximately 1620 to 1660, its associated yard space, a section of the palisade that surrounded the houses, and evidence of a Wampanoag activity just on the other side of the palisade and only a few feet from the English house (Beranek and Landon 2023).

The yard area contained features that documented plantings and several trash pits in proximity to each other and the house. The structure, like the Waterman House discussed below, was built with earthfast construction with one wall banked into the hillside. An intact section of a daub wall (made with clay or mud to form a type of plaster) was documented but based on the layout of the multiroom/multi-elevation structure, different construction techniques were probably used. This suggests that the building was completed in phases or was possibly built quickly in the earliest days of the settlement. A few bricks were recovered, but instead of a chimney or fireplace, one part of the building contained a hearth set directly on what was at least partly a subterranean floor. The artifacts found inside the structure include fragments of milk pans and storage vessels, and household ceramics, but also a range of trade items that would not typically be expected in a domestic building. These include a lead coin weight dated to between 1577 and 1603 based on its stamped mark; two cloth bale seals; and glass trade beads, possibly of Dutch manufacture (Beranek and Landon 2023). European beads and cloth were two of the most desired and commonly traded goods with Native Americans, and their presence in the building suggests that the structure may have served as the Pilgrims' storehouse (Beranek and Landon 2023).

The Plymouth excavation program benefited from public attention since it was tied to the 400th anniversary events occurring over several years around Plymouth and in England. The fieldwork site was open to visitors and the archaeologists provided interpretive information to interested visitors. Public and professional presentations about the work paid careful attention to the centuries of vernacular history surrounding the Pilgrims first settlement and how those narratives had affected American history. The concurrent "Our Story" interactive traveling exhibit created by Wampanoag historians and researchers utilized other ways of knowing to present Plymouth's history from a perspective that had long been subverted by white historians (https://www .plymouth400inc.org/our-story-exhibit-wampanoag-history/). The creators developed video segments with descendant community members portraying historical Wampanoag individuals. A second touring exhibit "Wampum: Stories from the Shells of North America," was co-curated by Wampanoag tribal members, Mayflower 400 UK, and the British Museum. A modern wampum belt created by Indigenous craftspeople was viewed by more than 6,000 people in Southampton, England and helped tell the story of a similar shell belt that was stolen from the body of Metacom, taken to England as a spoil of King Philip's War, and its location lost over time (Perley 2020). During this same period, Plymouth Plantation was renamed Plimoth Patuxet Museums to better reflect the Indigenous homelands on which it stands and the people whose material culture and history it archives.

The quadricentennial anniversary provided an opportunity to examine and reshape the narratives surrounding a time and place that are iconic in American history. On Thanksgiving Day in 1970, the United American Indians of New England organized the first annual National Day of Mourning in Plymouth as a day of remembrance to protest the lasting effects of settler colonialism, and to counter the venerated Pilgrim story. The Plymouth 400 archaeological studies and Indigenous-led programs and projects focused on the day-to-day lives and intentional actions of Native and English individuals just before the Pilgrim arrival and during the first years of the Plymouth Colony's existence. They replaced a mythologized and one-sided history with a more complex and complete understanding of cultural interaction told from multiple perspectives. The reexamination of Plymouth's history parallels other reckonings that have happened and are happening at historical sites across the country where previously marginalized peoples are making their voices and histories heard.

Seventeenth-Century English Households

Plymouth was just one of Massachusetts's seventeenth-century settlements, and archaeological studies of other immigrant sites across the Commonwealth provide data that help to individualize Massachusetts's early colonial history. Most of the people who arrived on Massachusetts's shores faced a difficult and uncertain fate and could not rely on regular supplies from Great Britain. Edward Winslow's 1624 *Good Newes from New England* advised would-be immigrants that they would need to possess some carpentry skills, build their own structures, and bring over all the tools, nails, and hardware they would need to survive (Wisecup 2013). They also needed cooking pots and storage vessels, grain and seeds, and farm animals for eggs, dairy, and meat. All these materials were cargo on small sailing vessels that also carried passengers and crew (Anderson 1991). Material lists, probate inventories, and letters to and from England from this period can be used to interpret and analyze the households of seventeenth-century settlers, sometimes provide clues about their relative socioeconomic status, their preparedness for life in the colonies, and the skills and knowledge they brought with them.

Early settler domestic sites are often characterized by small and ephemeral structural features built to provide basic shelter with very low densities of manufactured goods like ceramics and hardware. These structures included "wigwam" style bark-covered, cloth tent-like and wooden post structures that are described in contemporary sources but leave a very ephemeral archaeological footprint. One recent study documented the circa 1638 Waterman House site in Marshfield, a rare example of a Pilgrim-era structure that was not altered by later additions or archaeological reconstruction (Harper 2021). Evidence of a catastrophic fire indicated that the house stood for only a short period of time, essentially providing a seventeenth-century time capsule. The site was identified as part of a CRM project associated with airport improvements. The initial survey collected two redware pottery sherds, the only indication of a colonial-era site. A more substantial Native American component at the site necessitated a second phase of testing and the recovery of materials and features that suggested a more intact seventeenth-century component.

Marshfield is twelve miles north of Plymouth and was one of several Massachusetts towns established by "Old Comers," a term used to describe the first groups of European immigrants. As new settlers arrived in the years after Plymouth and Massachusetts Bay were first settled, the Old Comers were given large tracts of land outside the fortified village where they could establish farms to increase the supply of food and livestock. In the early decades of settlement, families were expected to return to the main colonies in the winter months for safety and security, leaving indentured servants to maintain the property.

It can be extremely difficult to associate a specific house site to a particular seventeenth-century colonist. Property and land records were not maintained until later in the century and many of those that did exist have been lost. The project team conducted archival and land evidence research and was able to trace the property from the nineteenth century back to circa 1700 when it was owned by Joseph Waterman, son of Robert Waterman. Family history and town records placed Robert Waterman in the Marshfield area sometime in the 1630s. An important document for the interpretation of the site was Robert Waterman's probate inventory, which included a detailed accounting of his household possessions that helped tie the more than 11,000 artifacts collected at the site to the Waterman occupation (Harper 2021).

The Waterman site excavation included the full exposure of the foundation which in shape and size resembled a "husbandman's cottage" typical of east England, where the family was from. The two-room structure measured fourteen by twenty feet and included two palisade-style exterior walls constructed of oak timbers that were set upright next to one another and anchored in a shallow trench. Handwrought rose head nails were concentrated along the structure walls and around the door. An interior wall separated a small pantry or "buttery" with a hearth set into the dirt floor from the main room where a storage pit was sunk into the earth. There was no evidence of a brick or stone chimney, and the fire was likely vented through a hole in a reed-thatched roof. This construction technique probably led to the fire that destroyed the house, documented by charred bulrush seeds and melted casement bottle glass and burned ceramic sherds. Bayberry seeds may have been remnants of candle-making.

Materials were discovered in discrete sections of the house and were used to reconstruct different activity areas. The third of the house used for food preparation contained redware and tin-glazed earthenware butter pots, bowls, and milk pans; latten spoons; Dutch brass kettle fragments; and burned food remains including shelled corn. European flint flakes found next to the hearth indicated use of a strike-a-light. The main living space contained the door with an attached entryway and a post that may have supported a sleeping loft. Artifacts were concentrated along the walls, indicating that objects were stored in the small multipurpose area for easy access when needed. The collected assemblage included 383 highly degraded pewter fragments (ten pewter dishes and three pewter basins were listed in Robert Waterman's probate inventory, indicating the family owned at least some pieces of fine serving ware). A high concentration of whole burned grapes and seeds indicated that foods were stored there, which further suggested that the house had burned down in the early fall after the grapes were harvested. The assemblage also included fragments of a Native-made pot and several tubular copper and glass beads. The Watermans could have purchased or acquired them through trade. An "Indian woman" was indentured to Joseph Waterman in the 1680s, so it is also possible that his father's household relied on forced Indigenous labor (Harper 2021) (see Chapter 4).

The Western Frontier

The influx of European settlers to the Plymouth and Massachusetts Bay colonies quickly overwhelmed available resources and it was not long before people began to look outward for new areas to establish farmsteads, industry, and new communities. By 1660, residents of the towns of Ipswich, Wenham, and Danvers had petitioned the Massachusetts General Court to settle Nipmuc lands around the ponds in present-day Brookfield and West

Brookfield in Worcester County. Like many other secondary settlement areas, West Brookfield was located along the Bay Path, a major trade and transportation route utilized by trappers and traders that extended from Boston west to Springfield and the Connecticut River.

The Connecticut River was Massachusetts's main north–south travel and trade corridor, connecting Quebec, Canada, and Long Island Sound. Beaver and deer were abundant, and anadromous fish runs at the many fall lines were important in the seventeenth century for food and commerce. By the early seventeenth century, the Connecticut River had become a place of diverse socioeconomic interaction. English, Dutch, and French explorers, traders, and militia encountered Sokoki, Pocumtuck, Nonotuck, Agawam, Woronoco, and Mohican Indigenous groups whose homelands encompassed the area (Paynter et al. 2019; Thomas 1984).

The coastal area of Massachusetts offered a seeming abundance of resources and easy water access for transportation, but it didn't take long for European settlers to realize that the land to the west, and particularly the Connecticut River Valley, had many of the same qualities. The lowland valley supported an oak-hickory-chestnut forest and contained sandy, clay-rich soils that were ideal for agriculture while the surrounding uplands were flush with fur-bearing mammals; beech, maple, and hemlock forests; and pasturage for sheep and cattle (Paynter et al. 2019). The region's extensive network of rivers, streams, and ponds were a ready source of power for mills and industry. English settlements were established on the river in present-day Wethersfield, Connecticut, and Springfield, Massachusetts, in the 1630s, and Deerfield in the 1670s. For the first time, permanent villages expanded across the landscape, a pattern that led to conflict with the Indigenous people whose homelands were invaded (see below).

The first colonists exploited the forests for ship building, turpentine and pine tar, and firewood and charcoal, all of which spawned commercial operations in western Massachusetts. Soapstone, marble, and lead were extracted commodities represented by quarries and processing sites (e.g., Haynes 1901). By the start of the eighteenth century, the surplus of agricultural products and the concentration of the most productive land in the hands of a few families created an enormous wealth and power disparity. In particular, the agricultural abundance of the Connecticut River Valley was integral to Massachusetts's early transcontinental trade and Caribbean plantation provisioning.

A seventeenth-century English settlement known as the "the Farms" or "Old Farms" has been documented near Hatfield, a town on the Connecticut

River north of Springfield. Town histories documented a fortified English enclave settled sometime before 1689 but had abandoned it by 1704 due to exposure along the western frontier and fear of French and Indian attacks during King William's and Queen Anne's Wars (1688–1713). "Ten or twelve old cellars" were still visible in the 1840s, but the exact location of the site had been largely forgotten (Daum 2014, 142). A local archaeologist noticed a scattering of seventeenth-century structural and domestic artifacts across a large, plowed field, and after completing some archival research identified the area as the likely location of the Old Farms settlement (Daum 2008).

Initial hand testing, geophysical survey, and coring over a ten-acre parcel identified several anomalies that appeared structural and provided a refined target for more extensive testing and excavation. The study documented ten spatially ordered house lots and the remains of structures lining both sides of a five-rod-wide (eight-two-foot) central lane, described in a 1720s deed as "the old road to Deerfield" (Daum 2008, 139). While the upper levels of the site had been disturbed by plowing, the lower portions were largely intact, allowing the archaeologists to reconstruct the original layout of the settlement and identify the individual house lots.

Twelve cellar features were documented, many with dry-laid fieldstone walls and remnant hearths or chimney bases. The researchers found that many of the structural stones, timbers, and virtually every complete brick had been removed from the site; almost certainly taken by the residents when they relocated as an efficient and necessary way to reuse resources that were expensive and difficult to replace. The nearly 2,000 artifacts collected at the site were mostly small and fragmentary portable artifacts, including German, English, and Dutch ceramic wares, hand wrought nails, brass spoons, iron horse harness hardware, English and French gunflints, and nearly 300 clay pipe fragments (Daum 2014). These materials firmly dated the site to the 1689–1704 period. Thirty musket balls, including fifteen that were flattened and had been fired, were collected at the site in all but one of the cellar holes. This led the researchers to speculate that the residents may have left the village shortly after an attack, possibly at about the same time as the well-documented 1704 French and Indian raid on nearby Deerfield. There was no evidence that the village had been burned, and the lack of complete objects as well as the removal of reusable structural materials suggest that the residents made a conscious decision to relocate, possibly to a larger and safer community (Daum 2014).

The Hatfield Old Farms site provides a rare opportunity to study an entire late seventeenth-century English settlement known to have existed for only a short period of time and largely undisturbed in the historic or modern periods. The site is extremely rare because almost every early European settlement in Massachusetts was continuously occupied in later historic periods and/or to the present day (for example, Plymouth, see above).

Religion as Colonization

The founding of the Massachusetts Bay Colony was closely tied, at least in theory, to the Christian conversion of the Indigenous population. This mandate was plainly evident in the charter for the Bay Colony, which stated that "the principall Ende of this Plantacion" was to "wynn and incite the Natives of [the] Country to . . . the Knowledg and Obedience of the onlie true God and Savior of Mankinde, and the Christian Fayth" (Shurtleff 1853–4, 1:17) and the official seal of the colony depicted a Native American holding a bow and arrow, uttering the phrase "COME OVER AND HELP US." In practice, however, few early settlers were interested in or involved with spreading Christianity.

As settlers streamed into New England, the Massachusetts General Court had two interrelated concerns with regard to the Native inhabitants: preventing hostile attacks and negotiating land transfers. The English minister John Eliot, known as "the Apostle to the Indians," became a critical link between the colonial government and the Native people whose homelands the colonists wanted. Eliot's congregation was in Roxbury, but by 1647 he and a handful of other ministers began traveling into Native communities to preach, and as the meetings became more regular, Eliot promoted the creation of missionary "towns" where Indigenous people could receive religious instruction, learn English, and adopt English customs, with the eventual goal of Christian conversion and the abandonment of Indigenous lifeways. Eliot skillfully promoted his work for the Society for the Propagation of the Gospel in New England (SPG) in a series of broadsides that were widely distributed in England to solicit funds that were given to colonial merchants for the purchase of goods and supplies (Cogley 1999; Copplestone 1998).

The historical narrative of the fourteen "praying towns" that Eliot initiated primarily in Nipmuc and Massachusett homelands across eastern Massachusetts ignored Indigenous agency and relied on English descriptions written to present the acculturation process as absolute (Gould et al. 2020; O'Brien 2010). Archaeologists have been frustrated by a lack of reliable historical documentation relating to these historic Native occupation areas, especially since they often encompassed thousands of acres and were poorly surveyed or documented (Carlson 1986). A more targeted effort to locate the first Christian Indian settlement at Natick produced little archaeological data, leading the researcher to suggest that seventeenth-century descriptions of these places as well-ordered English-style villages may have been written to persuade the English government and financial backers that the mission system was working (Brenner 1978, 1984, 1986).

Over the past twenty years, documentary research, archaeological investigations, and collaborative engagement with Nipmuc descendants have rediscovered the late seventeenth and early eighteenth-century events and individuals associated with Magunkaquog, one of Eliot's missions initiated in 1669. The general location had been known for centuries due to the appropriation of the Indigenous place name at Magunco Hill in present-day Ashland. When a residential development was planned for the undeveloped land around its slopes, a CRM survey documented a small assemblage of seventeenth-century artifacts, some chipped stone tools and flakes, two large, abandoned stone-lined wells, and what appeared to be a small, filled cellar hole (Gould et al. 2020).

The developer agreed to avoid the site area while UMB archaeologists and field school students enlarged the original excavation area and fully exposed a nine-by-twelve-foot dry-laid stone foundation set into the eastern slope of Magunco Hill. The detailed eyewitness accounts provided by colony agent Daniel Gookin and Eliot's missionary tracts had been used by researchers as reliable accounts of what the "praying towns" looked like, but the Magunkaquog site presented another version that incorporated some elements of English architecture and land use with more traditional Nipmuc use of space.

Rather than being an English-style residential village laid out with house lots around a central road (see discussion of Hatfield Old Farms, above), the structure at Magunkaquog was a solitary building and was likely the communal meeting or "fair house" where Eliot or other Englishmen would meet with Native communicants on their occasional visits. The structure did not include an interior hearth and there was no evidence of a brick or stone chimney. A large hearth outside the building contained charcoal; animal bones from processed beef, pork, sheep/goat, deer, and turtle; and quartz cobbles that had been heated, possibly to extract crystals, which were found around the site and purposely placed inside three of the foundation's corners. Burning on redware milk pans indicates they were placed directly on an open fire, a practice that was typical of Native food preparation but not English. Several gunflints manufactured from quartz were collected, and their method of manufacture was different from typical European chert gunflints. Quartz is a common lithic type used to make Native chipped stone tools in New England but is seldom used for gunflints (Gould et al. 2020; Kelly and McBride 2016).

This building may also have served as a storehouse for the mission's "common stock;" European tools and materials that were dedicated for use by the Native community to support their adoption of English cultural ways. A small collection of thimbles and buttons and part of a scissor found inside the foundation may have been communal supplies brought by Eliot. Curtain rings, a set of drawer pulls, and chair tacks suggest that the building contained a bed, storage chest of drawers, and some furniture. Small fragments of window glass found within and on the downs-slope side of the structure indicate it had at least one window. The building may have served multiple purposes and could have been where Magunkaquag's Nipmuc teacher stayed or where Eliot or Gookin slept and could have served as a communal gathering space for Nipmuc families when English missionaries were absent (Gould et al. 2020). In this interpretation, the mission site was probably recognized by Nipmuc people as a distinctly Indigenous place even though Eliot and others considered it to be the opposite. Documentary records also indicate that Nipmuc individuals repeatedly returned to Magunkaquog after their forced removal during King Philip's War, demonstrating the importance of this place to the community.

The Magunkaquog site provided a unique opportunity to critically examine seventeenth-century English narratives that have been used historically to describe Native acculturation. The site is a physical manifestation of Indigenous survivance in the face of repeated attempts to remove Nipmuc people from their homelands during King Philip's War, and from discouraging them to return after the conflict ended. The study also documented that the colonists were unsuccessful, and that the Christian Indian villages Eliot had hoped would acculturate Indigenous people were instead maintained as uniquely Native spaces.

Indigenous space has also been investigated at what could arguably be considered one the most English institutions in the Massachusetts Bay Colony. Harvard College, the first higher education institution in the United States, was founded in Cambridge (then "Newtowne") in 1636 as a place to educate future New England ministers. The college was initially funded by a substantial £395 bequest from the estate of minister John Harvard, whose library of 400 books was also included (Morison 1936). The first students and their tutors studied, ate, and lived in existing structures surrounded by cow pastures on two lots that had been purchased from colonists. The wooden two-and-a-half "Old College" completed in 1639 was the first new building constructed on the campus (Morison 1936). The "College Yard" continued to be used for grazing cattle but also served as a physically and socially ordered space where young men lived communally in accordance with strict rules enforced by academic overseers.

The SPG agreed to provide funds to Harvard at a time when the young institution was struggling financially, provided the College educated Native as well as English students (Hodge 2013, 227; Morison 1936). In return for the financial support, Harvard agreed to waive tuition and provide housing for up to six Indian students who would live in a separate building on the campus. The Indian College was housed in a brick building erected in 1655 to educate both English and Indian youth, because by this time the Old College building had fallen into disrepair (Hodge 2013; Loren and Capone 2022; Stubbs 1992). The first printing press in British North America had originally been housed in the president's house on the campus, but was moved to the Indian College building in 1659 before any students had arrived (Hodge et al. 2015). This press created the earliest printed government broadsides as well as the tracts that the SPG and John Eliot used to raise funds for his missionary effort. John Printer, a Nipmuc Indian, worked as an apprentice and set the type within this building for the first Bible printed in the Algonquin language in North America.

The first Native students were Caleb Cheeshahteaumuck and Joel Iacoombs, both Wampanoag men from Martha's Vineyard, who arrived in 1661. John Wampus, a Nipmuc Indian from Grafton, began his residence in 1665 and Eleazer, a Wampanoag student whose community is unknown, arrived in 1675. While a small number of additional Native students attended Harvard in the colonial era, these four were the only ones to live and study in the Indian College building. Caleb Cheeshahteaumuck graduated in 1655, but Joel Iacoombs and Eleazer died of smallpox before receiving their degrees and John Wampus left the college to work as a mariner. In 2011, Joel Iacoombs was posthumously awarded his degree (Hodge 2013, 228). By 1698, the Old College was no longer standing, and the Indian College had been torn down, its bricks repurposed for other new buildings on the expanding campus. As Harvard's focus moved away from religious education, the Indian College was largely forgotten, often excluded from Harvard's histories and campus tours that passed over its footprint (Loren and Capone 2022).

Archaeological studies were conducted on the campus in the 1970s prior to subway construction; in the 1980s as part of summer field schools; and in 1999 as part of facilities upgrades (Loren and Capone 2022; Stubbs 1992;

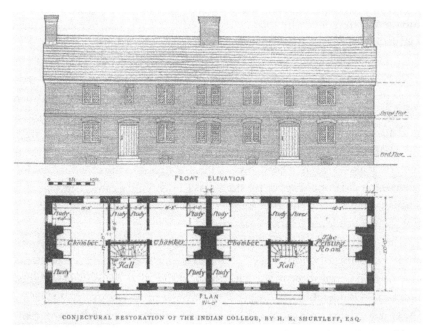

FRONT ELEVATION

PLAN

CONJECTURAL RESTORATION OF THE INDIAN COLLEGE, BY H. R. SHURTLEFF, ESQ.

Figure 2.1. Indian College at Harvard College conjectural image drawn by Harold Robert Shurtleff, 1883–1938 (Reproduced from Morison 1936: 344–345, courtesy of Harvard University Press).

Stubbs et al. 2010). The Harvard Yard Archaeology Project (HYAP) began in 2005 at the Indian College's 350th anniversary and was supported by the Harvard University Committee on Ethnic Studies and the Harvard University Native American Program (HUNAP). The Department of Anthropology, HUNAP, and the Peabody Museum of Archaeology and Ethnology cocreated and led a historical archaeology course called "The Archaeology of Harvard Yard" designed to explore public archaeology with an emphasis on collaborative and decolonized research, and as a way to explore the University's past and present relationships with Indigenous students and to investigate the visible and invisible use of space, institutional power dynamics, and colonialism (Stubbs et al. 2010; see Nassaney et al. 1996 for another example of campus archaeology in Massachusetts).

The archaeological investigations recovered approximately thirty pieces of lead printing type that were used in the original press, confirming their connection by comparing the unique characteristics and imperfections in the type fragments to surviving printed documents (Hodge 2013, 231). The archaeological remains include a portion of the seventeenth-century building foundation trench that has been interpreted as the east wall of the structure, and included foundation stones, red ceramic clay roof tiles, nails, broken window glass, and large quantities of brick (Hodge 2013, 218). This matches College records which describe the building as being a two-story, twenty-by-seventy-foot structure that could house up to twenty students. The Indian College artifact assemblages were compared to those collected from other mid-to-late seventeenth-century features in Harvard Yard. Interestingly, the only items that could be traditionally associated with Native students including glass and shell beads were collected in one of the other excavation sites which did not house Native students. The assemblages were remarkably similar, suggesting that order and structure applied equally to Native and non-Native students (Hodge et al. 2015).

The multiyear project included engagement with Harvard's Indigenous students (some of whom were Wampanoag and Nipmuc tribal members), the wider Harvard community and the general public. The project included outreach to Indigenous descendant communities in Massachusetts, including those whose ancestors attended the Indian College. Excavations, programming, articles, and interviews, and traveling exhibits have all been part of the project and multiple digital and web-based resources have been created to contextualize and anchor the archaeological work in both the past and present. The permanent "Digging Vertitas" exhibit at the Peabody Museum provides visitors with information about the HYAP, Harvard's historical associations with Native Americans, the material culture of the site, and the tribal students and community member collaborators. The exhibit can also be viewed online and via a mobile tour that allows visitors (in person at the Museum or remotely) to view a virtual excavation, meet seventeenth and twenty-first century Indigenous students, explore the materiality of the Indian College, and read content that connects Harvard's history and archaeology to the present day (https://peabody.harvard.edu/digging-veritas -gallery-exhibition).

Maritime Heritage

Massachusetts's early Indigenous and colonial heritage is not limited to land-based resources. Maritime and underwater archaeological resources include near-shore features like wharves, docks, and weirs as well as offshore shipwrecks, which can be hard to locate and even more difficult to investigate. Many wrecks are initially identified through documentary research, followed by nondestructive geophysical survey techniques like side-scan sonar and magnetometry to pinpoint the physical locations of materials resting on or below the seafloor. The waters of Cape Cod are known as the "Graveyard of the Atlantic" because of its shallow sandbars, dangerous shoals, and frequent nor'easter storms, and more than 3,500 ships are known to have been lost off its shores (https://www.mass.gov/orgs/board-of-underwater-archaeological -resources).

The first recorded Cape Cod shipwreck was the *Sparrow-Hawk,* which ran aground off the shore of Orleans in 1626. The twenty-five European passengers who were bound for Virginia but had been blown off course all survived, and the Wampanoag people who met them helped a small party get to Plymouth. Governor William Bradford recorded the event in his journal, noting that the passengers stayed with the Pilgrims for nine months before another Virginia-bound vessel picked them up. Bradford did not record the name of the ship, but the location he described matched a spot off the Orleans coast where storms occasionally exposed some ship timbers, and at some point, the wreck became known as the *Sparrow-Hawk.* In 1862, a large portion of the hull was exposed, the timbers were removed, and the reassembled ship traveled on exhibit around New England before being donated in 1889 to the Pilgrim Hall Museum in Plymouth where it has been in storage since that time (Daly et al. 2022).

The remains of the wooden forty-foot-long, thirty-six-ton ship were considered to be those of the 1626 wreck Bradford recorded. Its shape, size, and construction matched known descriptions of sailing vessels from the period, but until recently there was no definitive scientific evidence or associated artifacts to prove this was possibly the earliest and one of the only surviving seventeenth-century transatlantic vessels. A recent dendrochronological dating (tree-ring analysis) of the wood was undertaken to accurately date the age at which the timbers had been cut and, if possible, to identify where they had been harvested. While the results of the analysis varied for some of the different wood types that included elm and oak, the overall conclusion was that the ship was likely built of English timbers that were most likely cut between 1556 and 1646 (Daly et al. 2022). Although the technology available today cannot definitively pinpoint the date of the *Sparrow-Hawk,* its long-term preservation by the Pilgrim Society means that future technology may answer that question.

There is no ambiguity about the date of the *Whydah,* a Cape Cod shipwreck with a well-documented history, but its archaeological significance is tied to a controversy over ethics. The *Whydah* left London in 1715 for West

Africa where it collected nearly 500 enslaved people bound for the Caribbean. Named for the African port it operated out of (today Ouidah in the Republic of Benin) the *Whydah* was part of the Triangle Trade, the early colonial network that brought European materials to Africa where they were traded for enslaved people; the enslaved people transported to North American and Caribbean plantations; and the sugar, rum, and coffee produced by forced labor brought back to Europe and the colonies. As the *Whydah* set sail back for England, it was attacked and taken by Samuel "Black Sam" Bellamy, an early eighteenth-century pirate—a term applied to small crews of men who used captured vessels to attack and raid other vessels, taking their supplies and cargo for sale and profit. After raiding multiple ships in the Caribbean, Bellamy sailed the *Whydah* up the East Coast where the ship and most of the crew were lost in an April 1717 storm.

In 1982, treasure hunter Barry Clifford claimed title to the *Whydah* wreck in federal Admiralty Court, which would allow him to salvage the vessel and profit from the sale of recovered material. Clifford's claim that the *Whydah* carried precious metals and coins worth millions was an incentive to invest in the salvage. The Commonwealth of Massachusetts contested Clifford's request claiming it held title under its 1973 regulations that established the Massachusetts Board of Underwater Archaeological Resources as the sole trustee of sites of underwater archaeological heritage. The court ruled in favor of Clifford and the site was effectively no longer subject to state control or regulation.

In 1983, Clifford began exposing the wreck by removing the large amounts of sediment that covered the ship, and the Army Corps of Engineers found him in violation of federal environmental law because he had not obtained a permit for dredging. One consequence of the federal agency's involvement in assessing the penalties was a determination that the *Whydah* wreck was eligible for listing in the National Register of Historic Places. This in turn led to the creation of a binding agreement between the Corps, the Advisory Council on Historic Preservation, and the Massachusetts Historical Commission that ongoing excavation would have to follow certain archaeological performance standards and methodologies that would be monitored by the parties. The privately funded salvage team headed by Clifford was required to bring on a professional archaeologist and conservator who were required to submit annual reports (Hamilton et al. 1988, 1989, 1990; Roberts et al. 1987). Information about the recovery was presented at several national archaeological conferences in the 1980s, but many professional archaeologists felt that the *Whydah* project violated archaeological ethics and that by allowing the team a platform, for-profit treasure hunting was legitimized and presentations about the site were not allowed at later professional events (Elia 1992).

Clifford has continued to work at the site and in 2016 opened a museum on Cape Cod to display some of the thousands of objects recovered from the wreck. The *Whydah* archaeological team has changed frequently over time, and while stories about Clifford regularly appear in popular media and print, very little archaeological reporting on the site is available. Arguments about the ethics of the project and the participation of professional archaeologists are ongoing. Is it better to gain some scientific information that would otherwise be lost? Does working with salvagers legitimize their work and promote more disturbance? A difficult obstacle is the fact that archaeological resources are nonrenewable and archaeologists working today are charged with protecting sites for the future when they are not threatened. The only threat to the *Whydah* site is from the salvagers themselves, who continue to remove materials for display and/or to sell for profit (Elia 1992).

These discussions have become even more complicated by the recent identification of human remains in large concretions of hardened material that were removed from the wreck and have been slowly broken down at the museum. Most of the 146 men onboard who died washed ashore after the wreck, but some obviously went down with the ship. The *Whydah* crew likely included enslaved Africans, Native Americans, and European sailors, bringing issues of descendant community consultation, patrimony, and federal and state unmarked burial laws to the forefront and making it likely that the controversy surrounding this site will continue.

Conclusions

Today, archaeologists are investigating seventeenth-century English colonial sites with new research questions that are much less focused on the "who" and more interested in the "why" and "how." The opposite could be said of archaeology at Indigenous sites, where attention has shifted to the identification of individual and collective action and intentionality. Instead of examining sites as frozen moments in US history, archaeologists are interrogating how early colonists interacted with the environment and with the people whose homelands they had invaded, and how Indigenous responses to colonialism varied widely across space and time.

Traditional forms of Indigenous knowledge-sharing include storytelling and oral history, and these forms of cultural transmission persist, often with twenty-first century technology. Native Massachusetts's Native and archaeological collaborators have developed innovative methods to engage with audiences far beyond the typical academic and professional worlds. The Harvard Yard Archaeological Project and Project Mishoon serve as excellent examples of public archaeology efforts that are connecting tribal communities, local residents, and anyone with an internet connection across the country or world to Massachusetts's Native American history. Harvard's effort, which has included a significant commitment of capital, is part of a wider attempt to decolonize the institution and confront its treatment of people of color across the centuries. Project Mishoon operates without Ivy League funding but accomplishes the same goals of wide public engagement. In addition to helping raise interest and financial support for the project, Nipmuc Nation tribal members keep the practice of *mishoonash*-making alive and connect the Tribe's present generations with the non-Indigenous community members who live within their homelands.

Indigenous voices from the past are also being reclaimed from historical archives that so often silence them. The decades-long collaborative archaeological research with the Nipmuc Nation has identified seventeenth- and eighteenth-century Native-authored documents that challenge colonial attempts at authority and contradict the narratives of those in positions of power. The historical archive is being decolonized by the work of the Native Northeast Research Collaborative and its Native Northeast Portal database (http://nativenortheastportal.com/). This research repository began as the Yale Indian Paper Project in 2002 as a response, in part, to building political controversy surrounding the development of Indian casinos in the Northeast and racist rhetoric about Indian identity (Grant-Costa and Glaza 2017). Native leaders, educators, and scholars worked with historians and archivists to locate, organize, digitize, and make freely available tribal historical documents that include handwritten petitions, maps, journals, photographs, letters, and other records. As noted on the Portal, "Documents are digitized, transcribed, annotated, reviewed by the appropriate contemporary descendant community representatives, and brought together with scholarly annotations and academic/community commentary into one edited interactive digital collection. The Portal currently contains thousands of records associated with scores of Native communities" (http://nativenortheastportal .com/). The site is fully searchable and can be filtered by Native community. These archives illuminate the stories of the Indigenous people being told by their descendants who are actively reshaping the history of Massachusetts and the US.

Archaeologists have a responsibility to engage with the descendant communities whose ancestors are the focus of our research. In America, these communities include but are not limited to Indigenous peoples, and can vary depending on the location, resource, and time period of study. Archaeology as storytelling has been discussed in practical and theoretical frameworks for decades (Gibb and Beisaw 2000) and archaeologists can be effective advocates for more expansive and inclusive histories that draw in part from material culture. Our contributions need not be limited to active fieldwork and excavation. Even old artifact collections in museum displays and in boxes on shelves can and are being used to reinterpret sites that were excavated decades or even a half century ago.

The "Our Story" Wampanoag traveling and virtual multimedia exhibit and the Project 400 archaeological investigation of the original Pilgrim settlement were both significant components of the Plymouth 400 programming (https://www.plymouth400inc.org/) Guided by a board of directors that included Pilgrim descendants, Wampanoag elders and leaders, educators, historians, local and state officials, businesspeople, and tourism specialists, a Four Nations Commemoration included events in England, the Netherlands, in the spaces of the Mashpee and Aquinnah Wampanoag tribal nations, and in Plymouth. The multiyear commemoration of the 1620 Pilgrim landing created opportunities for investigating and amplifying the multiple histories that surround the first European settlement at Plymouth. The long-lasting effects of this effort on historical remembrance will be determined over time, but the ambitious project provides examples that can be adapted to other places. Americans take great pride in celebrating the anniversaries of significant events in the nation and in their communities, and these often include nostalgic remembrances and the reproduction of decades or even century old historical narratives about the people and places that are considered foundational. These histories, in many cases, present a story that is exclusive instead of inclusive and that often privileges placemaking narratives of discovery, settlement, and conquest over people and the land.

Archaeologists can and should engage with historic commemorations in the places where they work and live to offer support for commemorative events that consider multiple histories, liaison with the descendant communities with whom they collaborate, and, where appropriate, sponsor public programming that engages community members with a past they may not know about.

3

Globalism, Commercialism, and Gentility

There is robust evidence of globalism—meaning the interconnected nature of people beyond national borders—in the Massachusetts archaeological record from the seventeenth through the eighteenth centuries. The commercial evidence includes the presence of both imported and exported internationally traded goods, which illustrates that Massachusetts' residents were both consumers of foreign-produced goods as well as producers of goods that were sent abroad. Merchants ensured that in addition to physical goods, the people of Massachusetts spread around the world, and when they returned, they brought with them ideas and practices that would shape centuries of culture. One of the key movements that is highly visible in the archaeological record is gentility, a set of evolving social norms that codified moral superiority (Fitts 1999). This chapter explores how historical archaeology reveals Massachusetts as an engaged participant in global cultural, ecological, economic, and social changes.

Early Presence on a Global Stage

The Navigation Acts of the mid-seventeenth century specifically targeted the broad trade of goods between English colonies like Massachusetts and the outside world. The relative lack of regulations prior to this are abundantly clear in the archaeological record. The City of Boston Archaeology Program's recent re-cataloging of the circa 1635–1656 James Garrett site, a merchant household in Charlestown, revealed over 30,000 individual artifacts in one of the largest assemblages of early seventeenth-century artifacts in Massachusetts (Pendery 1999). The ceramics in this assemblage include

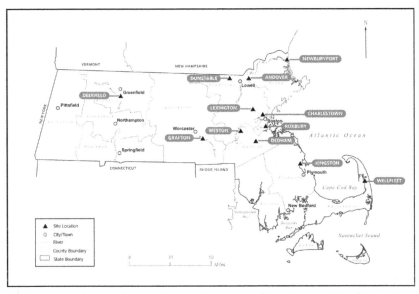

Map 3.1. Map of Massachusetts showing locations of sites discussed in Chapter 3.

Chinese porcelain, German Westerwald, and Renish stoneware; lead-glazed earthenware from the Netherlands, Germany, Italy, England, and Spain; and tin-glazed earthenwares from the Netherlands and Portugal. The Portuguese tin-glazed earthenwares are of particular note (Pendery 1999). Their presence is documented on many seventeenth-century Massachusetts sites in the Plymouth region (Deetz 1960; Traulis 2020), but the Garrett site, at 1,318 tin-glazed sherds, most of them Portuguese, represents one of if not the largest documented Portuguese tin-glazed earthenware assemblages in North America. While this is illustrative of the significance of Portuguese ceramics in early colonial trade in Massachusetts, it is more significantly indicative of the strong participation of Massachusetts merchants in the global market. The dramatic change in overall ceramic types present at a site following the Navigation Acts where only English earthenwares could enter the market is seen at the Parker-Emory House site in Boston's North End, less than a mile away from the Garrett site and separated by one century. At the Parker-Emery site, of the ninety-seven ceramic vessels recovered from the eighteenth-century barrel privy excavate at the site, only six represented ceramic vessels made outside of England or the American colonies, and of these, only one, a fragment of an Iberian vessel, represented earthenware made outside of the English sphere (Sharp 2023). These two sites, separated by a century, reflect the extreme shift in the availability of ceramic goods in the English colony of Massachusetts.

The Katherine Nanny Naylor Privy

During the Big Dig archaeological surveys at the Cross Street Back Lot project area, archaeologists encountered a roughly one-by-two-meter rectangular brick feature that would become one of the most important seventeenth-century features ever encountered in Massachusetts. This feature was a circa 1690 privy associated with Katherine Nanny Naylor, a wealthy resident of Boston in the mid- to late seventeenth century who was associated with the first recorded divorce in the state (Cook 1998).

The contents of the privy were remarkably well preserved due to the water-logged nature of the clay-lined feature (Heck and Balicki 1998). Recognizing the incredible opportunity this created for multidisciplinary analysis, the project team from CRM firms Timelines Inc. and John Milner included a wide variety of archaeological specialists (Heck and Balicki 1998). Although the exact artifact has not been compiled from the multiple reporting and post-excavation analysis efforts, the more than 150,000 recovered artifacts represent one of the most complete archaeological assemblages ever found in Massachusetts as well as one of the earliest. This remains one of the most intact and complete late seventeenth-century privy features recovered in Massachusetts and thus can provide significant information on this time period that can be compared to other early American sites.

Post-excavation specialized analyses included study of faunal, shoe, cloth-ing, pollen, and botanical artifacts, each with unique information about the late seventeenth century on a global and household scale. Alison Bain studied the beetle fauna totaling over 2,000 individual specimens (Bain 1998). Of the dozens of species identified within the privy contents, twenty-four spe-cies represented introduced beetles, and these represented between 64 and 80 percent of the individual beetles on the site (Bain 1998). Bain concluded that this dominance of introduced species by the 1690s represents an early establishment of "European biological imperialism" in Boston within a few decades of its founding (Bain 1998, 45). At the household scale, the beetles revealed the challenges in the Nanny Naylor residence with household beetle infestations including pests like the pea weevil and grain beetles (Bain 1998). Although Bain concludes that these infestations would have been relatively ubiquitous across households, the Nanny Naylor house had a particularly bad issue with flour. In addition to flour pests, Bain also found species of beetles associated with mold. Gerald Kelso (1998) also found unusually high concentrations of grain pollen, suggesting that large quantities of flour were discarded into the privy. Bain combines this data to indicate that the household had such a bad flour infestation and mold problems that it likely made this staple product unusable (Bain 1998).

Kelso's pollen analysis records the highest percentage of Eurasian grain presence of any archaeological site at the time of the publication (1998). This could not be accounted for by Kelso as fecal deposits of pollen or wind-blown deposits, resulting in his conclusion that not only was deliberate dumping of flour happening, but that it was happening with relative frequency (Kelso 1998). The relative wealth of the Nanny Naylor household could not prevent the infestation on their staple food products, but this same wealth also hid this food loss from the artifact and written records since there did not appear to be evidence that this food loss greatly impacted the family as much as it would have in households of lesser means.

Gregory Brown and Joanne Bowen (1998) studied the more than 13,000 animal bones from the Nanny Naylor privy. Their results demonstrated an established urbanization of Boston by the 1690s (Brown and Bowen 1998). Karen Friedman (1973) had previously used the historical record to prove that by 1640, just ten years after its founding, Boston had already outgrown its ability to produce enough food for its residents, necessitating the need to bring food to the city from nearby towns. This was supported through the archaeological record in the Nanny Naylor privy, but the privy provided more specific data on the various foodstuffs brought to the household and its reflection of the changing times. In the fish assemblage, Brown and Bowen (1998) found that there was more haddock at the highest levels in the privy, a higher percentage of cod than herring at the later upper deposits, and that the herring percentage increased with depth. The team concluded that these results reflect a broad trend in the region's fishing strategies: earlier time periods relied on a traditionally Native fishweir technology along rivers and streams that caught primarily anadromous fish such as herring. As fishing in Boston Harbor became well established, the fish in the Nanny Naylor privy reflected the increase in near-shore species (cod), which over time, transitioned to deeper water fish (haddock) (Brown and Bowen 1998). The team was unable to determine whether this transition to deeper water species was a reflection of cultural preference or fishing stock (Brown and Bowen 1998). In addition to the trends in fish types, Brown and Bowen documented that the presence of all parts of the fish in all species present showed that the Nanny Naylor household was purchasing predominantly fresh fish (1998). The salting process of fish, usually cod, began at sea with the removing and discarding or reuse of fish heads, meaning their presence on the site negates the presence of salted fish, despite its significant role in local and international trade in Massachusetts at the time (Brown and Bowen 1998). Lastly, the mammal bones of the privy show the dominance of local food items available at nearby farms, few wild game like deer and turtle, with a dominance of cow and sheep (Brown and Bowen 1998). This correlated well with the broader patterns established by David Landon (1996) whose study suggested that sheep in particular represented excessive meat production on farms that were readily able to be butchered and brought to market in cities like Boston before they spoiled.

To collect botanical remains, the project team used water screening making the visibility and recoverability of seeds significantly more likely. They also collected twenty-three liters of soil for processing via soil flotation (Dudek et al. 1998), a method of soil processing that collects seeds that float to the surface when the soil is processed in a pool of water. The botanical team recovered over 250,000 individual seeds from thirty-two species, a remarkably large sample from any site in New England (Dudek et al. 1998), much less an urban site from the seventeenth century.

The privy had multiple filling episodes (Cook 1998), and the seed remains were instrumental in interpreting and confirming their origins. For example, the deposits with the greatest numbers of seeds were believed to be fecal material based on the obvious smell and appearance, and the tens of thousands of seeds from those deposits that would pass through a person's digestive system (for example, blackberry and raspberry) helped confirm this (Dudek et al. 1998). The fecal deposits also had seeds that were not digestible (peach, cherry, etc.), which Dudek and team interpreted as food preparation waste. With fruit trees taking nearly a decade to reach fruit-producing maturity, these late seventeenth-century fruit pits likely represent some of the earliest harvests of fruit in New England (Dudek et al. 1998). Their large quantity also suggests that these fruits were used in the production of alcoholic beverages, an illegal act within homes. There was a significant presence of weed seeds (for example, smart-weed, pokeweed, dock, goosefoot/Chenopodium, etc.) within the privy (Dudek et al. 1998). These seeds indicate the presence of some Eurasian invasive plants as also documented in the beetle fauna (Dudek et al. 1998), but they also are strong indicators of the landscape of the property. Dudek and team found these seeds in higher concentration in filling or capping episodes signifying that weed-seed-rich soils from the nearby property and open spaces were carried into the privy and used to cap the deposits.

The Rural and Urban Contrast

Seventeenth-century historical archaeological sites in Massachusetts show how the colony experienced rapid growth in both its population and significance within the global economic world. While the influence of globalization continued toward the end of the century, the active resistance of the English leadership toward the unregulated markets of the American colonies and the resulting legal manipulation of the markets are clearly visible in the material culture record. This manipulation was never well received, resulting in clandestine trade and rebellion throughout the eighteenth century and ultimately leading to the American Revolution.

As the early seeds of the Revolution took root in the hearts and minds of Massachusetts residents, the Commonwealth underwent a rapid and permanent cultural transformation. Changes in religion and commerce modified the outwardly egalitarian Puritanical communities into a capitalist economy of haves and have-nots, a vast network of urban and rural spaces, and a rapidly diversifying economy and people.

The archaeology of pre-Revolutionary eighteenth-century Massachusetts reveals a western frontier where decimated Native peoples struggled to prevent the re-encroachment of European settlers they had recently driven out, at the same time as wealthy merchants in coastal metropolises one hundred miles away created cities full of imported goods, peoples, and ideas. At home, wealthy individuals adopted new practices and customs of their European counterparts, some of which spread into lower classes and rural spaces through the movements of merchants and minister classes into nearby towns. While the struggles of rural and urban people were fundamentally similar, their abilities to address and overcome these struggles diverged greatly during this time period. Geographic mobility, generational wealth, and the struggle to create new opportunities for newly born and recently arrived individuals in a tiny colony with dwindling and ever-dividing opportunities and resources lead to increasing resistance to rules and regulations from outside forces bent on tapping the success of Massachusetts in order to support English rulers (Taylor 2010).

Expansion West

The contrast between the tiny villages of rural, inland, Massachusetts and its urban coastal cities with their bustling commercial cores, mansions and hovels, and industrial shoreline is remarkable not just for the disparity of their sizes, but for the differences of the lived experiences of its residents. For a state with such significant contributions to seventeenth-century United States history including the founding of the Plymouth and Massachusetts colonies and the explosion of the American mercantile class in Boston, the vast majority of its non-coastal land remained undeveloped by European colonists until the beginning of the eighteenth century.

Indigenous communities that had already been decimated by the spread of European diseases were again impacted by the effects of fighting, lack of mobility, and forced internment during King Philip's War in 1675 and 1676 (see Chapter 5). The colonists used the disruption and dispossession of Native communities as an opportunity to create new towns and settlements westward across Massachusetts.

Eastern Massachusetts experienced rapid population growth during the first decades of the eighteenth century, with the region around the Fairbanks House in Dedham (see below), just west of Boston, quadrupling its population between 1700 and 1750 (McManis 1975; Meinig 1986; Parno 2013). This produced two key changes that differed from the previous century. First, large towns began to splinter as residents chose to build new meetinghouses at shorter distances from their farms. Second, large family farms began to divide over multiple generations, forcing some descendants to leave to find larger lots. Despite these changes, most new towns in Massachusetts still followed the seventeenth-century settlement pattern of first choosing the site of a meetinghouse, which defined the religious, political, physical, and cultural center of their town, then building the basic necessities of life including grist and lumber mills, clearing land for farms, and building homes.

The Fairbanks House

Archaeological research and analysis has been used to document the Fairbanks House in Dedham which was built in 1641 and is considered to be the oldest standing wooden house in the United States (Brown and Juli 1974; Cummings 1979). These investigations are supported by a detailed examination of divisions of land at the town and family level through four centuries of occupation by the Fairbanks family (Parno 2013).

Dedham was first settled in the 1630s, with a town center formed just ten miles southwest of Boston featuring a central meetinghouse and large farms surrounding it. In the early 1700s, the once massive 200-square-mile town began to break into the smaller towns of Wrentham, Needham, Bellingham, and Walpole as the increasing number of farmers living farther away from the original Dedham town center chose to build their own, closer, meetinghouses and form new towns.

As the town of Dedham shrunk around the Fairbanks family, their farm experienced a similar splintering effect including a reduction in the family's wealth and prospects. This resulted in an archaeological record that showed the Fairbanks family in the eighteenth century to be in reduced economic circumstances, illustrated by a relative lack of luxury goods and the house remaining relatively unchanged in shape from the late seventeenth century through the middle of the 1700s (Parno 2013).

In order to be self-sustaining, large family farms required a diversity of land, including areas for crops (tillage), mowing land for animal feed, orchards for productive use of less-tillable lands, and wood lots for heating and building needs. Parno discussed the fundamental flaw in large farm estate ecology: large farms are either given to one child or divided among several. Either way, farms will shrink until there is not enough land for self-sustainable farming or children will not inherit land and must find new occupations or new land to farm causing later generations to leave (Parno 2013).

In Andover, a town twenty miles north of Boston near the New Hampshire border, Parno showed that 39 percent of third generation male descendants of early farmers moved out of the town, compared to 22 percent of the generation before (Parno 2013). Parno concluded that by the early 1700s, farmland in eastern Massachusetts remained productive and sustainable for self-sufficient farms, but the division of land had made this nearly impossible (Parno 2013). As Native populations were concentrated into praying towns under English oversight, eastern rural farmers, urban pioneers, and fortune-seekers headed away from urban centers and eastern farms into areas recovering after the effects of King Philip's War (see Chapter 2 and Chapter 5).

The movement of people from increasingly urban areas to more rural ones reflects the overall movement of people across the country as individual towns and areas grew in size. These movements of people through relocation, settlement, and trade necessitated the improvement of transportation routes and the necessary infrastructure that supported people in transition.

Taverns were one of the key components of this infrastructure providing waypoints along routes for food and rest and providing key places to meet within towns for travelers and community building.

Archaeology of Tavern Sites

One of the key aspects of eighteenth-century archaeology in Massachusetts has been the focus on the differences between the urban cores of Boston, Salem, Newburyport, and other smaller eastern towns and the more rural towns mentioned above (Bower et al. 1987; Bragdon 1981; Elia 1989; Gallagher et al. 1994b; Gary and Randall 2006; Mrozowski et al. 2015). Archaeologists have sought sites where the differences between various groups of people may be represented through the material culture, especially at home. Taverns became an early target of historical archaeological research (Bragdon 1981) as they represented artifact-rich sites, in relative abundance, and they provided an opportunity to explore a single type of site in a variety of cultural spaces such as urban centers and rural outposts.

Taverns were present in nearly every Massachusetts community in the eighteenth century and provided at least two key services: a place to gather for drink and/or food, and a place to sleep for the night. In 1634, the General Court of Massachusetts gave itself the power to issue licenses to taverns, defining them as places to lodge travelers and traders and providing food and beverage to people doing business, explicitly forbidding the taverns from providing places for entertainment or serving lewd or idle people (which at the time included Native people, African Americans, apprentices, and seamen without captain approval) (Gallagher et al. 1994b).

In Boston, where tavern data is plentiful and well-compiled by the archaeologists who excavated the Three Cranes Tavern in Charlestown, historical data show the growth of taverns from just fifteen licenses in 1662 to thirty-six by the mid-eighteenth century. The latter served a population of 36,000 residents, or one tavern per thousand residents (Gallagher et al. 1994b), a similar proportion to present-day Boston (Alston and Tziperman Lotan 2024), a town known for its plentiful bars. The expansion of taverns, their goods, and growth reflects globalization. The expansion of trade resulted in the financial growth of families and towns necessitating the expansion of people into lesser developed areas to seek new opportunities for growth. The presence of an ever-expanding set of goods and people in the Massachusetts sphere is reflected also in the diversity of goods found at tavern sites, the availability of these goods as they spread into more rural spaces, and the specialization of taverns for clientele of varying socioeconomic status.

Throughout the eighteenth century, the function of taverns began to change as alternatives became available to residents, especially in urban areas. In the 1720s and 1730s, domestic production of rum increased dramatically, resulting in the presence of this cheap, high alcohol content, and relatively new spirit to the drinking experience (Gallagher et al. 1994b). While taverns historically served wine, locally made cider, and homemade beer, this new beverage presented a moral and economic challenge. Rum was prohibited by clergy (Rorabaugh 1979) and associated with public drunkenness, rebellion, and lower-class individuals. To differentiate themselves, many taverns avoided the sale of rum resulting in the formation of dram shops where rum was served in much smaller "dram" glasses, which look like small shot glasses with wine stems. The archaeological record of taverns including the Three Cranes Tavern in Charlestown and Pierpont Tavern in Roxbury, to Boston-area taverns in significantly different cultural settings, reflects these differences (Bower et al. 1987; Gallagher et al. 1994b).

These key community hubs shared more similarities than differences, but differences they had. Methodologically, archaeologists in the 1970s began to realize that there were enough taverns with enough excavations to begin to explore differences across multiple sites. Background research and analysis of two eighteenth-century sites in southeast Massachusetts, the Howland site in Kingston and the Wellfleet (Great Island) tavern indicated that there was a wide variety of drinking vessels available to the market in the eighteenth century, including tumblers, tygs, bellarmines, toby jugs, posset pots, black jacks, punch bowls, bombards, wine, and flip glasses (Bragdon 1981). Bragdon hypothesized that there would be a wider diversity of drinking vessel forms at Wellfleet where drinking was a priority. She also documented historical examples of tobacco pipe disposal practices in taverns that would produce a large quantity of pipe stems on tavern sites. From these data, she proposed a tavern site assemblage consisting of "a large number of vessels; a large percentage of drinking vessels in relation to the total ceramic sub-assemblage; a large percentage of those ceramic types most often found in the form of drinking vessels; large numbers of wine glasses; specialized glassware; and a large number of pipe stems" (Bragdon 1981, 36). The results of her archaeological analysis showed that the domestic Howland site had a high percentage of preparation vessels, low wine glass count, and pipestem counts in the hundreds (Bragdon 1981). The Wellfleet tavern site had the signature high percentage of specialized glass drinking vessels and thousands of pipe stems. Even though tavern sites can in theory have a similar artifact assemblage to domestic sites due to the tavern's function in many ways mimicking a home, Bragdon concluded that it is possible to differentiate a house site from a tavern site based on these relative percentages (Bragdon 1981). This was an important conclusion because it both proved that statistical archaeological data can be used to provide meaningful analytical results, and it presented a methodological approach for identifying site function based on statistical data alone, which has been used to interpret the function of historical sites without significant written records (Mrozowski et al. 2015).

The publication "City Tavern, Country Tavern: An Analysis of Four Colonial Sites," (Rockman and Rothschild 1984) which compared the Great Island/Wellfleet Tavern site (extremely rural) with three other late seventeenth- and early eighteenth-century assemblages in Pemaquid, Maine, (very rural); Jamestown, Viginia, (urban); and Lovelace, New York, (very urban). Rockman and Rothschild used the work of Stanley South (1977) to establish function classes of artifacts within the four assemblages, then used a Brainerd Robinson Coefficient of Agreement analysis to ask if the overall functions of the artifacts at the four sites were similar or different. This "solving culture with math" approach was popular at the time as part of the "new" or "processual" archaeology supported their hypothesis and others that urban taverns would have similar assemblages but differ in functional categories based on their urban/rural location, with the rural Wellfleet and Pemaquid taverns looking most similar to each other and most different from the urban taverns in Virginia and New York City.

Rockman and Rothschild (1984) agreed with Bragdon (1981) that ceramics and pipes were the most important and reliable indicators of activities occurring within taverns, but their results provided additional interpretation for why there was such a distinction between urban and rural taverns. They concluded that there was a fundamental difference between the function of rural and urban taverns. Their analysis showed that while all taverns provided food, drink, and a room to stay in for the night, the rural taverns had far more ceramics and lower percentage of tobacco pipes than urban taverns, suggesting that rural taverns were predominantly places for food and travelers to sleep, whereas urban taverns were predominantly places for community gathering with a less-significant component of traveler accommodation. Most of the tavern sites that have been excavated in Massachusetts including the Golden Ball Tavern in Weston (Elia 1989; Gary and Randall 2006), Pierpont Tavern in Roxbury (Bower et al. 1987), and Three Cranes Tavern in Charlestown (Gallagher et al. 1994b) have tested and confirmed this hypothesis and support the idea that an artifact-rich site with a high percentage of artifacts related to tobacco use and food consumption are likely to have functioned as taverns, even if they were not named as such. This model has further supported other site analysis including the early nineteenth-century Sarah Boston site in Grafton, which documents a Native Nipmuc woman whose home site had such great quantities of food production goods and tobacco pipes that it likely functioned more like a tavern or gathering place for the local Nipmuc community than strictly a house site for Sarah and her family (Mrozowski et al. 2015).

In Boston, the most urban core of Massachusetts, archaeologists have surveyed multiple tavern sites. The archaeological assemblages of the Three Cranes Tavern in the Charlestown neighborhood of Boston and Pierpont Tavern in the Roxbury neighborhood (both once their own independent towns) represent two different aspects of this urban/rural divide. The Three Cranes Tavern (which included portions of the 1629 Winthrop Great House) was located in the heart of the town of Charlestown, a moments' walk from Charlestown's town dock, and within sight of Boston. The Pierpont, however, was located on the edge of the town of Roxbury, today a bustling urban center within Boston. While neither tavern was the only establishment in the respective towns, the Three Cranes Tavern catered to wealthier clients within an urban setting (Gallagher et al. 1994b) whereas the Pierpont was located adjacent to an industrial area and frequented by laborers (Bower et al. 1987).

Running a tavern was considered one of the more respectable occupations for single or widowed women in eighteenth-century Massachusetts. At the Three Cranes, Mary Nowell Winslow Long inherited the tavern from her husband, John Long, when he died in 1683 and continued to own it until 1730, supported by an unnamed enslaved Black girl, Mary's mother-in-law, and at least four of Mary's children. Mr. Long's probate record includes a room-by-room inventory of the tavern, which provides a description of the layout of the institution: a large low room with tables, benches, and carpets known as a "hall" with an adjoining kitchen with a bar. Above the hall was a large bedroom with an additional two chambers accessible via a staircase in the kitchen. It is unclear how many of the rooms in the building were rented out (Gallagher et al. 1994b).

The tavern, still in operation under a different owner, burned in 1775 during the Battle of Bunker Hill. The residents of Charlestown voted to leave the place where the tavern once stood undeveloped indefinitely until it became an ideal location through which to place a highway tunnel during Boston's

Big Dig. Although they expected a much larger intact deposit, archaeologists excavated 228 square meters of the property finding 193 individual features, including five privies, multiple trash pits, and foundations of the original Long Ordinary (later Three Cranes Tavern) and the John Winthrop Great House foundations (Gallagher et al. 1994b).

While one privy at the site dated to the late seventeenth century, the other four spanned the mid-eighteenth century and one was clearly in use during the 1775 battle based on the burned and collapsed wood elements at the top of the privy deposit. The privies ranged in size and artifact assemblage quantities, but in general reflected a stable socioeconomic profile of their clientele (Gallagher et al. 1994b). In total, the archaeologists recovered 38,767 artifacts from the privies among a total assemblage of over 108,000 artifacts. Their analysis revealed that the privies at the Three Cranes contained better quality glassware and ceramics, including porcelain and a relative lack of dram glasses, than the items found in the deposits associated with the Long living quarters. This coupled with the large quantities of tobacco pipes, glassware, and serving ceramics all fit the tavern model first presented by Bragdon. In fact, the quality of the vessels found at the tavern suggested to the archaeologists that the Three Cranes Tavern attracted a wealthier clientele, perhaps the visiting and resident merchant class of the bustling harbor town adjacent to Boston, with the authors concluding that the Three Cranes Tavern was a "socially acceptable public substitute for an elegant private home" (Gallagher et al. 1994b, 185).

In Roxbury, a team of archaeologists from the Museum of Afro-American History (today the Museum of African American History) led the data recovery surveys of multiple archaeological sites along the eventually abandoned southwest corridor highway project. On the outskirts of "downtown" Roxbury about a half mile west of today's Dudley Square stood the Pierpont Homestead. Ebenezer Pierpont purchased the property in 1733, and his grandson inherited the house, converting it into a tavern in 1762. In 1788, the tavern closed but was soon reopened as the Williams Tavern in 1803 for a brief four years. In 1980, the archaeologists working on the project excavated a 3 percent sample of the property totaling 170 square meters uncovering a small stone-lined square structure that may have been a privy at one point (Bower et al. 1987). It contained a single depositional episode of artifacts including 194 ceramic and glass vessels. Analysis of the artifacts revealed that many of them were particularly incomplete, a relatively uncommon occurrence in privies where much or most of the fragments of a vessel tend to be thrown out together. The archaeologists concluded that the contents of the feature represented redeposited sheet midden on the site that had been gathered together and dumped into the stone-lined hole. The ceramics indicated a 1780s date for the deposit, which coincided nicely with the 1788 closing of the Pierpont Tavern and likely represented a cleaning episode at the end of the Pierpont occupation. A nearby feature dated to the later Williams Tavern (1803–1807). The comparison of these two features provides significant insights into later eighteenth-century tavern practices (Bower et al. 1987).

As discussed earlier, there was an increase in the consumption of rum during the eighteenth century that coincided with a negative impression on both those who drank and served it. There was a shift in the eighteenth century, especially after the Revolution, toward taverns functioning as primarily drinking establishments with the bifurcation of the once united services into the separate establishments of inns and bars. The glass and ceramics in the possible privy, the earlier Pierpont Tavern deposit, represented a higher percentage of kitchen, storage, and tableware (50 percent) than drinking vessels (25.8 percent) whereas the Williams Tavern deposit had fewer kitchen and tablewares (39.1 percent) and more drinking vessels (39.7 percent) supporting changes in activities over the mid-to-late eighteenth century. Finally, the dram glass, a predominantly rum-drinking vessel, accounted for 44.4 percent of the wine glasses in the Pierpont deposit and 85.7 percent at the Williams Tavern, further supporting the decreasing respectability of the Roxbury establishment as it became predominantly a place to consume alcohol (Bower et al. 1987).

Overall, the archaeology of eighteenth-century taverns shows that the urban-rural divide, the domestic-public spheres, and the differences between wealthy and poor are not always directly comparable due to the many factors that influence what makes it to the archaeological record. These tavern sites reflect the transitions not only of people across landscapes, but the broad differences between rural and urban spaces. On a smaller scale, domestic sites provide an opportunity to explore the complex and nuanced variability between urban and rural, as well as the impacts of globalization on the day-to-day lives of people at home.

The Domestic Sphere

Residents of eighteenth-century Massachusetts experienced rapid cultural changes at home as the area pivoted away from its Puritanical foundations. This switch was in part an effect of the influence of globalization on domestic tastes and the rise of gentility, but the decrease in Puritanical world views also increased the rate at which globalization and the influence of the outside world took effect. One of the major changes to occur this time is the transition from communalism to individualism. In the seventeenth century, Governor Winthrop's famous "Dreams of a City on a Hill" (1630) speech referred to the Puritans as "Members of the same body," threatened the colonists with jail time if they did not work together, and later called for town-wide fasts for Boston when crops performed poorly (Winthrop 1908). Deetz (1977) would study how the transition for this "body" to the individual was reflected in Boston-area architecture, dining practices, and gravestones.

In homes, Deetz demonstrated how the layout of early colonial homes transitioned from "hall and parlor" design with large rooms with many shared purposes such as dining, sleeping, and cooking in the same space to "Georgian" architecture where individual rooms had a more specific use such as dining rooms, bedrooms, and parlors (Deetz 1977). In dining practices, there was a clear switch from communal serving and food dishes (discussed in greater detail below) to individual dining settings and specialized wares (Deetz 1977). Lastly, the iconic slate gravestones that are seen throughout Massachusetts transition from skull designs to cherub and later willow and urn designs (Deetz 1977). Deetz interpreted these artistic styles to reflect the move from an emphasis on the universality of death (skull) to the individuality of the person and their soul (cherub), and then sentimentality and remembrance of an individual (urn and willow) (Deetz 1977).

As populations grew and wealth created greater economic disparity among neighbors, the spread of the availability of goods and ideas into the rural sphere somewhat blurred the differences between urban and rural home life and were instead replaced by the visible manifestation of a new social order: gentility. Gentility is a world view that "defined codes of proper behavior and imbued them with moral connotations" (Fitts 1999, 39). It was a necessary requirement for those who wanted to participate in the middle class and above, and was actively learned, taught, and enforced by within families (Fittz 1999).

Archaeological study of eighteenth-century Massachusetts home life in multiple settings in frontier spaces has been quite limited in central and western portions of the state, although the study of multiple historical house museums and sites across eastern Massachusetts has provided a strong foundation of data upon which to study the role of gentility at home.

Merchants in Boston and other shoreline cities were still heavily influenced by English and European trends of the early 1700s, especially luxury goods, which were still typically produced outside of the colonies (Cooke 2019). This naturally expanded consumerism (an emphasis on the acquisition of in-demand goods) and commercialism (the act of creating and expanding the demand for goods) with a pronounced visibility in the material archaeological record. As the wealthy adopted these new items and practices, these cultural brokers were able to translate the styles and new practices of the wealthy of Europe to Massachusetts through the introduction of new goods and ideas (Goodwin 1999). The colonies did not have the English birthright establishment of elite social status, wealth, and large landholdings. This created an opportunity for social mobility to the colonists that was not as present in England, because with enough resources, one could enter the elite class simply by acting the part. The emergence of the Georgian worldview (Deetz 1977) shifted a communal social organization to a more structured and hierarchical order resulting in stronger reflections of class, wealth, and consumer behavior. The mechanism for establishing that one had moved into or was living in an elite class in the colonies became gentility, the active and aspirational process of buying goods similar to their wealthy European counterparts, emulating cultural practices of the European elite, maintaining the awareness of new trends, and responding accordingly with the purchase of newer goods (Goodwin 1999; Hunter 2001; Kosack 2010).

Deetz's work on the communal aspects of early dining and its transition in the eighteenth century are a seminal part of early historical research (Deetz 1977). His work focused on the interaction of people with food, dining artifacts, and the spaces where these activities occurred. Deetz (1977) saw the hearth as the physical and social center of the home, around which cooking and dining took place in a communal and cooperative shared space. The dining space was egalitarian and servants, family members, and visitors all ate together, reflecting the seventeenth-century relative lack of social hierarchy. Deetz expanded on this to show that social structures within the seventeenth century were based more on functions than hierarchies (1977).

The Georgian worldview was a shift toward formality and structure with an emphasis on hierarchy. Deetz (1977) saw this reflected in homes through symmetry and dedicated kitchen and dining spaces. At the dining table, with its wealth of material culture, the shift toward structure and hierarchy came in the form of individual dining sets and servings for each person (Deetz 1977). Finally, dining became somewhat performative in the sense that while eating, the materials on the table and the food itself provided

opportunities to display wealth through the quality of the foods and serving wares as well as through the performance of refined rituals such as tea
consumption (Deetz 1977). Even the concept of the "head of the table"
arose out of the Georgian worldview as the physical location of a person
within the landscape of the dining table came to represent hierarchy and
status (Deetz 1977).

In the early eighteenth century, only the wealthiest residents of Massachusetts, usually merchants in major cities like Boston, were in a position
to be exposed to elite practices through their travels and interactions with
fashionable people from or in England, and were able to purchase actual
guidebooks and publications that instructed upwardly mobile hopefuls in
the latest practices of child rearing, domestic duties, public office, and religion (Bushman 1992; Goodwin 1999). In the following decades, these practices became established and highly visible among the Massachusetts elite,
spreading further to those with expendable income in cities as well as more
rural areas among individuals who had exposure to urban elites, including
lawyers, ministers, and doctors (Boushman 1992; Carson 1994; Dow 1935).
This also occurred in western Massachusetts where Paynter (1982) showed
that emergent elites in the Connecticut Valley created spaces that appeared
less peripheral and more core-like as they accumulated wealth.

The direct connection between material goods and gentility provides
an ideal lens through which Massachusetts archaeologists have studied
eighteenth-century domestic archaeological sites. Classes of artifacts that
are most discussed by archaeologists in the study of gentility are the artifacts
associated with the tea ceremony, the presence and absence of porcelain, and
artifacts associated with personal adornment (for example, buttons, jewelry,
clothing, hair decorations, etc.).

Tea and Gentility

Tea, coffee, and chocolate drinking all appeared in Europe roughly at the same
time in the mid-seventeenth century, and the triumvirate of liquid practices
made their way to New England by the 1690s. Tea, however, a Chinese export,
had the greatest cultural impact of the three in the eighteenth century. Coffee,
at first, was the most popular of the three and was seen as a public drink,
done in the tavern, with tea serving more medicinal purposes and drank in
a home setting. Tea was an expensive import, and the vessels associated with
it, which began as finely potted Chinese porcelain vessels, were extremely
expensive and difficult to replace if broken. Thus, the accoutrements of the
tea service (tea, tea drinking, and the tea service) became associated with

the new urban coastal elite class who were the only ones who could afford and have ready access to it (Roth 1961).

By the early eighteenth century, tea was still relatively uncommon. Judge Samuel Sewall made detailed recordings of daily life among the Boston elite in the early eighteenth century and only mentions tea once. By the mid-eighteenth century, however, tea became widely available, and it made frequent appearances in the logs of foreign travelers who also made comparisons to its heavy use in England (Roth 1961).

Of greatest impact to the archaeological record in Massachusetts was the ritual of the tea ceremony, which involved the introduction of a brand-new set of ceramic forms and cultural practices in most households. Tea required storage, often in tea canisters, steeping in pots, serving in tea bowls and saucers (teacups with handles were not yet introduced), and related dishes and furniture including sugar holders, waste bowls, creamers, tea tables, and table coverings.

The ritual of the tea ceremony included the gathering of individuals at a table often set specifically for the drinking of tea, the arrangement of the proper vessels, the making of the tea in the teapot, serving the tea, drinking the tea, and the socializing that occurred before, during, and after the ceremony. Gentility in the eighteenth century was not just about having and doing new things, but the performative nature and ritualism of the actions. For example, tea was not about the creating and drinking the new tea product, but the bodily control necessary to perform the tea ceremony, before an audience, using hot liquids and fragile ceramics, coupled with the delicate action of lifting the small bowls of tea with a thumb on the foot ring of the tea bowl and finger on the rim, drinking the tea, and returning the ceramics to the table, all of which required a level of slowness, care, and precision. These acts stood in stark contrast to the seventeenth-century communal aspects of dining (Deetz 1977) where foods were often stew-like meals served in limited communal bowls or trenchers, doled out into smaller bowls to be eaten almost exclusively with spoons, and consumed with a side of handheld bread (Cummings 1964; Kosack 2010; McCracken 1982).

The spread of ideas of gentility tended to flow east to west as books and ideas would enter the ports along the shore and then transmit through people and trade first into the port cities and then out into rural areas to the west (Cooke 2019). Because of this, there is an opportunity in archaeological research to examine both how this spread occurs as well as how it is modified and expressed in material culture as one explores sites further away from main cities and ports.

The Rev. John Hancock House Site

Reverend John Hancock lived in Lexington with his family from the end of the seventeenth century to 1752. Roland Robbins first excavated the Hancock-Clarke House site using a grid documenting five building cellars at the property. Later, UMass Boston's Fiske Center for Archaeological Research conducted a re-cataloging project in 2008 and 2009 for the Robbins artifacts following a 2007 restoration of the house by the Lexington Historical Society (Beranek and Kosack 2009). In her 2010 master's thesis, Katie Kosack (2010) reexamined the ceramic artifacts from the site in order to determine how they reflect Hancock's status in the Lexington community.

As a minister, Hancock's early eighteenth-century home was located at a cultural crossroads between public and private space. Ministers were often the most educated members of a rural community, though their status declined in the early eighteenth century as the Great Awakening caused some to question the cultural and political dominance of Puritan ministers, leading many eighteenth-century ministers to become poorly paid and less pivotal as their status declined. Despite this, they were still key members of their community, especially in rural communities, with frequent social visitors, and their home would have served as an alternative, more intimate meeting space than the nearby meetinghouse and a more refined location than a tavern (Kosack 2010).

Just twenty miles from Boston, Lexington was a small farming community that had grown large enough to support its own church and later the formal charter of the town in 1713. As a rural mostly farming community, there was little economic division within the town. While Lexington ministers were in the extreme minority, they averaged over twice the estate value of the farmers in the town (Kosack 2010; Main 1989).

As both a rural and relatively poor town, Lexington's residents would have had little access to tea wares and other luxury goods including porcelain and paintings in the early eighteenth century. This is clearly reflected in probate records, which have no recorded tea ware, porcelain/China, or portraits for any Lexington residents in the first quarter of the eighteenth century and just 3 percent of residences had these items by the mid-eighteenth century (Fuhrer 2004). The mere presence of tea wares in Lexington would have been a visible and culturally significant rarity.

Despite the relatively lower status of ministers in the eighteenth century, John Hancock was still from a relatively wealthy family and his pay made him fundamentally wealthier than his farmer neighbors allowing him to be the first Lexington resident to send their son to Harvard—which he did twice (Kosack 2010). The rural, elite status of the Hancock household was visible in the family's material goods. Kosack focused her analysis on the ceramics in the early eighteenth-century foundation features at the site finding that 68 percent of the vessels on the property were redware, an inexpensive domestically made ceramic type associated with food production, storage, and farming activities, indicating that the Hancock family produced their own food, and that John remained a part-time farmer in order to support his family's food needs. The presence of a North Devon plate and two Staffordshire slip-ware posset pots, all communal dining vessels, reflected a hold-over activity of the seventeenth-century communal dining practices in this transitional period. However, the site also contained a large quantity of mugs (fifteen), four of which were refined white salt-glazed and Nottingham stoneware type vessels and were more expensive than their redware and tin-glazed counterparts. The household assemblage also included twenty-four tin-glazed vessels (12 percent of the vessels), which were a Dutch and English pottery attempt to create ceramics that were porcelain-looking with white glazing and Chinese-style painting (Kosack 2010).

Most significant, however, were the presences of a Nottingham stoneware tea service slop or waste bowl, two dipped white salt-glazed teapots, and the ultimate ceramic status symbol: at least nine porcelain vessels including a bowl, tea bowls, and saucers representing at least two matched saucer sets. Kosack's analysis concludes that though the Rev. John Hancock was not able to achieve elite status in comparison to others in more urban areas, he demonstrated to his many visitors at his home that despite being middle class by economic status, he was aspirationally elite by material status, which embodied a relatively high status. The Hancock family members were able to demonstrate their refinement and gentility in their entertaining abilities to their community members who did not have the same access to luxury goods (Kosack 2010).

The Tyng Mansion Site

Nearly twice the distance from Boston as Lexington, the archaeological assemblage from the Tyng family of Dunstable (portions of which are now Tyngsborough) represents another nuance of this cultural and economic transition period in Massachusetts. The Tyngs were a wealthy merchant family who made part of their income from the buying and selling of enslaved

Native Americans and Africans in the seventeenth and eighteenth century, though their overall wealth was due to broader merchant activities and the products of their 6,000 acres of land along the Merrimack River.

Their property included two Tyng homes, the first built in the late seventeenth century and the second built in 1720 by Eleazer Tyng after he inherited the property. Eleazer Tyng was a merchant, town selectman, and representative of the General Court in Boston, which required his regular travel to and attendance in downtown Boston spaces. As a very wealthy family living in a very rural space, the Tyngs made many choices in their worldly possessions that left archaeological traces (Beranek 2007).

Prior to its burning in 1979, Boston University used the second Tyng mansion as a corporate education center. After the fire, the home was the site of multiple Boston University field surveys (Mrozowski 1980), a Boston University field school (Beaudry 1982), and a dissertation that included a complete catalog of all previous excavations (Beranek 2007).

Beranek's analysis (2007) approached the life and experiences of Eleazer Tyng from multiple types of material culture including his large Georgian house, a 1772 portrait painted of Tyng by John Singleton Copley in the collection of the National Gallery of Art, and domestic artifacts including dining wares and personal adornment (Beranek 2007).

The Tyng mansion was a massive Georgian-style home, built near the site of his father's home, which he had torn down. Beranek (2007) interpreted the new home as Tyng's opportunity to define his own presence in the architectural landscape of his hometown, while making a visible statement of his wealth and style. These houses, especially of this scale and style, were exceedingly rare in rural Dunstable, though they were relatively commonplace among more elite residences in urban centers of Salem and Boston as well as the seven mansions of mid-eighteenth-century wealthy merchants along the Connecticut River Valley known as the Connecticut Valley "River Gods" (St. George 1988).

Beranek's analysis of the ceramic assemblage at the site explored the difference between the family's ability to access refined goods and the knowledge of their appropriate use and meaning. Whereas a wealthy rural resident may be able to access new stylish goods, without the accompanying exposure to elite and stylish practices and social settings, they may not be able to access the social status that mere possession does not provide. At the Tyng house, more than half of the ceramics were redware, less needed by the Tyng's urban counterparts who lacked the space and land to produce, process, and store many of their own goods. The remaining goods were of a more refined type.

Figure 3.1. Portrait of Eleazer Tyng, 1772, by John Singleton Copley (Gift of the Avalon Foundation, courtesy of the National Gallery of Art).

Beranek was able to demonstrate the availability of refined tea wares in local stores through store ledgers, but many rural residents could not easily afford these goods (Beranek 2007).

The Tyng's dining table would have looked different from their poorer rural neighbors; they had porcelain and porcelain-mimicking tin-glazed ceramics, and a lack of large serving dishes suggested the presence of expensive pewter serving dishes. Still, it would have looked different from their urban counterparts in that it had fewer overall refined ceramics than would be found in urban elite homes. Beranek's analysis emphasized the ability of rural elites to make choices in their refinement and outward appearances that their rural neighbors were unable to afford and that were socially unacceptable to their urban counterparts (Beranek 2007).

While Tyng's home was an ostentatious expression of his wealth, he made more nuanced choices in his formal portrait, studied by Beranek's as a type of documentary archaeology given that nearly all aspects of formal portraiture represent conscious meaningful choices made by the artist and the person depicted. In his 1772 portrait, Eleazer chose to be painted wearing a modest brownish work coat of perhaps-local fabric (it was important to own domestic produced goods immediately prior to the Revolution), out of style black socks, and seated on a simple country-style chair. This was countered with the inclusion of stylish knee buckles for his breeches and high-fashion cloth-covered buttons. Though the mere existence of a portrait by one of the most prominent (and expensive) portrait artists in Boston at the time makes it clear that, ultimately, the painting was a luxury item meant to impress, Tyng deliberately chose to represent himself in a more modest manner than his finances could have allowed (Beranek 2007).

Beranek coupled the styles represented in Tyng's portrait with the clothing-related artifacts found during the multiple surveys on the property. She found strong association of the artifacts with prominent English styles, including coat, waistcoat, and sleeve buttons, which would have made their way to urban centers and remain almost inaccessible to rural communities without seeing visitors or elites like Tyng bringing them to their community. Eleazer's button assemblage did not include any bone core buttons, which were a less expensive form of cloth-covered button and instead represented an upper-middle class style. His buckles, too, were of upper-middle range of costs, similar to his portrait in style. Though the typical association of class and expense for clothing at this time was in the fabric type and quality, not necessarily the buttons and buckles, this datum coupled with the portrait suggests that Tyng represented himself through style as a modest rural person who had political power and was able to express refinement in subtle aspects of his appearance (Beranek 2007).

The Spencer-Pierce-Little House Site

In Newburyport, north of Boston, Mary Beaudry explored the evolving occupants of the Spencer-Peirce-Little House (Beaudry 1995). The original brick house at the core of the structure was built around 1690 with significant additions added in 1797 (Beaudry 1998). The property represents a large (230 acre) farm owned and occupied by six families over three centuries and remains a living farm museum today (Beaudry 1995). The history of the property traces the history of the profitable working farm through the changing ownership and the owner's perceptions of the farm. The seventeenth-century owners treated the farm similar to a medieval manor with the primary farm production of tenant farmers contributing to the owners' profits (Beaudry 1995). The eighteenth-century owners maintained relatively outdated farm structures and landscape and built new components in a nearly outdated Georgian style that "was resonant of the time-honored gentility and deeply rooted traditions of the landed class of English gentry" (Beaudry 1995, 43). The later nineteenth-century owners were less wealthy but inherited a beneficial public perception of the property's stately status (Beaudry 1995).

The vast collections of the property represented primarily redeposited contents of privies and trash piles with sealed primary deposits including a privy. Though slightly later than other sites in this chapter, this privy was associated with the Boardman family occupants of the early nineteenth century (Beaudry 1995). In addition to the privy contents, Beaudry had the benefit of the Offin Boardman diary to supplement missing data in the archaeological record. Together, she was able to describe dining experiences at the Boardman home as large meals with invited kinfolk (his immediate family was estranged) and his minister (Beaudry 2013). The dining room was well furnished, as documented in probate inventories, and the meals were eaten on undecorated creamware tablewares with shell-edged pearlware serving vessels (Beaudry 2013). She notes that this table setting reflects a middle-class household, but the inventory of the family includes a large silver serving set (Beaudry 2013). With more specialized and customized drinking vessels, including one with a "B" monogram, Beaudry concludes that this modest tablescape reflected a "Yankee" frugality with hints of refinement (2013). Beaudry reflects on the lack of faunal data in the Boardman privy, noting that without the diary evidence from the Boardman occupancy describing dinners and meals, the ceramic and glassware fragments would provide limited insight into dining practices (Beaudry 2013, 197). The tens of thousands of ceramic and glassware fragments and reconstructed vessels from the privy would have remained relatively insufficient in revealing information about dining habits and the sensory experiences of diners.

Unfortunately, the "analytical backlog of monumental proportions" Beaudry noted (1995, 43) is still very much present. As of the writing of this text, the Spencer-Pierce-Little collection is temporarily stored in the repository at the City of Boston's Mary C. Beaudry Community Archaeology Center pending a future transfer to Historic New England's (the owner of the property) storage facility in Haverhill. The 250-box collection is in desperate need of reorganizing, rehousing, and a complete catalog. This monumental task would create new opportunities for significant reanalysis of this assemblage, including comparisons to post mid-1990s excavation data on similar sites and a reexamination of the collection through the lens of the seventeenth-century enslaved people on the property (Beaudry 1995).

Gentility and gentrification were not limited to the eighteenth century. Nineteenth-century industrialization and the increasing availability of cheap long-distance commodities pushed many people out of subsistence farming, but those who did not need to rely on agriculture for their livelihood could afford to maintain large landholdings away from Massachusetts's urban centers. Ebenezer Hinsdale Williams was one of these "gentleman farmers" who, with his wife, Anna, maintained a large house with manicured and landscaped yard spaces, a large barn and outbuildings, and expansive fields along the Connecticut River in Deerfield (Reinke and Paynter 1984). Today, the Ebenezer and Anna Williams House is owned by Historic Deerfield and is open to visitors as a house museum.

Williams was part of a wealthy Deerfield family but was born and raised outside Boston. His father was a doctor and gentleman farmer, as well as a charter member of the Massachusetts Society for the Promotion of Agriculture, a nineteenth-century group devoted to progressive ideas about farming. The family bought some of the best land in the village at a bend in the Deerfield River, and between 1816 and 1820 Ebenezer improved the existing house that was already there and moved his family to Deerfield. Williams had the capital to improve his property and maintained tenant farmers who paid taxes on the land as well as rent to Williams. He also hired farm laborers to manage his own agricultural land and household servants, some of whom lived in the upper back rooms of the house. Williams held positions in the town and church, was a member of numerous clubs, invested in banks, and died as one of the richest men in Franklin County.

Archaeological investigations conducted in the 1980s and 1990s by the University of Massachusetts Amherst recovered tens of thousands of artifacts and documented features including privies, buried land surfaces, and agricultural structures (Paynter 2001; Reinke and Paynter 1984). The analysis of the Williams's material wealth is also documented in an 1838 room-by-room probate inventory of more than 1,000 items. A comprehensive study of the archaeological materials and landscapes was developed into an archaeology of rural "improvement" as a way to investigate nineteenth-century capitalism, materialism, and society in rural Massachusetts (Lewis 2016). The Williams's interior and exterior buildings, the landscaped grounds, and agricultural fields and farm structures were intentionally created and ordered to display the family's wealth. Ebenezer also improved his property by employing many of the progressive farming techniques he and other elite gentleman farmers read about and discussed. Among those documented archaeologically were several large, cobbled manure storing and processing platforms called "stercoraries" that were placed near the livestock barn. These features were designed to efficiently process animal waste into fertilizer and to store it for use as needed, which improved efficiencies across the agricultural operation. This system required a greater labor force, however, so less wealthy subsistence farmers could not afford to implement.

The rural-urban divide across these Massachusetts sites reflects how the urban lifestyle was often seen as aspirational. Rural elites were able to both experience and transmit their social status between urban centers to rural spaces through the material culture they chose to adopt and display. The ability of residents in both spaces to buy and present these goods was dependent on a network of merchants and artisans to create and distribute them.

Artisans and Trade

In the 1970s and 80s when massive transportation projects triggered numerous large-scale excavations on the eastern shoreline of the Commonwealth, archaeologists were able to examine several coastal trade infrastructure sites that were directly involved in Massachusetts import and export. In Boston, the Big Dig project included excavations at Charlestown's 1630s Town Dock and Dry Dock (Gallagher et al. 1994a) and Boston's early eighteenth-century Long Wharf (Bower et al. 1983). Later excavations under Faneuil Hall by archaeologists from Lewis Burger, URS Corporation (now AECOM), and UMass Boston were able to document the massive quantities of fill used in the 1630s town dock upon which Faneuil Hall was built as well as the eighteenth-century wharves built there to support early trade (Alterman and Affleck 1999; Cassedy et al. 2013). Elsewhere, eighteenth-century wharf excavations took place in Newburyport (Faulkner et al. 1978), Beverly (King 1992), and Salem (Garman et al. 1998), among other locations.

These surveys collectively produced ample evidence of the reliance of the colonists who invested significant time and resources into the modification of the original shoreline in support of boat construction, loading, and unloading. Most significantly, the excavations at Charlestown's town dock demonstrated that the architectural style of the eighteenth-century wharves resembled the fine carpentry skills of wharf building that dated to Medieval London with other coastal towns having less sophisticated backfilled crib log construction seen elsewhere including the portions of Boston's Town Dock under Faneuil Hall (Gallagher et al. 1994a; Cassedy et al. 2013).

These wharves allowed for the transportation of goods and ideas into Massachusetts, but also the products of its many craftspeople to be distributed elsewhere in the colonies and beyond. The world of artisan labor increased dramatically in the eighteenth century, spurred on by the growth of domestic production of goods and greatly supported by enslaved laborers (Cooke 2019). In seventeenth-century Massachusetts, many raw materials including wood, iron, and foodstuffs were gathered and sold off as export items, but the transformation of raw materials into the production of finished goods made from these raw materials, excluding ships, was relatively slow to occur. Primarily, this change required the presence of skilled artisans who needed to be convinced to leave the stability of their existing production sites to move to the US where the demand for goods was massive, but abilities to produce goods from raw materials and transform them into finished products were greatly limited by the lack of infrastructure.

The production of early ceramics by local artisans was aided by the presence of a massive clay deposit left behind by the receding glacier, which created the Presumpscot Formation extending from the eastern half of Maine to Boston. Over centuries, rivers cut into glacial deposits exposing this clay, which was ideal for the production of redware pottery. Although the first documented European-born potter arrived in Charlestown in 1635, it was not until the early eighteenth century that the pottery industry in eastern Massachusetts took off, following the development of the necessary demand and infrastructure for pottery production. By 1770, there were 175 documented Euro-American potters who lived and worked in Massachusetts (Watkins 1950).

Parker-Harris Pottery Site

Potter Isaac Parker purchased a shoreline lot in Charlestown in 1714, where he soon married Grace Hall, and began their large family and pottery business. The Parkers were one of nearly forty potters living and working along Charlestown's shorelines, which were lined with pottery kilns and wharves

Figure 3.2. Chamber pot excavated from a privy at the Three Cranes Tavern in Charlestown featuring the swags and bar slip decoration typical of ceramics made in Charlestown including the Parker-Harris Pottery (Photo by the author).

that pumped out "Charlestownware," as the local redware was known, to clients from Nova Scotia to South Carolina (Gallagher et al. 1992).

Already a successful potter, Issac Parker yearned to create domestic stoneware. Stoneware production required clays and kilns that could withstand the necessary heat to allow salt glazing without melting the pots or the kiln, and the technical challenges meant that until the mid-eighteenth century, nobody successfully produced stoneware in the western hemisphere. Isaac contracted with James Duché, a Pennsylvania potter who had just produced the first American stoneware, to help Parker meet his goals. Unfortunately, Isaac died in 1742 before the operation could begin (Gallagher et al. 1992).

Grace continued where Isaac left off, securing the funds, expertise, materials, and fuel to successfully fire multiple kiln-loads of forty forms of domestically produced stoneware, one of the first people in the colonies to do so by 1745 (Gallagher et al. 1992). Grace, her son John, and their enslaved potters, Jack and Acton, continued to produce red earthenwares in the factory until Grace's death in 1755.

The Parkers were likely the most prominent producers of Charlestown-ware. It is clear from the artifacts recovered from the Parker pottery productions that distinct decorations including a "swags and bars" motif and a fish-scale like decoration appear to be popular choices of slipware decoration in the Parker-owned workshop of the mid-eighteenth century.

The potters of Charlestown became a focus of the archaeology of the Big Dig project as plans placed the proposed tunnel running parallel to the original shoreline of the town where its many former redware potters were concentrated. In total, the surveys targeted four potteries, successfully finding and conducting data recovery investigations at two: the Town Dock pottery and the more-productive Parker-Harris Pottery (Gallagher et al. 1992; Gallagher et al. 1994a).

While these surveys produced massive quantities of redwares and extensive background histories, like many of the Big Dig surveys, the time and resources available to their analysis were fundamentally limited. With the unfulfilled expectation that many of the collections would be further researched over time, the results of the analysis of the red earthenwares at the Parker site were minimal. Of the 48,940 artifacts recovered at the site, only 29,929 were deemed to have been found in "significant" proveniences. Of the 24,925 redware fragments recovered from the site, the analysis of the redwares included a sample of just 645 sherds (2.6 percent) for analysis with an additional ninety-one fragments included for vessel identifications. From this very limited analysis, the archaeologists were able to identify thirteen individual forms, and many examples of kiln furniture, wasters, and other pottery-related artifacts recovered from the intact portions of the site and nearby Three Cranes Tavern (Gallagher et al. 1992). Today, these collections remain relatively understudied at the City of Boston Archaeology Lab but likely represent a significant opportunity to study enslaved labor and the influences of West African or Caribbean influence on design motifs.

Elsewhere, other pottery sites were targeted for archaeological survey in the 1970s and 1980s, including the Daniel Bayley (1763–1799) potter of Newburyport during a large-scale survey of the area's industrial and maritime shoreline (Faulkner et al. 1978), the Ebenezer Morrison kiln (1775–1785) in the same town (Scarlett 1994), the Hews Pottery (1765–1810) of Weston (Elia 1989), and many others covered by the Charlestown surveys including Battery Powers (1736–1807) (Gallagher et al. 1994a).

The redwares of Massachusetts remain understudied. With the increasing ability to identify individual potters in eighteenth- and nineteenth-century

New England redwares, these often-dominant artifact types will be able to provide archaeologists with the dating resolution and trade data currently possible with English ceramics. Furthermore, many of these sites represent diverse histories that have been understudied. Despite Grace Parker's important role as a woman entrepreneur in eighteenth-century Charlestown, the report on the Parker redwares make no mention of the enslaved African American boy and man at Grace and Isaac's workshop, Jack and Acton, who were themselves likely responsible for producing at least some of these wares. As with so many archaeological projects done in the twentieth century and presented in this book, the Parker pottery assemblage deserves reanalysis and interpretation.

Pottery was by no means the sole product created by Massachusetts artisans of the eighteenth century. Other products include furniture, silver, textiles, clockmaking, glassmaking, and others. The archaeological record of these remarkable craftspeople is fundamentally limited by the impacts of development and justification for large-scale archaeological surveys to recover their associated data. Without academic interest, the majority of sites that archaeologists are able to study are decided by developers through the CRM process. This process also means that some significant archaeological sites are rightly avoided due to their significance, limiting the excavations and potential data revealed.

The John Carnes Pewterer Site

One artisan site that happened to be located in the right-of-way of the Big Dig project was the John Carnes site, the home and workshop of a brazier, a maker of pewter and brass goods who lived and worked there from 1726 until his death in 1760. In 1992, a team of archaeologists working for John Milner and Associates Inc. excavated twenty-four five-by-five-foot units in an area located between Faneuil Hall and Boston's North End ahead of the Big Dig tunnel in the location where Carnes's home and workshop were once located (Cook and Balicki 1998). Their goals were to document the preserved features and yard deposits of the eighteenth-century landscape of a combined domestic and artisan back lot.

Carnes was born in Boston in 1698. He was a domestically trained artisan who, with other artisans, helped a flourishing urban metropolis be self-sufficient. This need for self-sufficiency came in direct response to the limitations placed upon international trade by the Crown beginning in the seventeenth century (Cook and Balicki 1998).

Though pewter was commonplace in nearly every home and far from a luxury good, demand was great for Carnes's wares, making him quite wealthy and allowing him to financially support a large family with fourteen children, his large stone house, two tenements, a shop, and a twenty-by-twenty-foot warehouse. The Carnes household also included an unnamed enslaved old Black woman and an unnamed enslaved Black man who likely worked at the pewter workshop. Carnes was even able to send one of his sons to Harvard College paying the tuition with an assortment of dining utensils. This wealth produced by the locally trained Carnes demonstrates the ability for adult white men to move upward in class and society, a feature of colonial American experience for these individuals in the eighteenth century (Cook and Balicki 1998).

The results of the 1992 archaeological survey produced evidence of the structure of Carnes's twenty-by-twenty-foot warehouse, a surprising assemblage of pewter-related production goods including turning devices and soldering irons related to pewter, a notoriously absent artifact class on historical archaeological sites, as well as ample evidence of the Carnes family's relative wealth and gentility including personalized wine bottles, porcelain tea wares, and wig curlers. In fact, when Carnes died a few years before the Revolution, he was one of the wealthiest men in Boston (Cook and Balicki 1998).

Conclusions

Wealth and access to goods and ideas is an inherently unequal concept. In order for one person to be wealthy and to have the most of something, there must be a corresponding and typically larger group of people who have less. English colonialism too was an inherently imbalanced concept of the English seeing themselves as possessing the right to land and resources because they have the ability to displace others through power, occupy a space, and then defend that land from others, all justified with religion. In the next chapter, we will explore how this worldview led to the rise of globalism, commercialism, and gentility, but also for the creation and maintenance of the institution of chattel slavery.

While white men were the ones often benefiting most from economic opportunities brought on by globalization and expanding markets for goods, these men were not successful on their own. They were supported in no small part by their wives and family members, and the households and businesses of many wealthy Massachusetts men benefited from slavery. Prior to 1783, the economy of Massachusetts and the lives of its residents was deeply entangled in the unpaid labor of enslaved men, women, and children. As will be seen in the following chapter, Massachusetts's African American histories are not defined by the period during which people of color were not free. Their diverse individual and communal expressions of culture from the seventeenth century to the present are documented at places across the Commonwealth.

4

Enslavement, Freedom, and Black Identity

African, African American, and Black histories are integral parts of Massachusetts's history and the American experience. These histories begin with the arrival of enslaved Africans in the earliest days of Massachusetts's colonial settlement, carry through the American Revolution and the end of legal bondage, expand in the nineteenth century with the formation of Black institutions led by prominent civic and religious leaders, and continue to the present in the form of community-based archaeological studies.

In a place that celebrates and venerates its historical ties to revolution and liberty, stories of unfreedom have not been widely told and only recently have archaeologists focused on this topic. Bondage took many forms in Massachusetts and was not limited to Africans and African American people. Large numbers of New England's Indigenous population were captured and sold into slavery in the English colonies, the Caribbean, and even Europe years before the first stolen Africans arrived on Massachusetts shores (Hardesty 2019; Newell 2015). Nor was slavery limited to Boston and eastern Massachusetts. In the early eighteenth century, many of the most prominent landowners, merchants, judges, military leaders, and even ministers in western Massachusetts's Connecticut River Valley were enslavers (Romer 2005). Slavery was not officially abolished in Massachusetts until 1783, but many people of color remained unfree after that period, laboring as indentured servants or in other forms of coerced or forced servitude. Massachusetts remained entwined with American slavery long after it was outlawed there. Massachusetts's nineteenth-century textile mills were dependent on southern cotton and also manufactured fabrics that were used to clothe enslaved workers, and factories in Worcester County produced inexpensive shoes and palm-leaf hats that were shipped to southern plantation owners (Rockman 2024).

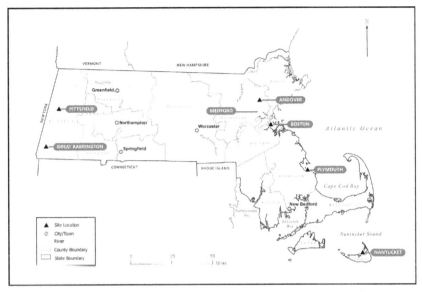

Map 4.1. Map of Massachusetts showing locations of sites discussed in Chapter 4.

To date, archaeologists have only investigated a few sites of enslavement in Massachusetts, most notably at the Boston-area Royall House discussed in detail below. The paucity of research may be due to a number of factors, including the low visibility of sites of bondage in the archaeological record. Unlike the highly structured plantation sites of the American mid-Atlantic and south, where large numbers of enslaved people lived in separate and distinct areas, most of those forced into bondage in seventeenth- and eighteenth-century New England lived and labored within white households in spaces that can be difficult to identify. Larger and more formalized sites of bondage in the northeastern United States have been identified on Long Island, New York, (Mrozowski et al. 2007; Mrozowski 2009; Trigg and Landon 2010) but to date similar sites have not been identified in Massachusetts. Future archaeological investigations at domestic sites can begin to address this disparity by developing research questions that seek to identify places of bondage. Careful analysis of historical records to seek out distinct cultural spaces and patterns in activity areas inside and around the home may help to define sites of unfreedom. Archaeologists can and should do more to bring the histories of slavery forward.

Free people of color experienced the impacts of bondage in different ways in the late eighteenth, nineteenth, and early twentieth centuries in Massachusetts. The case studies discussed in this chapter illustrate the ways in which African American and Black identity and community were maintained, transformed, and carried forward by formerly enslaved individuals and their descendants, and offer historical reminders of slavery's lasting legacy that make this history visible today.

The Origins of Massachusetts Slavery

Enslaved people were present in Massachusetts almost as soon as permanent settlement began. In 1637, Governor John Winthrop recorded the capture of more than 700 Pequot Indians during a conflict known as the Pequot War (Hardesty 2019; Newell 2015). In exchange for sending them to English plantations in the Caribbean, Massachusetts Bay received "cotton, tobacco, and negroes, etc." (Winthrop and Savage 1853, 305). The capture, transport, and sale of Native people was justified by the colonists who viewed them as combatants, but many households also held Indigenous people in indentured servitude. Many Native Americans sold into bondage were captured during seventeenth-century conflicts including the 1636–7 Pequot War and King Philip's War (see Chapter 5). Records indicate that Massachusetts Indians were sent to Africa, the Azores, and the Caribbean during this period, where descendants still live today (Hardesty 2018).

Massachusetts merchants were also heavily involved in the commodification of forced African labor. As early as 1644, Boston merchants were transporting slaves directly from Africa to the West Indies in what was known as the "carrying trade," moving humans as cargo for profit. Legislative records, merchant books, and letters document the presence of enslaved Africans in seventeenth-century settler homesteads and increasingly found as highly skilled unpaid laborers in the trades (Hardesty 2019). By the end of the seventeenth century, an estimated 800 enslaved persons were living in Massachusetts compared to approximately 16,000 in Virginia, however after 1700 that number began to expand in the growing urban centers and large-scale farms across Massachusetts. By the mid-eighteenth century, for example, Deerfield's population of 300 included twenty-one enslaved African Americans representing 7 percent of the total residents (Romer 2005, 98).

Massachusetts's involvement in the slave trade contributed to the development of American industrial capitalism and linked Massachusetts to

Figure 4.1. Photograph of Royall House *(left)* and Slave Quarters, Medford, Massachusetts (Photo by the author).

colonization efforts in other parts of the world, especially the Caribbean. Prior to the American Revolution, Massachusetts's most politically, socially, and economically powerful families developed connections to West Indian plantations that influenced the economy and culture of both places.

The Royall House

Isaac Royall Sr. was one of the wealthiest men in early eighteenth-century Massachusetts due to his active participation in the transatlantic Triangle Trade, including buying and selling African, Indian, and Afro-Indigenous individuals (Chan 2007). Born in New England, Royall Sr. raised a family and spent most of his life on the Caribbean island of Antigua where he owned a sugar plantation and rum distillery operated by a large work force of enslaved people. While still in the West Indies, Royall Sr. purchased three Massachusetts provisioning farms where at least thirteen enslaved people labored (Chan 2007). A slave uprising on the island led the Royall family to return to Massachusetts in 1737 where they settled at a 500-acre estate outside Boston in present-day Medford and became one of if not the largest slave-holding family in eighteenth-century Massachusetts (Chan 2007). Their three-story Georgian-style mansion house and landscaped yard spaces reflected design elements of their Caribbean plantation, but perhaps the most conspicuous inclusion was the construction of a free-standing "out kitchen" and slave quarters adjacent to and just behind the main house. This structure, now part of the Royall House and Slave Quarters house museum, is the only extant separate slave structure in the northern United States (https://royallhouse.org).

Boston University archaeologists Ricardo Elia and Alexandra Chan conducted excavations at the property between 1999 and 2001, and Chan published the results of the fieldwork, research, and analyses in *Slavery in the Age of Reason* (Chan 2007). Using documentary records, features, and artifacts, Chan tried to reconstruct the spatial and cultural landscapes of the site that were associated with the more than sixty enslaved people who lived on the property. Framing some of her analyses on comparisons between the Royall slave quarters and examples from southern plantations, Chan focused on trying to document the lived experiences of enslaved people who were present throughout Massachusetts at this time and whose histories are underrepresented in historical documents and archaeological sites.

Chan utilized the archaeological data to understand Black and white perspectives on the landscape interpreted through the lens of visibility and distance at the Royall estate. In Medford, the slave quarters were less than fifty feet from the Royall's mansion house, in a much closer physical relationship than that usually found at southern United States plantations. This meant that the enslaved people at the Royall House were more visible and observable to the Royalls and their neighbors and possibly under much more direct control by their enslavers (Fitts 1996). The patterning of artifacts and features indicated that the bulk of the work, construction, and waste-disposal activities carried out by enslaved people occurred in the side and back yards of the slave quarters which were out of sight of the main house, while the shared yard space between the two structures was swept clean and eventually cobbled (Chan 2007). The archaeological deposits indicate that the labor of enslaved people at the Royall House was intentionally hidden from the enslavers' (and their many guests') view, reinforcing the Royall's control over the physical landscape and those forced to labor there. At the same time, the back and side yard spaces were places where the enslaved could have some autonomy, social gatherings, private moments, and freedom to move about the landscape (Chan 2007). These private activities are documented by the presence of clay tobacco pipes, geometrical gaming pieces created from reworked ceramic sherds, and an expensive imported French faience plate that had broken into at least six pieces and been mended along visible seams with thick black tar. Chan noted that the latter object would certainly not have been used by the Royalls or their guests, but had likely been repaired by an enslaved person for use at mealtime in the slave quarters (Chan 2017).

Within the household artifact assemblage, 8,000 fragments representing 29 percent of the ceramic vessels were kitchen-related coarse earthenwares, reflecting the effort required to prepare and serve food for the more than thirty-seven Black and white residents. Chan observed that groups of women would likely have worked together in the kitchen and yard spaces to keep up with the demands of the residents, and afforded opportunities for creating and supporting social networks among the enslaved (Chan 2017).

Chan also interpreted African cultural elements in other objects found around the slave quarters. One of these was a stone flake worked into the shape of an arrowhead that had been notched at one end, possibly for suspension on a cord. Several of the enslaved individuals had names suggesting West African origins, and Chan found references to a traditional belief system that ascribed magical powers to prehistoric projectile points called *Nyame akuma*, or "god's axes," thought to bring or produce good luck to the holder (Ward 1958). Similar examples have been identified at southern plantation sites where West Africans were enslaved (Puckett 1926; Wilkie 1995).

The Royall House investigations offer a model for the archaeological study of sites of enslavement and unfree labor in Massachusetts. These places have been difficult to identify because the majority of those held in bondage did not occupy distinctly separate spaces from their enslavers and were not present in large numbers at most colonial sites. Chan's focus on identifying and interpreting the physical and material landscape, including work areas, may be an effective way to pinpoint sites of unfree labor at domestic sites. Thorough records research coupled with careful artifact analyses may allow Massachusetts archaeologists to discern African, African American, and Native American cultural elements that document unfree labor within an otherwise typical colonial site. As more of these places are rediscovered, the full extent of Massachusetts's role in the history of American slavery can be better understood and reckoned with.

Expressions of Black Identity

Although Massachusetts officially abolished slavery in 1783, institutional racism continued to limit opportunities for many African-descendant and Black residents. Archaeological studies at early and mid-nineteenth-century Black homesites and communities offer an opportunity to examine how individuals and families defined themselves and their spaces, and how they negotiated their identity and freedom in a state that was becoming increasingly ethnically and culturally diverse. In the past, archaeology conducted at enslaved and free Black residential sites usually relied on comparative analyses of material remains to interpret how Black and white residents were similar and different (e.g., Bullen and Bullen 1945; see below). These studies often looked for distinctive African signatures at a site—objects like beads and ceramics of African origin; objects like talismans and gaming pieces made or repurposed in traditional African ways—as a way to demonstrate the continuity of African cultural heritage in a white-dominant world (see Bullen and Bullen 1945; Baker 1980 [below]; Chan 2007 [above]; Chireau 1997; Handler 1997; Wilkie 1997). More recently, African diaspora studies and cultural critique have pushed archaeologists to examine Black homesites differently (Douyard 2014; Martin 2017, 2018; Paynter and Battle-Baptiste 2019). One approach uses archaeology to investigate the concept of "homeplace" as a way to understand how personal and communal spaces were created and utilized (hooks 1990). In this way the material culture, structural features, and yard spaces of nineteenth-century Black households provide clues about how individuals and families reinforced their own individual, family, and community identities. Taking a broader look at the archaeology of Black sites and individuals within the white-dominant world of nineteenth-century Massachusetts also sheds light on the institutionalized racism that persisted long after slavery ended.

Lucy Foster

The Lucy Foster homesite in Andover was one of the first archaeological studies of a Black homesite in Massachusetts. Lucy was born in Boston in 1767 and by age four was living in the home of white residents Job and Hannah Foster, who also housed an indentured white girl named Sarah. She spent most of her life enslaved, but in 1815 at age forty-eight established her own homesite on a one-acre parcel down the road from the Fosters. Lucy lived primarily alone in her house for thirty years until her death in 1845 (Martin 2018).

In 1942, Adelaide Bullen, a Radcliffe and Harvard-trained anthropological archaeologist associated with the Robert S. Peabody Museum of Archaeology, identified a historic house foundation and associated artifacts during a survey with her husband on a nearby ancient Native archaeological site (Bullen and Bullen 1945). Bullen conducted extensive documentary research and a thorough analysis of the collections, revealing them to be associated with Lucy Foster. Interest in this site and its archaeological interpretation (and reinterpretation) have now spanned more than eighty years. The site represents a significant intersectionality as a place associated with both Black and women's history, and the early and significant contributions of Adelaide Bullen as a female in historical archaeology (Battle-Baptiste 2011). The excavations by Adelaide and her husband Ripley Bullen (a founding member of the Massachusetts Archaeological Society) were also significant because MAS members focused most of their attention on ancient Native American sites. The Bullens' 1943 excavations at the site that became known as "Black Lucy's Garden," documented the cellar hole, well, vegetable garden, and dump (Bullen and Bullen 1945). In 1980, Vernon Baker conducted a detailed analysis of the ceramics from the site (Baker 1980). More recent reviews of the historical and archaeological record of Lucy Foster attempt to understand how she lived in her own space as a single Black woman, an unusual circumstance in the early nineteenth century (Martin 2018).

Battle-Baptiste (2011) conducted a reexamination of the existing Foster collections through the lens of Black feminism and documented some of the biases that had clouded early site interpretations, including a belief that a Black woman living alone would have significantly fewer material goods than a white household or that of a single white woman in the same circumstances. Battle-Baptiste's analysis determined that there was an abundance and diversity in the material assemblage at the site. Like many Black women in post-emancipation Massachusetts, Lucy supported herself by performing domestic work in her home that included sewing, mending, tailoring, and/or laundering; activities that she almost certainly had performed regularly while enslaved in the Foster home. Work-related items from her homesite include pins, scissors, a thimble, and a large and varied collection of buttons. There was a large assemblage of kitchenwares, more than a third of which were tea wares (see below), including different patterns and types, along with a large number of plates, bowls, glasses, and serving wares.

Some of the earlier studies speculated about how Lucy Foster acquired these objects and from whom, and what the material types say about her consumer patterns and status as a free Black woman. The site provides an opportunity to understand a space that was occupied and organized by a woman who was not part of a larger family, and also by a woman of color. Her material world and homesite organization were reflections of her individual taste and self-perception, formed after spending most of her life unfree and in domestic spaces controlled by others (Battle-Baptiste 2011).

Lucy was also part of a community of free Black people who lived in Andover during the early nineteenth century (including Cato Freeman, whose homesite has also been investigated by archaeologists) (Mrozowski and White 1982; Rotenstein et al. 2000). The large number of tea and serving wares may suggest her home functioned as a gathering place, where other Black Andover residents or people traveling through town may have visited and/or boarded (Battle-Baptiste 2011). More than 160 pipe stem fragments were found around the cellar hole and yard, and while Lucy may certainly have smoked, the large number of fragments suggests that although she is recorded as living alone, Lucy may have been surrounded by members of the local community in a distinctly Black space (Martin 2018).

Parting Ways

A small African American community known as Parting Ways has many parallels to the Lucy Foster homesite. Beginning in 1779, members of the Quash/Quande, Turner, Goodwin, and Howe families, most of whom had been formerly enslaved, settled on an outlying parcel of town-owned land along the Plymouth/Kingston line that had previously been occupied by transient, poor white families. Some of the men, like Cato Howe, had served in the Continental Army during the Revolutionary War and been given their freedom in return for their service (Deetz 1996; Hutchins 2013). Even though the land was never owned by these families, subsequent generations remained on the property, the last leaving sometime in the early twentieth century, and the land has remained undeveloped ever since (Hutchins 2013).

James Deetz undertook excavations at the Turner and Quash homesteads between 1975 and 1978 on behalf of the Bicentennial Committee on Afro-American History. Deetz had recently begun the first professional archaeological study of Pilgrim homesteads and included the Parting Ways results in his book *In Small Things Forgotten* (1977), which became a standard text for decades of historical archaeology students. African diaspora studies were new to archaeologists and Deetz's original interpretations included speculation about the house size and configuration resembling an African form and the presence of five large reddish earthenware "tamarind jars" as local wares similar to those used in African cultural practices. Deetz revisited his work in a revised version of his book (1996) which contained a more nuanced view of the Parting Ways site. Research had determined that the Turner family moved into a house they had purchased from a white resident, so they had not designed or built the house. The jars that had been found at both home sites were found to more closely resemble molasses drip jars made in the West Indies than forms found in Africa, and that the vessels may have even been made there (Hutchins-Keim 2015). Archaeologists have built on Deetz' work and like the study of Lucy Foster's homesite, have viewed Parting Ways in the larger context of community.

The broader contextualization of the artifacts from the Quah and Turner homesteads allowed the large earthenware drop jars to be reinterpreted. Plato Turner was a day laborer and mariner, and records indicate that at least once he sailed to the Caribbean Island of Martinique on a ship that returned to Plymouth with rum, sugar, molasses, coffee, and cotton (Hutchins-Keim 2015, 136). Turner's work meant he was often at the docks in Plymouth where imported goods from all over the world were imported. Similar "tamarind jars" found at archaeological sites in Salem, Massachusetts and Portsmouth, New Hampshire were thought to represent an African American presence, however like Plymouth both of these places were coastal ports where regular shipments to and from the Caribbean occurred (Hutchins-Keim 2015, 132–3). The Parting Ways jars could have been brought from the Caribbean or bought by Turner from Plymouth's waterfront merchants. Jars with the same shape and color were found on the island of Guadeloupe (Hutchins-Keim 2015). Comparative analysis with the Parting Ways vessels using techniques like x-ray fluorescence (XRF) of the clay may definitively identify the origin of the Parting Ways jars and how they came to Plymouth. Either way, the reexamination of these artifacts connects Plato Turner to the wider world of labor and a maritime economy where white and Black Americans interacted with people from other parts of the world.

The Quash, Howe, and Goodwin families who built and bought homes at Parting Ways included members who had formerly been enslaved in the homes of elite Plymouth residents. Plato Turner and his wife, Rachel, were from Roxbury and Bridgewater, Massachusetts. In 1818, all four male heads of household were placed under guardianship, at the same time Plato Turner, Quamony Quash, and Cato Howe became eligible for military pensions, giving town officials control over their income. In the 1820s, their widows, Lucy Howe and Lettice Goodwin, and families were evicted for failing to maintain and improve the property (Hutchins-Keim 2018).

The families at Parting Ways were unusual in that the majority of Plymouth County's emancipated Black individuals continued to live in white households where many were unable to gain financial independence (Melish 1998 cited in Hutchins-Keim 2018, 92). For some of the families, Parting Ways may have been the first time they lived together under the same roof. Although the land was located on poor agricultural soil and well outside the town centers of Kingston and Plymouth, the Turner, Quash, Howe, and Goodwin families created their own small community that may have served as a gathering place for other free African Americans in the region. Thousands of artifacts were collected at the Turner homestead including a large number of serving wares. Some of the ceramics may have been left in the house by the former owner, who had operated a tavern there (Hutchins-Keim 2018). Like Lucy Foster's homestead, their presence also speaks to the community of Black neighbors and visitors who would have gathered as they passed near Parting Ways along major travel routes.

The most recent investigations at Parting Ways were completed as part of a CRM project in advance of a proposed town cemetery expansion (Kelly 2024). The study documented the Prince Goodwin house's filled cellar, collapsed brick and stone chimney, a possible barn or outbuilding, and collected a mixture of eighteenth- to early nineteenth-century domestic and structural debris that match the 1783 to 1824 occupation dates of the Goodwin family (Kelly 2024). The analysis of the house layout suggested that it may have faced inward toward the other homes in the community, which may indicate the intentional creation of a communal space shared by the four families (Kelly 2024). Like Lucy Foster's house, Parting Ways may have served as a social and cultural hub for nonresident members of the families who lived there, and for other Black community members with whom they worked and worshipped.

Domestic spaces were one place where Massachusetts's African American and Black residents came together (see also below), but by the early nineteenth century dedicated institutional buildings also served as meeting places where political, religious, educational, and social activities were organized by and for the Black community.

African Meeting House and Boston Abiel Smith School

Perhaps no historic building in Massachusetts symbolizes Black community and identity more than the three-story brick African Meeting House in Boston's Beacon Hill neighborhood. Built in 1806, the Meeting House, which is a National Historic Landmark, is the oldest American extant Black church building in the country and is located in the heart of Boston's nineteenth-century free Black community (Bower 1990). The adjacent 1835 Abiel Smith School is the oldest surviving public school built solely for the education of African American children. Both buildings are main locations of the Museum of African American History, part of the Boston African American National Historic Site, and components of Boston's Black Heritage Trail. This area was the focus of Black communal social, political, religious, and educational activity for much of the nineteenth century. The property was also the site of several Black-owned and operated businesses including Domingo Williams's catering business which operated out of the Meeting House basement.

The African Meeting House, Abiel Smith School, and the yard and public spaces surrounding them have been studied by archaeologists for more than fifty years (e.g., Bower 1977, 1986, 1990; Bower and Charles 1986; Bower et al. 1984; Bower and Rushing 1980; Dujnic 2005; Landon 1996; Mead 1995; Pendery and Mead 1999). Beginning in the mid-1970s, investigations were spurred by Boston activist, and politician Bryon Rushing, who also served as the Museum's first president, and provide some of the earliest and most effective examples of community-based archaeology in Massachusetts. The archaeology was designed, from the beginning, by Black community leaders to educate and inform the Boston and wider Massachusetts Black community about the rich heritage of African Americans in the Beacon Hill area. These efforts brought forth histories that had previously been told from a white perspective of privilege or had simply been ignored (Landon and Bulger 2013; Melish 1998; Paynter 2001). The influence of this community-based program, which introduced archaeology to Black schoolchildren from Boston's neighborhoods, serves as an example that can be applied nationwide for the goals of descendant community-based studies, and of engaging constituents in the interpretation of their shared past (Herbster and Heitert 2007).

The most recent archaeological investigations at the Meeting House, Abiel Smith School, and surrounding public spaces were completed by the University of Massachusetts Boston Fiske Center in collaboration with the Museum and collected more than 38,000 artifacts (including fragments of more than 2,000 ceramic vessels). The archaeologists have drawn on the results of earlier projects while incorporating specialized studies (for example, zooarchaeological, macrobotanical, archaeoentomological, pollen, and archaeoparisitological analyses) to address new research questions about Beacon Hill's Black community (Landon 2007; Landon and Beranek 2014; Landon and Bulger 2013).

The archaeology has focused on examining the ways in which Boston's nineteenth-century Black residents expressed their individual and collective freedoms through physical and social community building as expressions of antiracist activism (Landon and Bulger 2013). The Meeting House and Abiel Smith School represented the visible and public identity of Boston's Black community and activities at both buildings were intentionally organized to highlight the successful, moral, hardworking, politically engaged members. Very few liquor bottles or drinking vessels were identified in the dense trash middens around the Meeting House, indicating that temperance was likely an ideal that community members and the caterer Domingo Williams held strongly. Pharmaceutical artifacts mostly contained medicinal compounds obtained from a doctor or apothecary shop rather than the high alcohol and opiate-content patent medicines that were more common. Smoking pipes were also relatively uncommon at the Meeting House compared to similar communal sites, which suggests that this activity was not condoned (Landon and Bulger 2013).

The findings from these public spaces were compared to those from a contemporaneous privy at a Black residential rental property adjacent to the Meeting House. The feature contained similar small quantities of liquor bottles and pipes, and more pharmaceutical than patent medicine bottles which suggests that the residents practiced the same behaviors in private, perhaps because they were encouraged by their religious and social community leaders.

Nantucket

Black residents of Boston were not only present in urban spaces. On the island of Nantucket, a Black community formed known as "New Guinea," creating a safe space for the island's Black community. The earliest Black land ownership on Nantucket dates to the second half of the eighteenth century, but freed enslaved people began to form a community on the island with more than 400 deeds recorded with Black owners from 1750 to 1850 and more than 500 people living in New Guinea by 1840. Despite being free, the residents of New Guinea were still subject to racism and denied many basic rights, segregated from white society, and lacked political representation or voice. The community grew over time to include other ethnic groups who were marginalized from white society and classified as Black by white people who did not differentiate, including people of mixed races, Native Americans, Pacific Islanders, and others (Muehlbauer 2021).

Previous archaeological research has occurred prior to restoration work at two Nantucket sites owned by the Museum of African American History (which also owns the Boston properties discussed above): the African Meeting House (Beaudry and Berkland 2007; Berkland 1999) and the Boston-Higginbotham House (Lee and Landon 2017). Both structures are located on a parcel of land purchased by Seneca Boston in 1802. Seneca, a free Black man, and his wife Thankful Micah, a Wampanoag woman, built their home in 1774, and their descendants lived in the house until 1918. Florence Higginbotham, a Black woman, bought the residence and the Meeting House and lived there until the 1970s. After her death, her descendants sold both properties to the Museum.

The archaeological deposits at the house were well-stratified, represented all periods of the home's occupation, and artifact rich, especially in the yard surrounding the house. Women's activities were well-represented and helped tell the story about activities that went unrecorded (Landon and Bulger 2013; Cacchione 2019; Lee 2019). Black households headed by women reached a peak on Nantucket in 1850 after the whaling industry collapsed, forcing men to travel further and longer on voyages to earn a living.

Archaeologist Jared Muehlbauer took a broader approach to the origin and growth of the New Guinea community using historic maps, census data, and demographic data to the origin and growth of the community. His research showed that Black land ownership within New Guinea supported the community and helped Black people enhance their economic opportunities when low-paying maritime trade jobs weren't enough. It also had the important benefit of creating generational wealth that maintained the community for centuries. While nineteenth-century Massachusetts voting laws were not as restrictive as some parts of the country, residency, literacy, and property all helped to enfranchise Black voters. The community created a geographic Black space that belonged to the Black community and had power in numbers. This power could not be denied by the white residents of Nantucket. This safe space allowed for political organizing and action around important causes including education and abolition, which were supported by the community and manifested at the Abiel Smith School in Boston (Muehlbauer 2021).

Black-owned spaces included a dance hall, a second church, several boarding houses, shops, and stores. These served multiple functions, but they were all places to come together and build community support networks. Many Black people didn't have access to banks or traditional forms of lending, so mortgaging property with individuals was a way to obtain capital and to keep wealth within the Black community. Douyard (2014) found the same practice in Pittsfield with the Freeman and Burghardt households (see below). Property ownership and the ability to raise capital (though a mortgage or multiple property ownership) increased the opportunities for Black-owned businesses on Nantucket. Black men were listed as weavers, shoemakers, and blacksmiths, and they all had shops on their land.

Black women contributed to the economic success of maritime households by doing domestic work in and outside their own homes and taking in boarders. This was especially important on Nantucket where there were often migrant laborers. The presence of Black women taking care of migrant members of the community can be seen as a form of "social mothering" (Lee 2019, 92) where cohesion of community could be enhanced.

Within yards, these spaces on their own property meant more freedom to have gardens and raise livestock as food for family, community, and surplus to be sold for income. The archaeology at the home suggests that Thankful Micah might have farmed and stored food (Lee 2019). Individual ownership meant there were more private spaces where Black families could organize their own space and do things differently from others.

This sense of privacy, individualism, freedom, and agency extends into the home itself. The Higginbotham investigations revealed one family's material objects. Analysis of these personal items showed how the family had the autonomy to construct outward identities while maintaining private spaces that were not visible to white outsiders (Bulger 2013; Cachione 2018; Lee and Landon 2017).

The nearby Meeting House was built sometime around 1825 and served as a school, church, and community center for Nantucket's free Black community. These surveys documented significant landscape features, food remains, and evidence that the Meeting House was the geographic and social center of the New Guinea community. One of the more impactful findings of the excavations at the Meeting House was the front yard, where the archaeologists found almost no artifacts, but they did find a very compact earthen surface. Archaeologist Ellen Berkland identified this landscape as a swept yard, a feature found on sites of African descent elsewhere (Beaudry and Berkland 2007; Berkland 1999). Battle-Baptiste (2011) has further interpreted these yardscapes as outdoor community social spaces that functioned as extensions of indoor living spaces as defined by the cleaned and prepared areas.

The resistance of the Black community was a particularly dissonant experience during the American Revolution when white Patriots were using the language and symbolism of slavery as a tool to combat their experience of injustice. From her home in Boston, Phillis Wheatley wrote the following in 1778:

"With thine own hand conduct them and defend
And bring the dreadful contest to an end—
Forever grateful let them live to thee
And keep them ever Virtuous, brave, and free—
But how, presumptuous shall we hope to find
Divine acceptance with the Almighty mind—
While yet (O deed ungenerous!) they disgrace
And hold in bondage Africa's blameless race;
Let virtue reign—And those accord our prayers
Be victory ours, and generous freedom theirs."
    (Wheatley 1778)

Wheatley was born in Africa, kidnapped from her parents, and taken to Boston where she was sold and enslaved by the Wheatley family. In 1773, Wheatley was freed upon the death of her enslaver following the publication of her first book of poems. It would be another decade before Massachusetts would legally abolish slavery. Wheatley's poem captures the irony of the ongoing Revolution while slavery remained legal. She calls upon a god's defense of those fighting for freedom but calls out these same people for enslaving Black and Indigenous people, hoping for victory for one and freedom for the other.

Social Agency and Activism

Archaeological studies at the western Massachusetts homesites of two prominent nineteenth-century Black social activists provide opportunities to examine the kinship and community networks that supported these men. The Reverend Samuel Harrison (1818–1900) was a formerly enslaved man who was a minister, an army chaplain during the Civil War, and a prominent abolitionist whose published orations and autobiography document his extraordinary life. His home in Berkshire County in western Massachusetts has been preserved as a museum. William Edward Burghardt (W.E.B.) Du Bois (1868–1963) was born and raised in an ethnically diverse area of Great Barrington, Massachusetts, three years after slavery was abolished. As an adult, he was the cofounder of the National Association for the Advancement of Colored People, the first African American to receive a doctorate from Harvard University, the author of several books and an autobiography, and a lifelong outspoken advocate of civil and human rights.

Reverend Samuel Harrison Homesite

The Reverend Samuel Harrison purchased land and built a house in Pittsfield, in 1852. The Harrison family included thirteen children and his daughter, Lydia, and her husband lived on the property until the 1950s (Martin 2019). Born enslaved in 1818, Samuel Harrison and his mother were freed in New York City and moved to Philadelphia where he eventually married and operated a shoemaking shop while he completed his ministerial studies. After accepting the pastorate at the Second Congregational Church in Pittsfield, Harrison was occasionally transferred to temporary duty at other churches and also traveled frequently to lecture with the Freedman's Society and was away while serving as a military chaplain during the Civil War. Harrison was an outspoken abolitionist, writing and lecturing on the subject often (Harrison 1876, 1877). His autobiography was published just before his death (Harrison 1899).

Today the house is preserved as a museum whose mission is to educate the public about Harrison's life and philosophy and to better understand the Black history of the region (https://samuelharrison.org/). Unlike the isolated setting of the Lucy Foster site and Parting Ways (see Chapter 4), the Harrison homestead was located in a mixed-race, working-class neighborhood (Martin 2019). The residents all shared similar socioeconomic backgrounds rather than ethnicity.

Testing and excavation at the Harrison site in 2008 focused on the areas around the standing house, yard, and workshop at the rear of the National Register-listed property (Manning-Sterling 2012). The archaeological assemblage at the site reflects some signs of Harrison's professions: a small assemblage of shoe tacks and leather around his workshop and an absence of liquor bottles (Harrison's involvement in the temperance movement dovetailed with his ministerial duties). Despite his prominence and varied roles in life, the majority of the artifacts and features at the site document the lives of the Harrison women rather than Samuel. This is not surprising given that they spent much more time at the homestead than the minister did. Samuel's wife Ellen's occupation in the 1880 census was listed as "keeping house," a common entry for both white and Black women in the period. This designation covered a wide range of duties including purchasing food, preparing meals, cleaning, making and mending clothing, raising children, maintaining a house garden, and entertaining guests when Samuel was at home. The artifact assemblage reflects these activities and includes mason jars for canning and preserving, children's toys including marbles and doll parts, medicine bottles, glass cosmetic bottles, and utilitarian and decorative table and serving wares. Two of the Harrison children were recorded as dressmakers and needles, pins, buttons, and clothing fasteners were found at the site (Martin 2019). These materials document the personal "homeplace" of the Harrisons as a Black family but also identify it as a place where Black women carried out paid and unpaid labor for their own kin as well as other members of the community. In this sense, the Harrisons were like many other Black families who incorporated domestic workspaces into their homeplace (Martin 2019, 318).

W.E.B. Du Bois Boyhood Homesite

The five-acre W.E.B. Du Bois Boyhood Homesite in Great Barrington is a National Historic Site. Documentary and deed research (as well as Du Bois' own written family history) indicates that the property was occupied by the Burghardt family by at least 1820 in a house that may have been built by a family member even earlier. W.E.B. Du Bois' great or great-great-grandfather had been enslaved by Coonrad Burghardt, one of the first European settlers of Great Barrington, and the family may have settled part of or adjacent to Burghardt's lands. Their house likely stood in the same location as a later house based on the identification of several dateable foundation features and trash middens (Paynter et al. 2008). By 1870 two-year-old W.E.B. Du Bois was living on the homesite with a number of relatives and four members of a white family who were boarders. Members of the Burghardt family continued to live on the property which passed through maternal family members until the 1950s, an occupation spanning more than a century.

The site has been investigated by archaeologists since the 1980s and like the Andover and Plymouth sites discussed in Chapter 4, some of that work focused on what the artifacts could communicate about Black identity. Several seasons of field school survey at the site collected more than 31,000 artifacts, mostly around the remains of the house Du Bois lived in as a child and again as an adult (Paynter and Baptiste 2019). Like the Harrison Homesite, the material remains around the homesite say more about generations of Burghart woman than they do about the famous man who lived there. Du Bois's autobiography describes his relatives as engaged in a wide variety of professions including farm laborer, whitewasher, waiter, cook, maid, and barber—all common occupations for nineteenth and early twentieth-century Black Americans. Evidence of women's work is visible in the wide variety of food preparation, storage, and serving wares, the large number of sewing-related items, children's toys and writing slates, and personal items. The materials indicate that the Burghardts purchased mass-produced and marketed goods including ceramics, tinned foods, medicines, and beauty products and that some possessions were curated and passed on over generations while new items were brought into the household (Martin 2019; Paynter et al. 2008).

The Harrison and Du Bois sites were studied because of their association with historical figures, but they are only two of the many Black households in nineteenth-century Berkshire County. Many African Americans came to this part of Massachusetts to escape bondage in neighboring New York and Connecticut, which did not officially outlaw slavery until 1827 and 1848, respectively. Between 1810 and 1860, Great Barrington and Berkshire County had larger percentages of Black residents than the Commonwealth of Massachusetts as a whole (Paynter and Baptiste 2019). While several African American communities developed in rural areas, the majority of Black families lived in densely settled urban neighborhoods like the Harrisons. Additional research using census and land evidence records, family history, and community studies may help to identify more sites where individual households can be linked to one another through religious, social, and commercial ties. Public interest in the archaeology at the W.E.B. Du Bois Site has led to the creation of a walking trail and interpretive panels at the property, now owned and preserved by the University of Massachusetts, and ongoing and future studies may work to consider how African American history and archaeology can be interpreted and understood at the regional level (https://www.duboisnhs.org/). Early efforts at commemoration were met with resistance by the local community, some of it attributed to Du Bois's politics, which speaks to the challenges of recognizing minority groups in historical narratives (Paynter 2014).

Conclusions

Massachusetts takes great pride in being the birthplace of the Revolution, but in 1641 it was the first American colony to legalize the institution of slavery. Over the last century, archaeologists have devoted considerable energy to investigating sites associated with the fight for American independence (see Chapter 5) that tell one story of the struggle for freedom, but considerably less documenting the many sites of unfreedom that existed before and continued after the Revolution. Fortunately, Massachusetts contains many places that document African American and Black history, and an abundance of material culture that can help make visible a history that has gone under told and under celebrated.

In the early 2000s, Everett G. Tall Oak Weeden Jr. (now deceased), an Indigenous historian and descendant of the Wampanoag, Mashantucket Pequot, and Narragansett tribes, reestablished connections with people on the island of Bermuda who descended from captives stolen and transported there in bondage during King Philip's War (Deetz 2023). What began as a small outreach effort has grown over the years into a biannual gathering at the St. David's Reconnection Day where New England tribal members come together with their kin and other people of color in Bermuda. This reaffirmation of culture and Afro-Indigenous identity combats the historical erasure of forced relocation and enslavement of both Native American and African American individuals and families in the sixteenth and early seventeenth centuries. This legacy is not only obscured in Massachusetts history but also in Bermuda, where one of the only visible reminders is a seventeenth-century church cemetery with a section reserved for enslaved Africans and Native Americans (Deetz 2023). If descendants wish to engage in additional research, archaeologists may be able to identify some of the material culture that ties Massachusetts to Bermuda.

In 2023, a Community Preservation Act-funded project at Boston's Faneuil Hall was installed to create an exhibit on slavery in the city (City of Boston Archaeology 2023). This project was designed around the artifacts of enslavement recovered at archaeological sites across Boston and serves as a showcase for how historical archaeology is capable of supporting storytelling and new data on broad and significant issues like slavery. These artifacts are small parts of the story of resistance in Massachusetts and reflect a broader American experience of struggle against injustice and oppression.

5

War and Revolution

Conflicts can reshape towns, disperse communities, and alter history. In Massachusetts, the archaeological record of war ranges from a lone gunflint on Boston Common (Pendery 1988) to the devastation of the Three Cranes Tavern in Charlestown (Gallagher et al. 1994b). This chapter examines how historical archaeology has explored warfare and the American Revolution, uncovering new insights into these events.

Early Conflicts

King Philip's War (1675–1676), also known as Metacom's Rebellion, has historically been interpreted from a settler colonial perspective that depicts Indigenous communities as defeated and dissolved in its aftermath. Relative to population size, King Philip's War is considered the deadliest conflict in American history with thousands of Native and Euro-American settlers killed. Building tensions between the Massachusetts Bay and Plymouth colonists and Indigenous groups broke into a series of armed raids and retaliation after tentative alliances were broken (Brooks 2018). The colonial government responded by forcing entire Indigenous groups from their homelands north, south, and west of Boston into confined Native "Praying Towns" and to internment camps located on the Boston Harbor Islands (Brooks 2018; Delucia 2019; Seasholes et al. 2008). Thousands of Native people died on the exposed islands where a lack of food and shelter and foreign disease decimated entire kin groups. Many Indigenous people consider the actions of Massachusetts's leaders and residents during this period as cultural genocide and refer to the areas of confinement as concentration camps (Riley 2009; Tiernan 2018).

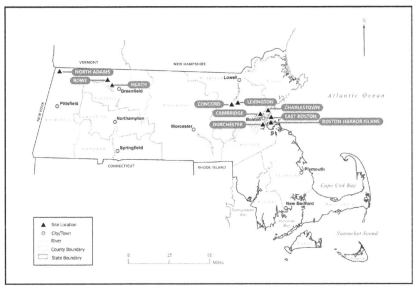

Map 5.1. Map of Massachusetts showing locations of sites discussed in Chapter 5.

In the early 1980s, archaeologists surveyed Deer and Long Islands in Boston Harbor for a proposed wastewater treatment plant (Ritchie et al. 1984).
This treatment plant would aid in cleanup efforts of Boston Harbor over the
next two decades. Both of these islands are known to have Massachuset
and other Native prisoners. The survey on Deer Island showed that the area
of potential development had been previously disturbed whereas the Long
Island project area had intact Native deposits. Archaeologists did not find
seventeenth-century Native burials in either space. Unfortunately, neither
the Massachuset nor Nipmuc were consulted in this project as they are not
federally recognized tribes. Collaborative work with the tribes today (see
Chapter 8) has shown that Native people would have likely objected to the
placement of a sewage treatment place on these islands, regardless of documented intact burials or intact archaeological deposits given their historical
connections to the atrocities committed on their people and the likelihood
that ancestors are buried nearby or within now-disturbed soils.

Recent historical scholarship (Brooks 2018; DeLucia 2019) has brought the
Indigenous history of King Philip's War to the forefront, and multidisciplinary
studies are combining traditional battlefield archaeology with eyewitness

accounts and historical records to document the movements of Native and Indigenous participants with a level of detail not previously thought possible. While largely centered around eastern Massachusetts, western Massachusetts communities were also scenes of violent encounters during King Philip's War. The National Park Service American Battlefield Protection Program, through a grant to the Town of Montague, has supported study at the Battle of Great Falls or Wissatinnewag-Peskeompskut. In the early morning hours of May 19, 1676, English residents from Hadley, Northampton, and Hatfield attacked the multi-tribal village area of Wissatinnewag on the Connecticut River in present-day Montague. The Peskeompskut Great Falls were an important fishing, gathering and ceremonial place for Indigenous groups including the Pocumtuck, Narragansett, Wampanoag, Nipmuc, Norrotuck, and Nonotuck. The colonists killed more than 200 Native people, most of whom were women and children. The English attackers retreated to Hatfield, and Native people pursued and fought as the English retreated. This deadly battle was one of the most significant in King Philip's War and signaled the beginning of the end of the conflict.

The Battle of Great Falls/Wissatinnewag-Peskeompskut archaeological project utilizes the KOCOA military terrain analysis system, which has typically been used to interpret dominant culture conflict archaeological sites, including the American Revolutionary and Civil Wars (McBride et al. 2016). The term is an acronym that stands for: Key terrain, Observation, and fields of fire, Cover and concealment, Obstacles, and Avenues of approach/withdrawal. For this phase of the project, archaeologists at the Mashantucket Pequot Museum and Research Center wanted to understand Native and Euro-American movements, tactics, and techniques. The team conducted extensive documentary, cartographic, and primary source research; consulted and partnered with the Narragansett Indian Tribe, Wampanoag Tribe of Gay Head (Aquinnah), Nipmuc Tribe, and Stockbridge-Munsee Community Band of Mohican Indians whose ancestors were among those attacked; collected tribal oral history; analyzed local artifact collections; conducted visual inspections and viewshed analyses; and completed limited excavation (McBride et al. 2016).

The project utilized a geographic information system (GIS) to identify and map areas of likely archaeological sites and landscape features, travel routes of attack and retreat, Native villages and camps, and the actual locations where fighting occurred. The study site area covered more than thirty square miles across several towns. The analyses determined that terrain and natural environment played a significant role in how the battle occurred, and that documenting the natural landscape across this large area was critical for understanding the Native American history and archaeology (McBride et al. 2016). This landscape-level approach to archaeological identification and documentation has advantages that can be relevant to nonmilitary sites. Although the built environment is entirely different than it was in 1675, geographic landforms such as hills, valleys, rock outcrops and streams are still present in many places and can be used to understand the setting of the battle and to reconstruct individual sites of engagement and activity (McBride et al. 2016). The results of the initial project will be used to guide future investigations consisting of metal detection, remote sensing, and survey and excavation, and to engage local stakeholder groups to help protect and preserve important sites and landscapes associated with the event (McBride et al. 2016).

Massachusetts's seventeenth-century defensive works were focused on the eastern coastline and major river drainages, but they weren't the only places that needed protection. During Queen Anne's War, English settlers built stockade walls, garrisons, and watchtowers to defend from French and Native fighters. These were burned in February of 1704. Three major forts were erected along Massachusetts's western boundary during King William's War, a short-lived conflict between 1744 and 1748 that ended with a short peace and then exploded into the Seven Years' War (1755–1763). Archaeological investigations at two of the three major defensive works produced important documentation of military structures that were built and used for less than ten years and were manned primarily by community members and their families. Fort Shirley in Heath and Fort Pelham in Rowe were first investigated in the 1970s and the results published several decades later after analyses were completed (Coe 2006). The briefly occupied forts had no evidence of Native artifacts or creations, but did contain an abundance of new European-made goods despite their remote locations. The remains of the third site, Fort Massachusetts in North Adams, sit under a parking lot. Smaller forts and garrison houses were placed between the major installations forming a "Line of Forts" from the Connecticut to New Hampshire boundaries to protect the Connecticut River Valley and the major English settlement areas lining the river from attack by the French and their Abenaki and Mohawk allies (Coe 2006). Massachusetts Royal Governor William Shirley ordered the defensive works to be built in 1744 and placed the elite merchants of the Connecticut River family "River Gods" in the region in charge of the project.

While the earlier conflicts in Massachusetts tended to be between colonists and Native people, that changed in the mid-eighteenth century. With the rising rebellion toward the Crown, Massachusetts took a more offensive approach to defending their rights as colonists. These acts would eventually lead to the American Revolution.

Historical Archaeology of the Revolutionary War in Massachusetts

Massachusetts was the location of many pivotal events that would ultimately lead to the outbreak of full warfare in the American Revolution. While this history is far too detailed to include in full here, a summarized narrative, below, provides context for the archaeological studies mentioned throughout. In response to resistance to a series of taxes and duties on the American colonies, King George III ordered British troops to Boston. In the fall of 1768, troops landed on Long Wharf and marched through the city in occupation (Nash 1979). Though troop leaders took private homes for their use, the majority of the troops camped on Boston Common prior to the events of the Battles of Lexington and Concord (Pendery 1988).

In 1986, then-Boston City Archaeologist Stephen Pendery (1988) conducted a broad survey of Boston Common ahead of a massive lighting installation project. Dividing the park into blocks delineated by paths, Pendery and his team of volunteers and short-term staff excavated shovel test pits and one-by-one-meter units everywhere a new light pole was to be installed (Pendery 1988). While the spacing between these excavations exceeded what would now be thought of as an adequate locational survey methodology, the team nevertheless found multiple archaeological sites that had survived years of park use and a massive revamping of the soils by the Olmsted Brothers company in the early twentieth century that disturbed the Common in most places to a depth of three feet (or so the Olmsted Brothers said) (Pendery 1988).

Fortunately, not all of the Olmsted excavations went according to design and the archaeologists were able to find a British troop occupation area near the Parkman Bandstand. This area was identified by the presence of three lead musket balls and six D-shaped Dutch spall gunflints of the type typically used by British troops during the Revolution, all within a small twenty-by-five-meter area (Pendery 1988). Only one other musket ball and five gunflints, most of the blade type, were recovered among all of the 68,525 artifacts found on Boston Common during the survey. A later survey by The Public Archaeology Laboratory in 2015 confirmed the integrity of the site and produced additional evidence of the encampment including a historic midden with white salt-glazed ceramics dating to the period of troop occupation (Bannister and Cherau 2015). These troops would remain camped on the Common from 1768 to Evacuation Day on March 17, 1776 (Nash 1979).

British troops camped on the Common lived there with their wives and families brought over from England. The gunflints and musket balls provide an ideal comparison to similar artifacts at Lexington and Concord as the British troops there came from the Common camps, though this analysis has not yet been done. On the Common, food presumably was prepared by the spouses of the soldiers. The presence of a dense, midden-like deposit with clear indications dating to the Siege of Boston may provide an opportunity to study the lives and actions of these women living remotely from their homes in hostile territory during one of the most intense periods of late eighteenth-century English culture (Bannister and Cherau 2015).

At 9 p.m. on April 18, 1775, around seven hundred troops left Boston Common "by sea" boarding boats on the western edge of the Common and rowing northwest up the Charles River to Cambridge where they began their march toward Lexington and Concord (Watters Wilkes 2016). The initial plan was to seize a rumored cache of weapons in the rural towns, destroy them, and return to Boston in order to prevent further uprising. However, tipped off to their departure, various riders left that evening on a quest to pre-warn local townspeople of the marching troops.

In a show of visible defiance, Captain John Parker and about eighty militiamen lined the road near Lexington's Common in parade formation (Watters Wilkes 2016). These men were part of the training band of Lexington, the rural equivalent of the Charlestown training band who would have mustered on their previously mentioned Training Field. As leaders from both sides yelled orders at their own troops, a shot rang out triggering gunfire (Watters Wilkes 2016). The well-trained Regulars fired multiple volleys as the militiamen fled, and then they charged with bayonets (Watters Wilkes 2016). At no point were either side ordered to fire by their leader. In the end, eight Lexington men were killed and ten wounded (Watters Wilkes 2016). Only one British regular was wounded.

After the Regulars reformed following the skirmish, they continued their march to Concord where the village was searched for weapons and goods that could support the rebellion. Meanwhile, Minutemen and militiamen from multiple towns gathered in Concord, confronting and outnumbering the Regulars. After another errant shot, the "shot heard 'round the world," the Battle of Lexington and Concord began (Watters Wilkes 2016). Outnumbered and unaware of the local landscape, the Regulars retreated the way they came back toward Boston (Watters Wilkes 2016).

Now numbering over 2,000, the local militia forces chased the Regulars back to Boston inflicting several casualties. One of these ambushes was led by John Parker, who had rallied his wounded troops and marched west toward the Regulars whom they did not know were now retreating (Watters Wilkes 2016). This event, known as "Parker's Revenge," was well recorded, but details did not survive of precisely where the event happened and how the events unfolded (Watters Wilkes 2016).

In 2013, archaeologist Margaret Watters Wilkes led the Parker's Revenge Archaeological Project (PRAP) on a multiyear research and survey project to document the location and events surrounding the event. This was a research project funded by the NPS, Lexington's Community Preservation Fund, and other history organizations. The PRAP was conducted as a collaborative venture between the Friends of Minute Man National Historical Park, Minute Man National Historical Park, the National Park Service Northeast Regional Archaeology Program, the Town of Lexington's Community Preservation Fund, the Lexington Minute Men and other living history experts, Save Our Heritage, the Civil War Trust's Campaign 1776 project, the American Revolution Institute of the Society of the Cincinnati and numerous local supporters. Watters Wilkes employed an innovative collaborative approach using lidar and geophysical survey techniques and teamed up with metal detectorists who were specially trained in survey and field methods on a broad twenty-five-acre field survey of the supposed area of the skirmish that ultimately led to a full reconstruction of the event (Watters Wilkes 2016).

Watters Wilkes was able to use the detectorists skills in differentiating between British and militia musket balls in order to identify which side fired any ammunition found in the survey area. Generally, the British musket balls were higher caliber and therefore heavier. Watters Wilkes was able to identify two concentrations of musket balls in the project area: a colonist cluster near a water seep at the base of a hill and a slightly more scattered assemblage of British musket balls along the slope of the hill (Watters Wilkes 2016).

This pattern coupled with detailed landscape study and historic research allowed for the reconstruction of the events surrounding Parker's Revenge. Parker's troops were stationed along a small finger ridge, just north of a stone outcrop that was believed to be Parker's hiding place prior to the survey. Watters Wilkes was further able to establish that light from behind the militiamen would have revealed their position from the top of the outcrop, and the outcrop would have been far harder to retreat from due to the steep drops and unfavorable topography. From here, the militia could see down Battle

Road at a bend, and there was an easy route to another potential ambush point if needed further down the road (Watters Wilkes 2016).

When the British arrived, they formed a three-hundred-meter-long parade of approximately 768 men marching eight-wide eastward to Boston. When they had crossed the nearby Nelson Bridge, an advanced guard or vanguard likely noticed the militiamen in the woods and advanced faster, turning to flank the minutemen and inadvertently lining up in front of the militiamen at the base of the hill in a seep. When they were around forty meters away and still flanking, the militia fired a single shot upon the vanguard embedding their musket balls (the ones that missed) into the ground of the seep. After firing, the militiamen turned and then fled uphill (Watters Wilkes 2016).

The vanguard stopped and returned fire at the slightly scattered fleeing militiamen, embedding their musket balls in a wider scatter upon the hillside above their position. The fleeing militiamen then headed east toward Bloody Bluff and Fisk Hill, the site of further battles during the British retreat back to Boston. (Watters Wilkes 2016)

Scared, tired, and injured, the still-large number of British troops continued to march east, sometimes at an unorganized run due to ambushes, until they reached a brigade of 1,000 supporting troops in Lexington where the battle ceased, seventeen hours after they began to assemble on the Common.

The combined 1,700 troops marched east and stayed north of the Charles River, ending up in Charlestown where they were able to rest, some for the first time in two days. Though there were relatively few casualties on both sides, the ability and willingness of the colonists to attack British regular forces and for them to fire upon colonists came as a shock to everyone and aided in gaining support for the rebels across multiple colonies as war appeared to be unavoidable. Public discussion at the time focused on the injustice of the British firing upon the colonists and deliberately suppressed the unknown nature of the origins of multiple first shots and emphasized the "innocence" of the American colonists (Nash 1979). Today, much of the western portions of the land where the events of the Battle of Lexington and Concord occurred are protected archaeological resources as part of the Minute Man National Historical Park.

The returning British troops in April 1775 faced a major problem: The angered and alerted militias around Boston had all marched toward Boston, effectively surrounding the city and preventing any British troops from leaving (Nash 1979). They were soon reinforced by rebels from neighboring states. There, the British Army was only able to be supplied by water, and the Massachusetts colonists had to rely on supplying themselves without their largest port.

In the eight weeks between the Battles of Lexington and Concord and the Battle of Bunker Hill, the British Army consolidated to Boston proper, abandoning Charlestown to the north and Dorchester to the south, and fortifying Roxbury neck, the only route by land to Boston, and building fortifications on all hills within the town and making Castle William on Castle Island in Boston Harbor a primary place of fortified refuge (Nash 1979). The relatively uninhabited Dorchester Neck (now South Boston) remained empty, and the people of Charlestown, seeing their proximity to potential conflict, fled, leaving the town mostly abandoned (Nash 1979).

The Siege of Boston

With the stalemate that accompanied the Siege of Boston, both sides began to focus on ways in which they could both repel any advances by their enemy and also increase the ability to advance themselves (Nash 1979). The western-most island in Boston Harbor, Castle Island, is today attached to the mainland of South Boston by a road but was formerly positioned in an ideal location at the transition between the inner and outer Boston Harbor (Nash 1979). Owned by the Commonwealth, the property has been the site of numerous archaeological surveys resulting in a detailed accounting of the evolution of its use and stories of its occupants.

As early as 1634, Royal Governor John Winthrop ordered a fortification on the island. Since then, it has remained one of the longest continually fortified sites in the US (Turnbaugh 1974). This early fort consists of a castle-like structure made of mud bricks and oyster shell lime mortar, which rapidly began to fail. With the support of local towns, the fort was expanded into a brick and wooden structure in 1644, named Castle William at the end of the seventeenth century, and rebuilt in the early eighteenth century with stone following a fire. By the mid-eighteenth century, Castle William was armed with one hundred cannons.

This heavy fortification allowed for the Royal leaders of the Massachusetts Bay Colony to both retreat to this location during the troubles ahead of the Revolution as well as to store significant and problematic items within its walls. The riots following the Stamp Act and later Boston Massacre prompted the fleeing of Royal leaders to the Castle and it was the chosen location to store the stamps when they finally arrived. During the Siege of Boston, the fort served as one of the safest places for loyalists and British troop leaders until they fled during Evacuation Day leaving the fort burned and the ammunition destroyed (Nash 1979). Not far from the location in Cambridge from which British Regulars departed boats on their way to Lexington, the American rebel forces began to build their own fortifications. In November 1775, George Washington, headquartered in Cambridge, ordered the construction of a series of forts along the Charles River that could prevent any advancing west from the far-superior marine forces of the British (Nash 1979).

Far from the largest construction during the war, Fort Washington was a modest fortification consisting of a half-circle earthwork ridge approximately ten feet high, with three openings cut through the ring for the placement of cannon (Davis 1975). In front of each of the four ring segments were four moats to further protect both the cannon and those behind the walls (Davis 1975).

Castle William and Fort Washington would have vastly different histories following the war, expanding multiple times (see below), and eventually becoming a large tourist and recreation destination, and the latter falling into disrepair and eventually becoming a modest city park. Despite these differences in use, scale, and later history, they both were caught up in the overall excitement and interest of the 300th anniversary of the Revolution in and around 1975 when many Revolution-era sites became the target of various levels of archaeological investigation.

Castle William, similar to Fort Washington's relative scale, received more attention with a large-scale survey, but due to its later renovations and expansions the project team could not focus exclusively on its Revolutionary history (Turnbaugh 1974). The Massachusetts Department of Conservation (now Department of Conservation and Recreation [DCR]) hired William Turnbaugh in 1974 as an archaeological consultant to survey what is now known as Fort Independence on Castle Island.

Upon the evacuation of the British in 1776, the fleeing Brits did not just burn the fort but used eighty-seven mines and bombs to blow it up (Turnbaugh 1974). Following the Revolution, George Washington took control of the fort and then levied a day's work upon every man in Boston to come to the site and clear the ruble. He then ordered the sunk British man-o-war, the *HMS Somerset*, to be looted, bringing the ship's twenty-one cannons to the island to replace the far larger number of weapons taken by the British when they left (Turnbaugh 1974). Washington made a garrison within the newly built fort, whose commanders included Paul Revere, John Hancock, and Samuel Adams. Fortunately for Boston and Castle Island, the city saw almost no military action for the rest of the Revolution (Turnbaugh 1974).

In 1972, the planting of several trees within the Fort Williams property revealed artifacts and the likelihood of a significantly well-preserved archaeological site on the property. In the year prior to the 1975 Bicentennial, a team of archaeologists including Quincy High School students and the Peabody Museum at Harvard excavated a series of two-by-four-foot trenches across visible features on the property. Frustratingly, though not unusual, the excavations revealed that period maps did not correlate well to the archaeological realities found in the ground (Turnbaugh 1974).

These earlier surveys first concluded that prior phases of the fort, including early seventeenth- and eighteenth-century deposits, features, and structures, were destroyed by later expansions and the blowing-up of the fort following the war (Turnbaugh 1974). Later surveys by The Public Archaeology Laboratory revealed primarily early nineteenth-century deposits (see below), but there was an area of potential earlier earthworks under the sixth and seventh casements on the southeast bastion of the current "star" fort. These survived as little more than small rises in topography under larger constructions, but the archaeologists concluded that the earlier four seventeenth-century forts may also survive in various areas of the property, which have yet to be surveyed (Stokinger and Moran 1978).

Buoyed by a sense of righteousness and their unexpected abilities, colonial forces began to take more aggressive action toward the British during the Siege of Boston. One month after Lexington and Concord, the surrounded British forces in the besieged Boston had only the resources available in Boston proper and the Harbor Islands, as well as whatever their ships could supply to feed and support what would be over a year of occupation. The rebels, knowing this reality, attempted to sabotage the troops by destroying crops and livestock, formerly their own, on the islands, in an attempt to force the British to leave.

Somewhat successful raids on Grape Island emboldened the rebels, and plans were made to sneak onto Noddle's Island, today part of East Boston, to kill hundreds of livestock and burn all stored hay (Mastone et al. 2011). Smoke from the initiating raid alerted the British, who sent the warship *Diana* up Chelsea Creek in order to be stationed near the likely rebel escape route at the shallow end of the island (Mastone et al. 2011). Two other warships, the *Cerberus* and the *Somerset,* set out to land troops on the islands to stop the raid (Mastone et al. 2011).

As over 150 British troops landed on Noddle's Island, the *Diana* found itself in a narrow inlet surrounded on three sides by a nearby shoreline rapidly filling with local armed rebels who began firing on the ship and its occupants. As the ships and fighters on both sides exchanged fire in a heated but slightly distanced battle, the lowering tide began to trap *Diana*, which was towed by longboats under constant fire from the shore until it reached deeper water. Next, it headed to the ferry dock in Chelsea at the mouth of Chelsea Creek where it again took fire, and the longboats fled. Untethered, *Diana* drifted into the shallow flats where, as night fell, the ship rolled onto its side. The troops on board abandoned ship and fled for the nearby *Britannia*, which recovered them and sailed to safer waters (Mastone et al. 2011).

Having managed to disable an approximately 150-foot British warship without their own boat, the rebels rushed to the abandoned ship, captured it, and plundered its cannon guns, money, and other supplies. At midnight, the ship was set afire and eventually exploded. Over the following months, local rebel forces continued to remove supplies from Noddle's Island without British recourse (Mastone et al. 2011).

In 2009, the National Parks Service coordinated with then-director of the Massachusetts Board of Underwater Archaeological Resources Vic Mastone who conducted a broad survey to reconstruct the details and battlefield boundaries of what had become known as the Battle of Chelsea Creek, the first naval engagement of the American Revolution (Mastone et al. 2011). The project also sought any new means to determine the precise location of the various landscape features that played pivotal roles in the Battle and also to attempt to determine where the *Diana* may have run aground and if that location retained archaeological integrity (Mastone et al. 2011).

Mastone and a team of underwater archaeologists from the University of Massachusetts Boston created a detailed GIS dataset of the specific timed events and locations of the events of the Battle (Mastone et al. 2011). They were also able to reconstruct the landscape of the area of the Battle, which had drastically changed due to massive filling episodes that resulted in Noddle's Island no longer being an island. One particularly transferable and effective technique was the use of historical topographical analysis to reconstruct the topography of the heavily modified landforms and reconstruct via viewshed analysis the sightlines and historical battleground area using documented events (Mastone et al. 2011). Today, many of the historical shoreline features are located dozens of meters inland from the shore due to filling, and there are significant topographical and structural changes to the battleground. This made the digital reconstructive visual analysis particularly valuable and otherwise unachievable even though physical access to the location of the event remained possible.

Though much of the battlefield had been disturbed or destroyed by development and dredging, their work documented three sites from the Battle where archaeological integrity may still be present including the ferry site where *Diana* was first fired upon, the mouth of the smaller creek where *Diana* fired upon by the retreating rebels, and the neck of Chelsea where another engagement with the *Diana* occurred from the shoreline. Most significantly, the team documented the area where the *Diana* likely ran aground, today within a filled-in industrial zone. While this filling may have impacted the shipwreck site and today makes survey of the area challenging, it is likely that without this fill, the frequent dredging of the river that has since occurred in the area would have likely included the site, so there is still a possibility that the *Diana* can be found (Mastone et al. 2011).

A month after the Battle of Chelsea Creek, rebels would try their boldest action in Boston. On the night of June 16, 1775, a group of over 1,000 rebels secretly fortified what would later be known as Breed's Hill on the back pastures of the town of Charlestown, built a redoubt by digging a roughly oval shaped trench around the crest of the hill and fortifying it with wood, and built additional smaller fortifications along the hills of the town (Philbrick 2014).

The following morning, the British saw the fortification above them and decided to both attack the redoubt and fire incendiary ammunition upon the mostly abandoned town of Charlestown. The fires raged below the fighting on the hill, and by the end of the day the Battle of Bunker Hill had ended, the British had recaptured Charlestown, and the town itself was burned to the ground (Philbrick 2014).

While this seems like a major defeat, both sides were relatively surprised by the success of the rebel forces, who despite their smaller numbers had far fewer casualties than the British. The psychological damage was yet another considerable show of force by the rebels against the might of the British Army.

Centuries later, many of the areas impacted by the Battle were faced with the combined impacts of the Bicentennial and the largest tunneling project ever attempted. Portions of the project would replace a raised highway that traveled through downtown and the Charlestown neighborhood of Boston with a tunnel (Boston University 1987). This required excavation through and under existing buildings. Underground within the project area were two sites that burned during the Battle of Bunker Hill, the Three Cranes Tavern, and the Parker-Harris Pottery, both discussed earlier, but both suffering the same fate during the Battle. One of the most distinctive signatures of the Battle were significant burned wood remains, which had been pushed or collapsed into basements, including the Three Cranes Tavern and nearby Privy 2 (Gallagher et al. 1994b). This particular privy, one of five found on the site associated with the Tavern, still had its charred superstructure collapsed into the well-preserved vault when the archaeologists excavated it. The contents of this privy are the key deposits mentioned in the earlier tavern discussion.

On Breed's Hill, today the site of the Bunker Hill Monument, archaeological surveys over several decades have revealed that much of the site's archaeological signature is ephemeral and difficult to find through relatively small trenches and shovel test pits (Heitert 2009). Three surveys in the 1990s used ground-penetrating radar and excavations to provide the first evidence for the potential preservation of the redoubt trench on top of the hill: a vague oval surrounding the top of the hill (Heitert 2009). Later NPS excavations included sixteen hand and machine-excavated trenches (Heitert 2009; Pendery and Griswold 1996). While most of the trenches produced no evidence of the redoubt trench, one trench on the southwest side of the hill had a flat-bottomed ditch feature with a sloped scarp and artifacts including white salt-glazed stoneware and Staffordshire (North Midlands) combed slipware, both typical circa 1775 artifacts, suggesting portions of the hill contain intact redoubt trench or related features (Pendery and Griswold 1996, Heitert 2009). As of the writing of this text, the City of Boston Archaeology Program is in the planning stages to return to Breeds Hill for another round of GPR survey with closer-spaced survey intervals that are intended to provide a better idea of the redoubt trench location and conditions (City of Boston Archaeology 2024).

Ultimately, the British recaptured Charlestown and the siege continued. Over the winter of 1775–76, a team of engineers transported captured cannon and other heavy artillery from Fort Ticonderoga in New York south and east to Boston (Nash 1979). These new weapons extended the firing range of the rebels to fire upon the British within the town of Boston. Similar to their successful overnight defense of Breed's Hill, on March 5, 1776, thousands of rebels moved the cannon and prefabricated wooden fence structures through the Dorchester neighborhood to its highest hill, Dorchester Heights, now in South Boston. Overnight, the rebel forces led by General George Washington had gained the ability to fire upon the British, whose range was inferior. Outgunned and unable to effectively return fire, the British realized they were incapable of staying in Boston, triggering the evacuation of troops and loyalists on March 17, 1776 (Pendery and Griswold 1995).

Unlike in Charlestown, the British left Boston relatively intact. Over three centuries later, a team of archaeologists from the National Park Service investigated the site of the fortifications on Dorchester Heights, now a National Historic Site (Pendery and Griswold 1995). Their investigations focused on determining the extent of the redoubts, structures, and artifacts associated with the fortifications. A challenging aspect of this project was the later 1814 construction of a wooden star fortress on top of the original fort, with extensive impacts to the earlier deposits as well as historical significance itself, requiring the maintenance of the later historic landscape.

In 1995, the team used GPR to survey the overall site and then excavated eight five-by-five-foot excavation units guided by the radar findings. Their testing revealed that many of the GPR signatures that appeared promising, when excavated, did not turn up much significant data. Despite this, the team were able to find a filled 1776 trench and evidence of significant grading of the historic site, including the removal of upward of six feet of topography in the mid-nineteenth century to build the later 1901 church-steeple-like monument on the site. Like many Revolutionary sites in the Boston region, this site had few artifacts. It appears that an emerging pattern among Revolutionary-era battle-related sites is a sparse artifact signature almost exclusively made up of gun-related artifacts, and only sites with more established longer-term occupation have additional artifacts (Pendery and Griswold 1995).

Conclusions

Conflict and war are integral to the history of Massachusetts from Puritan separatists to Native conflict, to the fight against oppression. Resistance and the struggle against oppression are far from exclusive to wartime conflicts (see Chapter 4 and Chapter 8). Still, these conflicts loom large in the historical narratives of American history. Historical archaeology of war and the Revolution provides nuance to the broader stories of military leaders and troop movements, providing instead a moment-by-moment account of action and a personal view of the battlefield experience. These are valuable contributions to the larger story of the American experience.

As Massachusetts moved beyond its colonial conflicts, the Commonwealth became a center for industrial innovation, reshaping both the physical and social landscape. The transition to mechanical production techniques reshaped the landscape, labor, class, and daily life. The next chapter explores how industrialization transformed Massachusetts, influencing everything from urban development to the material culture of its people.

6

Labor and Industry

Material evidence of industry and labor is common in the archaeological record of Massachusetts and appears in the form of stone quarry sites; one of the earliest iron works in the country; hundreds of water-powered mill sites dating from the seventeenth through twentieth centuries; shipbuilding, fishing, and whaling industries that were tied to international commerce; and the water, rail, and overland transportation corridors that moved raw materials and finished products. Many of America's most exemplary early factories were built in Massachusetts, and the Commonwealth's textile mills and factory towns served as templates that were adapted by other manufacturing industries across the country (Gordon and Malone 1994). The American System of Manufacturing that utilized interchangeable parts and mechanized production developed in the early nineteenth-century firearms industry at armories in Springfield, Massachusetts, and Harper's Ferry, Virginia, and revolutionized the manufacture of sewing machines, cutlery, furniture, and eventually automobiles (Hounshell 1984).

From its earliest colonial settlement, Massachusetts was ideally suited for industry. It benefited from abundant natural waterpower along hundreds of rivers and streams, English capital available for investment, and experienced artisans who planned and built mills and the machinery within them. As new technologies were developed, many of the earliest industrial sites were improved, expanded, and/or redeveloped over the centuries to the present. A number of sites discussed below document the repeated use of environmentally rich areas in Massachusetts that supported communities and sent products across the country and overseas for hundreds of years. As many of Massachusetts's aging and outdated nineteenth- and twentieth-century industrial sites are being removed, industrial archaeologists are documenting the hidden and often forgotten development of these sites and the individuals who labored there. Studies provide new and sometimes surprising information about technological innovation, resistance to wage labor, environmental impacts, and the diversity of populations who worked to make Massachusetts a world leader in industrial enterprise.

The case studies below highlight research that contributes to a greater understanding of our industrial past and how it developed in a uniquely American way. In addition to these sites, Massachusetts's industrial heritage has been documented archaeologically at sites of all scales and time periods: rattan-processing facilities in Wakefield (Marlatt and Wheeler 2002); a gunpowder manufacturing mill in Concord (Russo and Garman 1998); nail factories in Mansfield (Donta and Wendt 2002); a tidal gristmill in Quincy (Spencer-Wood 2001); granite quarries in Quincy (Holmes et al. 1994; Ritchie and Herbster 1997, 1998) and Milford (Elam and Heitert 2012); a cordage factory in Plymouth (Herbster et al. 1995); shoe production in Beverly (Garman 1996); a cranberry picking and packing industry in Truro (Dimmick 2006); leather tanning in Petersham (Doucette 2015); and dozens more.

The archaeology of industrial sites in Massachusetts, much like industrial archaeology elsewhere, once focused on understanding the mechanics of labor through the analysis of remnant buildings, machinery, artifacts, and documents including company records, operating manuals and catalogs, and plans. This type of study characterized the mid-twentieth-century work of Roland Robbins at the Saugus Iron Works (Griswold and Linebaugh 2011; see below). More recently, archaeologists have studied sites of labor to understand how capitalism and class structure were experienced by individuals and groups. Multidisciplinary studies of the Lowell factories, and specifically the Boott Mills, and smaller projects like the Russell Cutlery demonstrate the potential for industrial sites to illuminate human stories of dominance, resistance, innovation, and perseverance that are common to all Americans. As former industrial sites are repurposed and/ or removed to restore natural habitat, industrial archaeology has increasingly focused on the relationships between technology and the environment and on social and environmental justice issues. These modern-day issues affect community members directly and are providing new opportunities for the archaeology of industry to engage and inform decisions about the future.

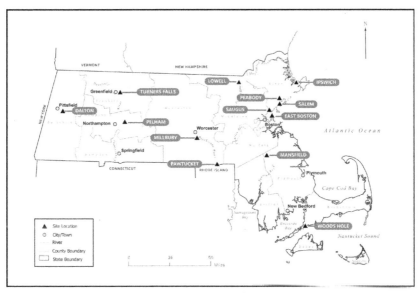

Map 6.1. Map of Massachusetts showing locations of sites discussed in Chapter 6.

Early Water-Powered Industries

The seventeenth-century British North American colonies depended on English shipments for everything they could not produce themselves (Innes 1983). The earliest industrial sites were developed to help support a new town or community and included small water-powered mills established along the rivers and streams that were abundant in Massachusetts. These provided essential services like grinding corn and grain (gristmills), cutting shingles and timber (sawmills), and finishing nails and hardware. When built at a natural fall line the waterway required little modification. If stream flow was not sufficient to power a wheel, an earthen dam and cut channels, head, and tailraces were built to impound and control water flow. Tidal mills established at coastal estuaries included flood gates that would let water come in with the rising tide then closed to hold it for later use. As communities expanded, more resource-specific mills were built to process and manufacture a wider range of materials and water privileges were enlarged, diversified, and often supported multiple mills.

The first commercial industry to develop in seventeenth-century Massachusetts was processing wood for shipment to England. Wood species were diverse and there were plenty of rivers and streams to power sawmills and then move wood and timber to the coast for shipping. The Pilgrims sent a load of clapboards and two hogsheads of furs on the first cargo ship to return to England, marking the earliest commercial export from the English colonies (Gordon and Malone 1994, 58). Massachusetts's abundant great white pines were ideal for masts and were harvested for early shipbuilding enterprises along the coast and for export to Great Britain. A man could cut enough wood for himself then sell any surplus to a local sawmill which would then for a ready market as well as to export to market using draft animals overland or waterpower to float downstream. Pit sawing or cutting by hand was slow and labor-intensive so water-powered sawmills were often built in a new settlement before the houses. "Up-and-down" sawmills were operating in Massachusetts by 1634 and remained critical through all stages of colonial development. By 1830, the town of Sturbridge had sixteen sawmills (Englund 1982 cited in Gordon and Malone 1994, 64). This produced an early need for edge tools (axes and saws) that were at first produced individually by blacksmiths but then became one of the first American factory industries (Nassaney and Abel 1993, see below).

Saugus Iron Works

As the population quickly grew in the early seventeenth century, access to resources became increasingly important. Building supplies, including fasteners, hardware, and tools, were among the most essential. In 1641, the General Court enacted legislation that anyone who discovered mineral deposits in the colony would be given exclusive rights to their extraction for twenty-one years. John Winthrop Jr., son of the Massachusetts Bay Colony leader, had received training in alchemy and metallurgy in England and solicited investors in England to form the Company of Undertakers of the Iron Works in New England (the Company) (Hartley 1957). Winthrop used some of the funds to purchase a small supply of tools and indentured a group of iron workers from England to return with him to Massachusetts Bay. The Company was granted a twenty-one-year monopoly provided they were able to produce enough iron to meet the colony's demands within two years (Carlson 1973, 9).

The colonists planned to produce wrought iron using Europe's most modern technology at the time. It involved a two-part process where a blast furnace was used to convert raw ore into cast iron, which was then refined in a forge to produce wrought iron. Casting required larger amounts of ore than the older bloomery process, where only a forge was necessary, and it also required both great amounts of charcoal to fire the furnace and water to power a bellows and forge hammer.

Winthrop had scouted iron sources before he went to England and one of the best was in Braintree (present-day Quincy), just south of Boston, where a rich deposit of natural bog ore was located along a waterway renamed Furnace Brook. In 1644, Winthrop purchased the Braintree land for the Company and built a blast furnace the following year, producing both iron bars and cast-iron wares (Bates 1898; Hartley 1957). Furnace Brook could not provide enough waterpower for the furnace and forge, so the latter was established about two miles away on the Monatiquot River (Carlson 1973). Today the short-lived industrial site is documented with an interpretive panel and an above ground portion of the original blast furnace.

Soon after a new location for iron manufacturing was identified just below a natural fall line on the Saugus River in Lynn, a coastal town ideally situated halfway between the growing seventeenth-century settlements at Boston and Salem. This area also contained bog iron deposits and a much more powerful river that drained into Boston Harbor, which meant ships could bring equipment, supplies, and raw materials to the site and carry away finished products. The 600-acre parcel acquired by the Company included a natural terrace that dropped steeply to the waterfront below and was ideally suited for the construction of the large top-loading blast furnace and waterwheels needed to power the forges. Work began on the blast furnace in 1646, and the seventeenth-century works, known as "Hammersmith," also contained a forge, rolling and slitting mill, as well as two blacksmith shops, a coal house, an agent's house that may also have served as a warehouse, and a wooden bulkhead and dock (Regan and White 2011a). A massive earthen and stone-faced dam was constructed upstream on the Saugus River, and the impounded water was channeled through a canal to the water wheels that powered equipment in the three main ironworking buildings.

The yearly production of the Saugus works in the 1650s included more than one hundred tons of wrought-iron bars, at least twelve tons of which were turned into nail rods for use in the colony (Carlson 1973). The bars and finished goods were loaded onto company vessels and moved to a Boston warehouse where they were shipped to other towns in the New England colonies including Portsmouth and Kittery, Maine, as well as to London and to plantations in Barbados (Regan and White 2011a). The on-site blacksmith shop repaired forging equipment and produced tools for the iron works (tongs, shears, shovels, hooks), hardware for the buildings, and agricultural tools for the adjacent farm. A saw pit or mill at the site made boards for Hammersmith's structures and buildings, to line the canals, channels, and sluiceways, and to make carts and storage containers. Cutler Joseph Jenks was granted a patent in 1646 and established a mill on the blast furnace tail race where he manufactured saw blades, axes and edge tools, drawn wire used for wool cards and fishhooks (Regan and White 2011a). Son Joseph Jenks Jr. learned the trade from his father and later operated his own forge at the Pawtucket Falls on the Blackstone River (present-day Pawtucket, Rhode Island) at the site that would later be developed into the first American textile mill by Samuel Slater (Regan and White 2011a; see below).

The English and Scottish iron workers who ran the original Braintree operation were joined by newly arrived indentured workmen and their families who lived in a clustered settlement across the Saugus River from the iron works. The Company paid for the construction and maintenance of the housing, and families who boarded single men were reimbursed for their food and lodging (Regan and White 2011a). Ironmaking was considered critical to the colony's success, and once it begun a blast furnace operated twenty-four hours a day, so workers were excused from military service (Regan and White 2011b, 254). In addition to approximately thirty-five full-time iron workers, almost 200 part-time workers were paid over the life of the ironworks operation. They included local yeoman farmers, tradesmen, merchants, and boatsmen as well as women who laundered and mended clothing and at least two Native Americans who were paid to cut and haul wood.

Researchers have noted that some of the finished objects located through archaeological testing at the Saugus works are nearly identical to iron and brass items identified in Wampanoag graves at the seventeenth-century Burrs Hill burial ground in Warren, Rhode Island, suggesting the possibility that items such as kettles, axes, and hoe blades manufactured there were sold or traded to Indigenous people (Gibson 1980; Regan and White 2011a, 34). Hammersmith also employed at least ten colliers who produced charcoal from the woodlots west of the iron works, and miners who extracted bog ore, clay, and sand from dry bogs and shallow ponds and gabbro rock used for flux from outcrops around the Boston basin (Regan and White 2011a).

Incredibly, the extensive industrial complex developed at Hammersmith only operated for about twenty-four years. The Company went bankrupt in 1670 after high production and maintenance costs, mismanagement, and lawsuits halted production, and the works were shut down. Gordon and Malone (1994, 68, 73, 75) posit that the extensive economic and social networks necessary to support such a complex industrial site were not yet established in seventeenth-century Massachusetts, and in fact it was nearly a century before an industrial operation of the same technological complexity was attempted in America. The iron workers who had honed their craft at Hammersmith went on to establish or operate new iron works in Connecticut, New Jersey, and other seaboard colonies and helped spread the technology that created the American iron industry (Regan and White 2011a).

Some elements of the iron works site remained visible on the landscape, and in 1943, the newly formed First Iron Works Association (headed by a former executive at Bethlehem Steel) purchased the property with the intention of restoring it as a heritage site to promote its significance in the history of American industry (Griswold 2011a). Avocational archaeologist Roland Robbins was hired in 1948 to locate and document the blast furnace and forge. Robbins hired a part-time civil engineer and a professional photographer to help document the site, along with Robbins's own extensive notes and plans, for the eventual reconstruction. Professor E. Neal Hartley from the Massachusetts Institute of Technology (MIT), who specialized in the history of science and technology, was hired to complete a detailed historical study of the iron works (Linebaugh 2011). Hartley researched Company records including correspondence, inventories, and account books related to the construction, operation, litigation, and 1670 bankruptcy of Hammersmith archived at Harvard University's Baker Library to document the site history and to help locate and interpret the seventeenth-century landscapes, features, and artifacts (Hartley 1957; Regan and White 2011a).

The blast furnace was buried by only a small amount of fill, so it was quickly exposed and determined to be relatively well preserved and complete, which generated excitement about the excavations and more funding to continue (Griswold 2011b). Within a few months, he had delineated the masonry furnace foundation and was also excavating the furnace tailrace, casting beds, crucible pit, and bellows base (Linebaugh 2011; Pineo et al. 2016). Robbins identified the forge hammer base and 500-pound iron triphammer head within the refinery forge area. Over the six years he was involved with the project, Robbins and his team identified and documented the furnace waterwheel tailrace, wheel pit (and approximately 40 percent of the wooden overshot waterwheel), and headrace; portions of the forge; the wharf and boat basin; and an intact deposit of slag used to fill an area along the adjacent Saugus River.

More than 4,000 artifacts collected by Robbins's team are curated at the Saugus Iron Works National Historic Site (Regan and White 2011b). The materials document early seventeenth-century ironmaking processes and mechanical techniques, defective and finished iron goods produced at Hammersmith, and materials that document the daily lives of the men and women who lived and worked at the complex. The assemblage includes metal, wood, leather, and bone. Identified artifacts and features include the wooden water wheel and hutch enclosure complete with iron hardware and cow-hair caulking; worker's tools including crucibles and ladles; structural components including furnace bricks, the oak sills and wrought-iron nozzle from the bellow; sow and pig iron bars, holloware wasters from kettles, Dutch ovens, and cauldrons; hammerheads, cams, and replacement parts for the works; and samples of raw materials including gabbro, bog ore, charcoal, and slag (Regan and White 2011b). In addition to personal tools, the assemblage also includes domestic objects like ceramics, glass, and leather shoe fragments. Records indicate that the Company supplied tobacco to the workers and numerous pipe fragments were collected including regionally manufactured terra cotta examples (Regan and White 2011b, 254).

Although Robbins did not find the structural remains of the rolling and slitting mill, he did collect several flat bars produced there as well as nail rods which would have been sold to blacksmiths to make finished nails. The limited excavations at the Jenks blacksmithing forge located edge tools including knives, a scythe blade, axes, adzes, chisels, and an extremely rare example of a seventeenth-century sawmill blade. Blacksmithing and other tools including tongs, hammers, a wrench, and a tool rest were collected. Several latten spoons were excavated along with brass sheets. Iron products included horse and ox shoes, a stirrup, a spur, a pitchfork fragment, and a cow bell. The forge produced drawn wire and hundreds of brass straight pins, and two brooches were identified (Regan and White 2011b).

After Robbins's extensive excavations, a large portion of the main industrial complex was reconstructed, and the First Iron Works Association operated the site as a private museum. The excavation of the main industrial ironworking site at Saugus helped archaeologists and industrial historians better understand America's seventeenth-century colonial ironworking technology and the specific development of the integrated works at Hammersmith.

Today the twelve-acre site is managed by the National Park Service and includes a museum and visitor center, a working water wheel, reconstructed industrial buildings, and the restored seventeenth-century Iron Works House. Since Robbins's time, archaeological investigations have been conducted around the original complex as part of compliance studies prior to ground disturbance, reinterpretations of the original excavations, and collections studies all contributed to a more humanistic understanding of seventeenth-century life at Hammersmith (e.g., John Milner Associates 1978; Johnson 1997; MacMahon 1988; McManamon 1978; Moran 1976a, 1976b; Parson and Cassedy 2007; Piechota 1973). The data collected by Robbins and his team in the 1950s continues to provide opportunities to understand the development of industrial archaeology and to stimulate new research about the people who lived and worked at this unique industrial site.

Hammersmith was the first sustained integrated ironworks in America, producing cast iron, refined bars, and nails at one location (Griswold 2011). The self-contained industrial complex was the first Massachusetts precursor to the "company towns" that would be established after the Industrial Revolution in places like Lowell (see below) (Hartley 1957). The site was listed as a National Historic Landmark in 1963, and the twelve-acre Saugus Iron Works National Historic Site is promoted as the "Birthplace of the American Iron and Steel Industry" (https://www.nps.gov/sair/index.htm). The operation was integral to the development of the American iron industry, contributed to the emergent colonial economy, and played a critical role in reducing colonial dependence on British raw materials, technology, and finished goods. When the iron works ceased operating in 1670, the men who had been involved in its construction and operation went on to set up other ironmaking sites in the expanding colonial territories and taught the next generations of ironworkers (Pineo et al. 2016).

Roland Robbins's extensive archaeological investigations were completed several decades before an academic "industrial archaeology" was practiced in the United States. He pioneered techniques that would later characterize the discipline including the use of machine-assisted excavation to expose large industrial features; the use of professional survey and large-format photography; and collaborative research with specialists including conservators, metallurgists, a dendrochronologist, a faunal analyst, and a ceramics expert (Linebaugh 2000, 2011; Pineo et al. 2016). In other ways, Robbins's work highlighted the shortcomings of early industrial archaeology. From the beginning, the goals of the archaeological work were to identify the seventeenth-century industrial complex and collect information that could be used to reconstruct and interpret the site. Robbins focused on mechanics and materials; he was not particularly interested in the lives or working conditions of the people who built, supervised, and labored at Hammersmith (Linebaugh 2011, 60). As the discipline evolved, archaeologists would increasingly see industrial sites as places to examine labor, class, ethnicity, and gender.

As one of the first and largest commercial production sites in colonial Massachusetts, the Hammersmith complex included a variety of support industries designed to feed and house workers, harvest raw materials, and transport finished goods to consumers. Most early industrial sites in Massachusetts were initially built for a single purpose like sawmills to produce lumber or gristmills to process grain, often enlarging and expanding over time as new technologies were developed. One constant for all of these industrial sites was the need for a steady source of power, for which Massachusetts's networks of coastal and interior rivers and streams provided a seemingly unlimited supply.

Pelham Timber Dam

While some mills were built at fall lines where waterpower was concentrated, many industrial sites were impounded to regulate and increase water flow across a wheel. This often included damming a tributary stream or brook to create a holding pond or to create an artificial barrier to concentrate flow. The circa 1739 Amethyst Brook Timber Dam was identified in Pelham in west-central Massachusetts in 2013 after the removal of another historic dam downstream exposed the structure that had been completely buried under sediments (Banister et al. 2016; Stantec 2013). Archaeological investigations at this historic dam and others across Massachusetts were completed as part of a state and federal ecological restoration program. Documentary research, archaeological excavation, and monitoring and documentation were completed as part of project mitigation prior to and during the dam removal process.

Amethyst Brook is a tributary of the Connecticut River with a vertical drop of approximately sixty feet. Between 1729 and 1931, at least four different industrial sites were developed and operated along a one-third mile stretch of this waterway (Banister et al. 2016; Bigelow 1993). The Timber Dam's visible remains consisted of a spillway structure that extended approximately fifty feet across Amethyst Brook and extended beyond the eroded stream banks. Noninvasive geotechnical study had determined that the dam was approximately eleven feet high and extended beyond the current stream channel approximately 100 to 200 feet in total, indicating the dam had been built with an existing valley prior to the construction of the downstream dam (Stantec 2013). The vertical section of the dam, which was at least five feet tall, consisted of a wood crib, gravity-type spillway structure with a vertical downstream face and sloping upstream face. It was assembled from a matrix of barkless tree trunks (boles) cut into logs with saw and axe and laid in regular courses that alternately ran transversely (up- and downstream) and longitudinally through the structure. Field stones and rocks were visible at some places within the dam matrix—stones were presumed to have filled the entire dam before being removed by stream action (Banister et al. 2016).

Machine-assisted excavation was completed on a portion of the dam located within the existing brook channel and one stream bank. The dam was breached by removing several of the central bolts and planking, then when the upstream water level had dropped, sediment and debris that had accumulated were removed by machine and excavation into the south bank revealed a well-preserved and undisturbed abutment buried under 3.5 feet of sediment from the impoundment. The dam's structural components were recorded and documented by the archaeologists as it was removed, providing a great amount of detail about the dam's original construction. The exposed dam consisted of a fifty-foot-long timber crib spillway with a cross section right triangle shape that ran across the brook channel and then terminated at a five-foot-long stone and wood abutment. The sloping upstream side of the spillway was sheathed in heavy pit-sawn planking to form the face of the dam. The archaeologists were able to record shims and saddles placed during the dam's construction to account for the uneven size of the wooden timbers and to keep the spillway level. The wooden dam timbers were pegged together entirely with wooden tree nails and mortise and tenon construction; no metal fasteners were identified anywhere in the structure. Carpenters' marks cut with a race knife or other edge tool were visible on the planks (Banister et al. 2014, 21–50). An "X" to denote peg locations appeared frequently, and the end of one plank, adjacent to a rabbet or groove, was marked with a "φ" symbol, which appears to be a variation on the use of Roman numeral that a carpenter often made to aid assembly (Mercer 1960).

The requirement to entirely remove the dam structure from the current stream channel provided an opportunity for the archaeological team to carefully study the dam's construction techniques and materials and to better understand this specific type of wooden industrial structure. The study allowed the team to date the dam's construction to the period between 1740 and 1820 based primarily on the cut and saw marks on the timbers and planks, the methods of joinery, and the carpenter's marks which indicated the dam was built before factory-cut lumber was readily available (Banister et al. 2014, 51). The pit-sawn wood likely came from either Pelham or Amherst; both towns established their first sawmills between 1740 and 1745. Pit or reciprocating saws began to be replaced by circular saws in limited applications such as shingle manufacture in the 1830s and entered wide use by the 1870s, although rural areas such as Pelham might have maintained sawmills with the older reciprocating blades several decades after this (Bigelow 1993, 10; Garvin 2001, 26; Carpenter and Morehouse 1896, 59).

The lack of any metal fasteners and use of pegged joints did not correlate with a specific date of construction but provided a strong indication that the dam was built in the 1700s when bolts and spikes were scarce or more costly. Particularly noteworthy was the use of pegs for the attachment of the spillway planking, an instance where metal spikes would have provided a much more rapid means of construction. Wood dam construction requires a large number of connections and attendant fasteners, and a review of trade publications suggested that engineers and builders shifted to metal fasteners as soon as it was feasible (given available supplies, cost, etc.) (Evans 1850). By the late nineteenth century, books on waterpower were describing the use of metal fasteners throughout wood dams, and use of this hardware was associated with "modern methods" of wood dam construction that eschewed traditional carpentry techniques (Frizell 1901, 45–46). Based on this trade literature, it was assumed that some metal fasteners would have been used in Pelham's mill dams as soon as possible. Machine-cut nails and spikes became widely available circa 1800 in main population centers in New England but might not have been readily available in a more rural area like Pelham (Banister et al. 2014; Garvin 2001, 76; James Leffel and Co. 1874, 33–34).

The archaeological analysis supported an interpretation that the dam was a run-of-the-river (weir) structure typically used for small-scale milling and manufacturing in New England between the seventeenth and early nineteenth centuries, and that it had been built to power the documented forge or gristmill located near the site. The careful excavation of the dam components confirmed that it was built using vernacular design elements that were modeled after British and European examples. The use of wood, combined with rubble stone ballast, made the structures cost-effective and relatively easy to construct, particularly in this part of western Massachusetts which was still heavily wooded. This dam design was published as early as 1795 in Oliver Evans's *The Young Mill-Wright and Miller's Guide,* but the contractor or millwright had some knowledge of dam construction techniques and carpentry (Banister et al. 2014; Evans 1850, Plate X; Frizell 1901, 61–63; James Leffel and Co. 1874, 26–31; Schnitter 1994, 147–150; Smith 1972: 146–148; Wegmann 1899, 140).

No evidence of a downstream apron for the spillway could be located, and the absence of such a substructure is noteworthy because dam engineering treatises generally recommend the use of a spillway apron to control water flow (Evans 1850, 207; James Leffel and Co. 1874). The lack of a spillway apron indicates that the dam builder either miscalculated the brook's power because of insufficient knowledge of the waterway or inexperience, was not an expert, or else was limited in means. The presence of uneven cap logs on the dam's crest runs counter to accepted dam design, further suggesting that the builder had limited experience in dam construction (Banister et al. 2014, 54). The professional guides recommended a crest without obstructions or anything that might catch debris in the water and result in damage to the structure.

Few, if any other, examples of largely intact eighteenth- or early nineteenth-century dams have been documented in Massachusetts, and the Pelham Timber Dam may be the oldest. At the time of the study, the state inventory contained approximately 241 dams that were built or reconstructed before 1900 and thus may reasonably be expected to employ timber construction. Only five are recorded as timber structures with dates of construction between 1790 to 1833. Substantial portions of timber crib dams were archaeo logically recorded in Dalton and Millbury, Massachusetts (Johnson 2007; MHC 2014, 2016; NE Historical Services Inc. 1987; Parsons 1994; Stott 1988). Recordation of intact historic timber dams in other New England states seems to be equally limited (Banister et al. 2014). The archaeological study of the timber dam not only documented important details about this type of early industrial feature and offered a methodology for examining similar sites in other parts of the country but provided comparative data to be used with other waterpower features from this time period. Dating the timber dam within the period of industrial development along Amethyst Brook provides a better understanding of how the craft village of West Pelham expanded with new technology over time.

The Industrial Revolution and the Rise of American Factories

The Blackstone River Valley in Massachusetts and Rhode Island is often labeled as the "Birthplace of the American Industrial Revolution." In 1671, Joseph Jenkes Jr. built a forge and mill at the Blackstone's Pawtucket Falls located in present-day Rhode Island on the Massachusetts border. Jenkes had helped establish the Saugus Ironworks in 1645 (see above) but moved to Pawtucket after the Saugus enterprise ended. Wealthy merchant and early industrialist Moses Brown purchased the water privilege at the thirty-foot fall line and in 1783 hired Samuel Slater to develop a textile manufactory. Slater had recently emigrated from England and made improvements to Brown's water-powered fulling mill based on the emerging British factory system. Slater innovated the process by hiring local artisans to build or modify machines using his own designs to approximate the mechanized process in England that included carding, drawing, and the first fully power-driven machine for spinning yarn. The resulting facility, known as Slater Mill, was considered the first true factory in America and stands today as a National Historic Landmark (Gordon and Malone 1994).

Unlike the typical brick or masonry factories in England, Slater's mill was a rectangular wooden building that incorporated post-and-beam construction (some of which still survives) with nailed vertical-plank framing. Receipts from the plasterer indicate that the interior was whitewashed to help light from the windows get to the work spaces in the center of the building. The interior was ordered with the machines in horizontal lines along the long building axis separated by aisles that made it easy to transport materials and gave managers unobstructed views of workers. Bolt holes and marks left on the floorboards at the mill document the placement of machinery and shafts in the original Slater Mill factory, and mapping the wear patterns in the original floorboards was used to identify workstations and the flow of materials (Gordon and Malone 1994). This type of forensic examination of extant early nineteenth-century industrial labor sites is extremely useful in the absence of the construction drawings that often survive for later nineteenth and early twentieth-century factories (Gordon and Malone 1994, 312; Gross 1988).

Slater's technological innovations coupled with the 1807 American embargo on British textile imports led to an explosion in mill factory development utilizing what became known as "the Rhode Island System," mainly built and run by men who had trained under Slater in Pawtucket (Gordon and Malone 1994). An 1809 manufactory census identified forty cotton mills in operation within thirty miles of Providence, accounting for almost two-thirds of all such mills in New England. By 1832, there were 119 mills in Rhode Island alone (NPS 2011). For much of the nineteenth century, the Blackstone River had the most intense industrial development of any waterway in New England. The Blackstone dropped 438 feet between its headwaters in Worcester, Massachusetts and its terminus in Providence, Rhode Island, and of that total an estimated 400 feet were utilized by industrial operations according to a report in the 1880 federal census that also stated, "it would be hard, in fact, to find another stream in the country so completely utilized" (US Bureau of the Census 1880 cited in Gordon and Malone 1994, 63).

The Public and Private Lives of Factory Workers

By the mid-nineteenth century almost every American city and town situated on a major waterway had developed some type of commercial factory, but

Massachusetts textile mills were among the largest and most successful in the nation. Major industrial textile sites were established in the coastal cities of Fall River and New Bedford, on the Merrimack River in Lowell, and along the Connecticut River in Springfield, Holyoke, and Greenfield.

In 1813, Francis Cabot Lowell, a wealthy merchant from an elite generational Boston family, led a group of associates in a new effort to make cotton textiles at a larger scale than had previously been attempted. They worked to mechanize the process, creating larger structures with multiple floors, adding additional water turbines to power multiple machines at the same time, and expanding on Samuel Slater's successful mechanization. Lowell and his fellow industrialists used their profits to build and control much of Massachusetts pre–Civil War economy, social institutions, and politics. They funded and developed the Boston and Lowell Railroad and other railroad lines across New England that brought raw materials to their factories and finished goods to market. They owned controlling stock in a number of banks, allowing them to finance and insure new ventures and expansions of their own companies. They supported Whig Party politicians and funded the construction of hospitals and schools, many of which still bear their names (Dublin 1992).

The City of Lowell is located at the confluence of the Concord and Merrimack Rivers near the New Hampshire border along a natural thirty-foot fall line. This location was a significant cultural landscape and gathering place for Native Americans for millennia, and prior to the early nineteenth century was almost exclusively farmland. In 1825, Lowell was founded as the first planned industrial community in America where everything was located on-site: mills, housing, support services, transportation, and power, including the Middlesex Canal which had just been built to supply hydropower. Initially, the factories recruited young women from surrounding rural towns to provide unskilled labor in cloth weaving mills under a very closely supervised setting where they lived in nearby boardinghouses. By the mid-nineteenth century, immigrants began to replace the "mill girls" with Irish and French Canadian laborers and then later in the nineteenth century eastern European immigrants (Mrozowski et al. 1996). The Boott Corporation operated thirty-two boardinghouses for unskilled, unmarried workers and thirty-two tenements for supervisors and skilled workers and their families, all arranged in eight blocks adjacent to the mill.

While industrial archaeologists have studied the buildings and machinery at many of these sites, the people who kept the mills operating have not been as well documented. One of the most comprehensive studies of the groups who labored and lived at these sites was completed as part of multiyear archaeological and interdisciplinary research and analyses at the Boott Cotton Mills Corporation which operated from 1830 to 1950 and is partially preserved as part of the Lowell National Historical Park. Excavations were conducted behind one boardinghouse and one tenement built between 1835 and 1839, and at an agent's house built in 1845 (Beaudry and Mrozowski 1987a, 1987b, 1989). The results of the multidisciplinary study were published in numerous professional reports and journals as well as in a popular book (Beaudry and Mrozowski 1988; Mrozowski et al. 1996).

The archaeology focused on the backlots of two nineteenth-century boarding houses and tenements and the yard space around the factory agent's house. The information collected at the sites was used to understand and document the home and work lives of the mill employees and to highlight the differences between the working and supervisory classes. The tenement and boardinghouse buildings had been torn down in the early twentieth century and the site paved over rather than redeveloped, so the yard spaces were essentially capped deposits. Records and fire insurance maps were used to reconstruct the nineteenth-century layout of the buildings, each with an enclosed backlot with a privy and a woodshed which was also used to store coal, wood, and garbage.

The artifact assemblages at the boardinghouses confirmed that the agents purchased goods and supplies in bulk and used the cheapest, most utilitarian wares. Workers were provided with three meals a day served family-style in the boardinghouses. Fragments of more than 300 dishes were collected from the backlots. Those that were decorated were unmatched—probably assembled piecemeal as hand-me-down or seconds. At the agent's house, a high proportion of the ceramics were transfer print wares with matching table and serving wares and fine glassware. The excavations in the tenement yard produced middle range consumer goods and evidence that the residents used tea wares (Beaudry and Mrozowski 1987a).

Workers' meals were generous but not always of high nutritional value. Beef dominated the faunal assemblage but bones from chicken, sheep, goat, and pig were also recovered, indicating at least some variety. Fatty meats were more common than lean ones, and workers were served home baked breads and pastries and canned goods which were made on site, all cheaper for the mill owners than buying prepared goods from suppliers. Account books indicate that vegetables and grains were bought in bulk and stored in the cellar, where gnawed bones and rodent remains suggest at least some infestation. Seeds found in the privies indicate that strawberries, blueberries, and blackberries were eaten and may have even been grown in the yards.

The agents' meats and foodstuffs were very similar to those found at the boardinghouses with beef bones also the most common and not from the best cuts, although no rat bones and only a few gnawed bone fragments were found. The main difference appears to be in how the meals were delivered: on fancy matching wares brought to the table by servants versus communal meals on utilitarian plates (Beaudry and Mrozowski 1987a).

Clay pipes were a socioeconomic indicator for working-class people and both men and women smoked (Cook 1989). Workers generally smoked short clay pipes called "cutties" because they could be easily gripped in the teeth, freeing hands as they worked, unlike the long thin clay pipes that were a sign of leisure and luxury. Cigars were preferred by middle and upper classes and limited to men. Many of the pipes found during the boardinghouse excavations showed markings that they had intentionally been made into short pipes with the stem scored and then snapped off or ground down, and teeth marks on the stubby stems. Nearly 500 pipe fragments were collected behind the boarding houses, most of which were "TD" stamped types—a very common and inexpensive pipe. Some pipes were stamped "HOME RULE" which advertised for the Irish fight for independence, and one fragment was stamped "Wolf Tone," the name of an Irish political martyr and likely a reflection of ethnic pride for some of the mill workers (Cook 1989).

Alcohol was prohibited on Boott Company grounds by policy, and while drinking was not outright prohibited, the owners discouraged the use of alcohol and sent letters to keepers stating drunkenness and disorderly behavior would not be tolerated from workers in the boardinghouses. The upper classes associated alcohol consumption with lower classes, vices, and crime. Ample evidence of alcohol consumed by workers was found at the boardinghouse, although broken liquor bottles were primarily found in out-of-sight locations including at the corners of buildings, along fence lines, in crawlspaces, and within the enclosed privies. Alcohol-related artifacts included wine glasses, beer mugs, and at least seventy-two alcohol bottles, including flasks for hard liquor and wine and beer bottles. This total represents only a small percentage of what was probably consumed since bottles had deposits and would have been returned and refilled. Most of those collected at the site were locally made cheaper brands (Beaudry and Mrozowski 1987a, 1989).

Clothing and personal adornment items were some of the only material goods workers purchased for themselves. Several finely made brooches were found at the site, along with a copper and rhinestone pin with glass stones. Many women's hair combs and a few designed for lice removal were recovered. Buttons and studs were the most common items, and more than

two-thirds were plain white porcelain. A pattern observed in these personal items showed that although the mill workers couldn't afford expensive
materials, they purchased items that looked fashionable but were cheaper
than the fancier counterparts. Plastic (a new material in the 1870s) combs
imitated tortoiseshell, white porcelain resembled shell, and cut black glass
was a substitute for "jet" which was made from coal and cost considerably
more (Beaudry and Mrozowski 1989).

The analyses of soils and floral remains from the yard spaces provided a
means to examine and understand industrial ecology and worker health and
hygiene outside the workplace. The excavations in the small, enclosed boarding house yards indicated that sanitary conditions grew worse over time.
Drinking water came from wells or was pumped from the nearby canal, but
both sources were contaminated by the backlot privies, which were used by
many people and were infrequently cleaned out. Piped water was introduced
in the 1870s but most boardinghouses still used wells into the 1890s, possibly to avoid the cost of installing plumbing. In 1890, the Board of Health
ordered that all privies be closed, sealed with sand, and replaced with indoor
water closets hooked up to sewers. The archaeological investigations proved
that mill owners did not immediately comply. More than 700 machine-made
bottle fragments with manufacturing dates after 1910 were found in two of
the excavated privies, confirming that they were still open and in use twenty
years after the order was posted (Beaudry and Mrozowski 1987a).

At the agent's house, soil chemistry revealed that rather than a landscaped
yard surface, the backyard space was initially a work area for slaughtering or
butchering animals by the servants who attended the agent and his family.
Refuse had been allowed to decay there, and the yard was probably used
for laundry as well. Yet, over time the yards were transformed into orna-
mental spaces as indicated by the grassy landscapes that replaced the weeds
(Mrozowski 2000; Mrozowski et al. 1996, 44).

A major goal of the investigations was understanding corporate paternal-
ism in a nineteenth-century mill "company town" located in an urban industrial community. The mill owners' focus on economy and efficiency affected
every aspect of the mill operation and extended to the company-owned and
-operated boardinghouses. Factory workers owned their own clothes and
personal items, but almost everything else in their daily lives was provided
and/or controlled by the company and appointed keepers and agents: the
rooms they lived in and the furnishings that adorned them, the food they
ate and the dishes it was served on, the beds they slept in and the linens that
covered them. The keepers' purchasing decisions were reflected in the faunal

remains and discarded serving and table wares, while the individual residents' decisions are reflected in the personal items they lost or discarded including buttons, beads, combs, jewelry, pipes, marbles, and bottles. The archaeologists hoped that by thoroughly studying the boardinghouse yard spaces and the artifacts within them, they could interpret the worker's social and domestic lives because these were some of the only areas where they could exercise control over their surroundings (Beaudry and Mrozowski 1989).

Other Nineteenth-Century Industries

The mill operations at the Boott Mill in Lowell and at many textile factories across Massachusetts represent the largest and most complex end of Massachusetts's nineteenth-century industrial past. The rapid mechanization of production in the nineteenth century led to an increased use of what was considered by managers to be "unskilled" labor, but craft production was not entirely replaced in every industry. In many settings, work was completed by an individual who operated a specific machine or completed specific tasks that resulted in a finished good. The autonomy of a laborer was often tied to the scale of the production and the degree to which labor was managed (Fennell 2021). Many other industries incorporated some elements of craft and artisanal production into smaller factory operations that also provide opportunities for archaeological analyses.

The Cutlery Industry

The Russell Cutlery Factory site in Turner's Falls the Connecticut River Valley provided an opportunity to study technological innovation in a metalworking trade; how it changed the need for skilled labor, and worker's reactions to mechanization in the early years of the Industrial Revolution (Nassaney and Abel 1993, 2000). Cutlery and metal edge tools were generally imported to America from England, Germany, and France prior to the nineteenth century. By the 1830s, mechanization and standardization/interchangeability, two hallmarks of what became known as the "American System of Manufacturing" had revolutionized the production of firearms at Massachusetts's Springfield Armory, and the technology quickly spread up the Connecticut River to other metalworking trades including the cutlery industry (Cooper 1988; Smith 1985). John E. Russell formed a manufacturing company on the Green River in Greenfield, Massachusetts, in 1833, and he is often described as the first cutlery manufacturer in America (Nassaney and Abel 1993; Stone 1930). Russell utilized a mechanical triphammer in the forging process which was considered a technological breakthrough and dramatically increased production in a trade that had been almost exclusively performed by hand. By the 1840s, Russell's products were recognized around the world and the company's knives were a favorite of American frontiersmen. By 1860, the Russell Cutlery was one of two Franklin County firms that accounted for nearly half of all cutlery produced in the United States (Nassaney and Abel 1993, 259; Taber 1955).

In 1868, Russell began construction of a new factory for his growing business and moved a short distance north to the planned factory village of Turner's Falls on the Connecticut River in Montague. The concentration of industry at Turner's Falls required a large labor force increasingly drawn from Irish, German, English, Polish, and French Canadian immigrants who made up 32 percent of the Montague population by 1880 (Abel 1987; Nassaney and Abel 1993, 260). The Russell Cutlery was the largest manufacturing firm in the village, employing six hundred people who represented more than half of the manufacturing workforce in the village (Nassaney and Abel 1993, 260). When completed in 1870, Russell's factory was reportedly the largest of its kind in the world comprising 160,000 square feet of workspace and capable of utilizing 1,200 laborers (Nassaney and Abel 1993, 261; Merriam et al.1976, 23). Like many of the late-nineteenth-century industrialists, John Russell built a boardinghouse for his workers when housing in Turner's Falls was limited, increasing his wealth by collecting rent money or deducting the cost from his worker's pay. The business underwent a modernization, but by the 1900s, more competition in the national and worldwide cutlery industry led to the merger of Russell's business with a Southbridge, Massachusetts, cutlery and the relocation there in 1936. The abandoned buildings were demolished in 1958 although foundations and portions of the raceways were still visible until the 1970s (Nassaney and Abel 1993).

Archaeological survey of the site was conducted in 1986 and 1987 and at that time, the only visible factory elements were concrete floor sections, a steel penstock along the canal, and architectural debris scattered across the surface (Nassaney and Abel 1993, 2000). The team developed a set of research questions to investigate the American Manufacturing System and laborer reactions to it (Nassaney and Abel 2000). The field investigations documented a water tank and turbine that were part of the power system, and the archaeologists collected a sample of more than 200 objects from a 100 square meter artifact concentration near the former cutting room and triphammer shop. The assemblage included scraps of raw material, cut metal, and cutlery wasters representing various stages of the manufacturing process.

Most of the objects including forks, dessert and steak knives, putty knives, skinning knives, and a distinctive pocketknife, were identified using an 1884 Russell Cutlery Sales catalog (Nassaney and Abel 1993, 264).

The materials documented all stages of the mechanized forging process where steel was cut and hammered between dies to produce the finished product, and sheet metal stamping which was a much less labor-intensive process and produced parts that were assembled to complete the tool or item. The researchers closely examined and categorized the items to learn why they had been rejected and noted that most had been discarded early in the production process. They combined the archaeological data with their documentary research to question whether the workers had intentionally discarded items out the shop window due to errors or carelessness or as acts of resistance and defiance. The archaeological assemblage was also a means to investigate intentional spatial and social control within the factory hierarchy, and whether managers were aware of material losses or disciplined inefficient or non-compliant laborers (Nassaney and Abel 2000).

The documentary research indicated that John Russell preferred immigrant factory workers who could recruit relatives and others from their home countries over American-born men who were quick to leave the operation for other pursuits. There were also clear labor divisions in the cutlery industry, with men employed in most of the skilled and semi-skilled jobs like grinding while women were generally confined to the sorting and packaging areas within the factory. Company literature and plans indicated that Russell utilized the American system to mechanize the cutlery production process and to design his factory so that specific standardized and routine tasks were completed in a highly efficient and organized circular flow with each worker performing a specific task in the manufacturing process (Nassaney and Abel 2000).

The need for a skilled workforce diminished as more tasks were mechanized and as labor was segmented into narrow categories such as grinding and polishing. Russell Cutlery employees demonstrated their resistance through a variety of actions including strikes in 1884 and 1885. Some of the retired cutlery workers interviewed as part of the archaeological project reported that they made custom knives for personal use during their breaks (authorized or not) at the factory (Nassaney and Abel 2000, 269). Despite the constraints that management placed on workers, employees at the Russell Cutlery sought to regain some autonomy in their daily activities both on and off the job. Worker agency can be identified in many industrial settings where the aspirations of operatives and managers often came into conflict.

Industrial Pottery Production

Massachusetts clays were utilized for millennia by Native Americans and have been a significant extractive resource in Massachusetts for centuries (see the Charlestown potters discussed in Chapter 3). Archaeological investigations at the Osborn-Read-Page Pottery site in Peabody included comprehensive archival and land evidence research and documented the individual potters who worked there (Garman et al. 1998; Heitert et al. 2002).

Many of the larger waster piles (which included broken, misfired, or damaged pottery pieces) toward the back of the site contained materials generated by Moses B. Paige (active from 1883 to 1944), the last in a long line of potters at the site. His tenure represents a definable shift away from "traditional" pottery and toward a retail establishment offering mass-marketed ceramics, many of which were imported from the massive stoneware potteries of the Midwest. An analysis of column samples taken from the waster piles showed the majority were of stamped and molded flowerpots and undecorated bowl forms, all dating from Paige's occupation of the site. Wares produced by the Osborn family of potters were less numerous, and their distribution helped explain the pottery's structural and organizational evolution as a gradual movement of the means of production from the front of the lot toward the back, with the original Osborn pottery developing from a locus of production to a retail center.

Analysis of the kiln deposit and associated artifacts indicate that the original kiln structure was incorporated into later iterations of the pottery complex. This deliberate effort to build around the original kiln indicates that it was valued as an efficient and cost-effective piece of production equipment even as the pottery grew and was mechanized. Analysis of the stratified waster deposits determined that vessel loss during firing was largely a consequence of improper clay preparation, which increased over time and likely was a cost-cutting response to intense competition from other New England pottery factories. Competition may also have contributed to the decision to streamline the production and finishing processes by transitioning from domestic utilitarian wares in the early nineteenth century to mass-produced flowerpots, field tiles, sewer pipe, and retail goods in the late nineteenth to twentieth centuries. Analysis of raw clay samples indicates that the potters utilized the same clay beds along the Danvers and Waters rivers over the entire 150-year span of redware production at the site.

The research and excavation helped document the development of the pottery through its structural and marketing transformations in response to larger socioeconomic changes in the Massachusetts North Shore potting industry. These changes were documented archaeologically as spatial modifications to the pottery itself, changes in labor organization and the ethnic profile of the laborers, and a dramatic increase in labor mechanization. The pottery investigations also provided an opportunity to document examples of craft specialization that continued to be visible in the increasingly mechanized industry. Discarded wares that display nonstandard form, design or decoration could indicate a craftsperson's attempts at creative change. Reused, repaired, and recycled objects could indicate that the individuals who labored at the site were innovative and resourceful (Fennell 2021).

Commercial Baking

While farming and food production was always a significant aspect of the Massachusetts economy, the late nineteenth century saw an increase in industrial food processing and packaging. The background research and an archaeological survey conducted as part of a proposed retail development project in Mansfield identified components of the circa 1890 George P. and Mary Bailey House site and barn as well as structural elements of the circa 1883 Bailey Cracker Bakery and a circa 1897 mincemeat factory operated by the Bailey's on their property (Cherau et al. 2018). The project included a review of town histories and maps; aerial images; land evidence, census, tax, and business directory records; technical literature, patents and designs pertaining to nineteenth- and early twentieth-century bakery ovens and mincemeat ovens/factories; and local informant interviews. The half-acre site boundaries were determined using a combination of documentary data (primarily Sanborn insurance maps), visual survey (locations of oven mounds and visible foundation remains), and hand and machine excavation. The extensive research provided contextual information on bakery development and the rapid technological changes in this industry in Massachusetts over time, and the fieldwork helped document how these technologies were adapted for the specific needs of the Bailey family businesses.

The Bailey family established a farmstead on the property in 1710, and in 1848, Jacob Bailey reportedly began a bread baking business on his farm which was run by his son-in-law and later his son George Edson Bailey, who built his own house on the property and became one of the most prominent businessmen in Mansfield. Deeds indicate that between 1847 and 1888, the Baileys acquired additional land around the original farm where the bakery and later the mincemeat factory were built along with a boarding house for workers, an office, and several family homes including George Palmer's house that was standing until 2008. The bakery operated between 1848 and 1897 and produced crackers, bread, and baked goods, during which time the Baileys transformed the business from a traditional craft shop relying on a version of a traditional brick peel oven into a mechanized, technically modern facility (Cherau et al. 2018).

During this period, most bakeries transitioned to a reel oven where baked goods were suspended on a wheel that revolved over a firebox. George Bailey refined the peel oven to separate the firebox from the baking chamber and build in a series of flues, which resulted in an indirectly heated oven that could operate continuously with no need to relight the fire or reheat the oven. The business expanded with other patented and unpatented innovations including traveling ovens, an "endless steel pan," and new buildings and equipment. Bailey ovens were displayed at numerous fairs and exhibitions, including the Paris Exhibition of 1889 and the 1893 World's Columbian Exhibition in Chicago, and were sold nationally and globally until about 1915 (Copeland 1936, 129–130).

Bailey and his sons also sold his patented oven designs between 1871 and about 1900. Secondary accounts indicate that his ovens were particularly suited for baking bread, cakes, and pastries. Bailey had two sales agents, one for New England and one for the remainder of the United States and they distributed these ovens throughout the United States and in Canada in the early 1880s. Massachusetts public institutions including the State Prison at Concord and the Reformatory at Sherborn also adopted Bailey ovens. By 1890, Joseph Baker and Sons (later Baker Perkins), a prominent British manufacturer of baking machinery, had obtained a license for Bailey's oven and sold it as the "Bailey-Baker Oven" (Bailey 1871, 1872; Copeland 1936, 124; Hurd 1883, 461).

In the early 1880s, the business underwent a rapid expansion. George's sons joined the business, which was incorporated as George E. Bailey and Sons and continued as the sole bakery in town. The spatial configuration of the old bakery was apparently inadequate for Bailey's new traveling oven, and so in 1883 the firm added a large, cracker-baking building to the premises that more than doubled their floor space. A new office was also built, and the old office was converted for storing spices and other baking supplies (Copeland 1936; Foss and Co. 1887; Mansfield News 1888; Sanborn Fire Insurance Company 1887).

The bakery sold its products including crackers, fancy biscuits, and cakes throughout the region. Transport was mostly by bread carts going out from the factory to Boston, Taunton, Fall River, New Bedford, Lowell, and Providence,

Rhode Island. Some of the Bailey baked products were also shipped by train to New York and other parts of New England where Bailey had sales agents. Raw materials including flour, spices, and eggs were most likely obtained locally or transported in by train. The local foundries and machine shops likely supplied the iron components of the ovens and other machinery used in the factory (Copeland 1936, 125; Hurd 1883, 461; Mansfield News 1888).

The cracker bakery building was destroyed by fire in 1888 although newspaper accounts indicate that the ovens survived. By 1897, the Baileys had rebuilt the west portion of the 1883 cracker bakery building and were using it for "Baking and Preserving," and, by 1903, for a mincemeat factory which operated until sometime between 1916 and 1924. The circa 1897 mincemeat factory's oven appears to have been similar to the earlier cracker ovens, utilizing the same "traveling tray" system to bake the mincemeat. Preserved meat was probably acquired for use in the mincemeat pies and chopped at the factory, as there is no evidence for on-site butchering of animals. The other ingredients were probably purchased wholesale as well, and some of these ingredients may have been stored in the stoneware jugs like the one recovered during the excavations.

The bakery employed as many as thirty men in the 1870s and seventy or seventy-five men by 1883. The early shop ran two shifts every day, and the bakers would share beds at the boardinghouse located near the factory on Bailey family property. In addition to the bakers, the shop also utilized wagon drivers. These were not strictly employees but instead operated as quasi-independent contractors who paid the bakery for the goods they sold and then pocketed the profit (Copeland 1936). Bread making was reportedly a separate department and the work was done at night when none of the other workers were around. Census records indicate that the employees and boarders were all men and while most were from Massachusetts, at least three were second generation Irish immigrants. All of the boarders were under age thirty, and several appeared to be related or from the same families. Neighboring households to the bakery included bread salesmen or bakery employees (Cherau et al. 2018, 42–44).

Data recovery investigations at the site focused on two oven mound features and were designed to collect information related to technological innovations in and adaptations to late nineteenth- and early twentieth-century baking and food manufacturing processes. Two perpendicular machine-assisted trenches were excavated into the elevations of each oven feature to obtain cross section profile and plan views. The archaeological research questions explored specific issues relating to the history of development and utilization of the two ovens within the bakery/factory complex. One question focused on what the cracker oven remains could reveal about known contemporaneous technological baking oven advances. The excavations exposed the partial remains of the cracker bakery oven's structure, including brick-faced walls and domed brick oven arches, a cinder-filled ash pit below the cast-iron grate of the oven, as well as the brick base of a rectangular brick chimney or oven draft stack. An unmarked clay pipe bowl collected in the ash pit is one of the few domestic items found in the oven area and was likely deposited by a baker or one of the workmen who would have regularly cleaned out the waste. Recovered hardware parts included an iron rod, an iron disk, an iron bracket, and five short lengths of an iron roller drive chain (Cherau et al. 2019). The excavations indicated that the cracker oven in use at the circa 1883 bakery was similar to Bailey's patented "Bailey Oven" from 1879, designed to incorporate new mechanical innovations to facilitate a continuous baking process. The oven was not fully mechanized, as it still required loading and unloading of baking trays by hand. The oven's structural elements also indicated that Bailey was still experimenting with oven configurations, as some of its features did not precisely match his patented designs (Cherau et al. 2018).

Excavation and analyses were also used to investigate whether the remains of the ovens showed any obvious signs of adaptation or reuse of earlier structures or materials. Despite evidence for some reuse of bricks and refractory materials, the majority of the material observed during excavation and collected for laboratory analysis indicated that construction at the site largely relied on new materials, especially construction of the new ovens. The firebricks identified at the site largely originated from the Presbrey Stove Lining Company of Taunton, Massachusetts, which was one of the largest of its kind in the United States in the late nineteenth century (Elstner Publishing Company 1891, 191). Bailey likely relied on the company to provide the materials for his new ovens, given their geographic proximity to the complex and their ability to produce special order materials. The latter would have been particularly advantageous considering that Bailey appears to have constantly been incorporating new oven innovations and utilizing slightly altered designs with each new oven at the bakery complex, based on the differences observed between the 1879 and 1883 cracker ovens (Cherau et al. 2018, 129).

Hand excavation was completed in the ancillary work rooms associated with the ovens. These included the cracker bakery building foundation which had intact sections of the baking department, storeroom, storage stock, and packing rooms. Artifacts collected from the burn layer below demolition fill largely consisted of architectural debris such as machine-cut and wire nails,

Figure 6.1. Photograph of the partially excavated cracker oven, Bailey Bakery and Mincemeat Factory site (Courtesy of The Public Archaeology Laboratory, Inc.).

brick fragments, window glass, and building slate. The material types and densities suggested that portions of the building may have collapsed in on itself after one of the fires at the complex, then was subsequently filled over during construction of the mincemeat factory (Cherau et al. 2010). Artifacts collected in the storeroom included a glass button and the bowl from a ball clay smoking pipe.

The archaeological investigations documented the technology at a site that is significant for its associations with the emergent market for mass-produced crackers and biscuits in America in the mid- and late nineteenth century. George E. Bailey's patented improvements to the baker's oven are documented as having helped revolutionize the manufacture of baked goods including crackers, biscuits, breads, and pies in the United States and around the world (Cherau et al. 2010). The comparison of the physical machinery and building layouts with written plans and specifications provided information about the technological innovations in and adaptations Bailey and his laborers contributed to late nineteenth- and early twentieth-century baking and food manufacturing processes.

The site did not yield many artifacts relating to other activities at the bakery and mincemeat factory, or to the living and working conditions of the

Bailey family's employees at the complex. As a result, information on these aspects of the bakery and mincemeat factory was largely gleaned through the documentary record. It is likely that the cracker baking and later mincemeat production that took place on site conformed to the standard practices of the late nineteenth century, which were evolving as new technological innovations like oven mechanization were introduced. The employees that carried out these practices probably lived working-class but comfortable lives, some in the boardinghouse at the complex, and their ability to smoke and eat at work suggests that working conditions were not particularly harsh at the factory. The data may be useful for comparison with industrial sites of similar size and scale, to see if Bailey's workers enjoyed more or less autonomy than those at other food production factory sites.

Maritime Industries

Despite the rise of inland industries in the 1820s through 1840s, coastal towns in Massachusetts did not see a corresponding decline in economic success. If anything, towns like Salem, New Bedford, and Gloucester experienced a boom following the success of international trade networks for merchants and the increased capacity and technology for fishing and whaling. Colonial settlers were engaged in near-shore whaling almost immediately and numerous seventeenth-century records relating to the ownership and dispersal of drift whale oil and blubber attests to the importance of this resource (Dow 1925, 1–40). Massachusetts's Indigenous people had harvested whales from shore and in near-shore watercraft for millennia, and the residents of many coastal towns in both the Plymouth and Massachusetts Bay colonies recognized the whale's value as a source of revenue. As early as 1639, the Massachusetts Bay Colony passed an act that encouraged and regulated fisheries, including a provision for drift whales that divided the sum into three parts: one portion for the colonial government, one to the town having jurisdiction, and the third part to the finder (Starbuck 1989).

The organized and deliberate pursuit of offshore whales began in the colonies during the third quarter of the seventeenth century. Communities on the eastern end of Long Island, Martha's Vineyard, Cape Cod, the Bermudas, and Nantucket were the first to outfit boats for coastal expeditions that would usually last one or two weeks. English merchants employed Native Americans as the labor force, who would be paid in turn with a stipulated portion of oil (Starbuck 1989). By the early 1700s, Nantucket had taken the lead in the system of boat whaling from the shore, which characterized the earliest American phase of the fishery, and by 1755, the town of New Bedford entered the industry (Hohman 1928).

During the first half of the eighteenth century, the American whale fishery, with Nantucket in the lead, underwent a steady development in technique, in range of operations, and in size. The tool kit of the whaler was enlarged and improved to include harpoons, lances, whale line, cutting spades, and other articles of whaling craft and gear. Vessels became larger, heavier, and underwent gradual changes in rig and hull which transformed them from small boats and sloops to ocean going schooners and brigs. Massachusetts whaling crews frequently included Native Americans recruited from Cape Cod, Martha's Vineyard, and Nantucket (Kugler 1980). A comprehensive ethnographic study documented the critical contributions of Wampanoag, Black, and Portuguese men to the success of New Bedford's whaling economy (Handsman et al. 2021). Two important advances in whale industry technology that profoundly altered the scope and shape of whale hunting in America occurred in the early 1750s, namely the installation of tryworks on board ships and the separation and utilization of spermaceti, a waxy substance found in the head of sperm whales. Tryworks permitted whalers to immediately process whale blubber and store oil without fear of spoilage, which in turn allowed ships to be at sea for years in pursuit of the highly lucrative sperm whale. Waxy spermaceti, known as "head matter," proved to be an ideal material for candles, and in the late eighteenth and early nineteenth centuries became the most important subsidiary industry in the whale fishery (Kugler 1980).

A thirty-four-acre National Historical Park in downtown New Bedford encompasses more than seventy historic structures and resources associated with the operation of the business (including a custom house, warehouses, candle and rope works, wharves, shops, and offices). To date, no substantive archaeological studies have been conducted in the urban center, however archaeological study of smaller land-based whaling sites has provided important information about how the industry worked. The construction of new buildings and infrastructure within a section of the historic whaling port of Woods Hole Village in Falmouth on Cape Cod required archaeological investigations prior to the start of construction (Glover and Feighner 1991). The work area was adjacent to the circa 1836 stone candle house, built by the town's nineteenth-century whaling industry founder Elijah Swift. Initial background research and historic map review suggested the site could contain deposits and features associated with shipbuilding, salt manufacturing, and supply and support facilities for the whaling industry, including the remains of a bake shop, try and bleaching house, and several storage structures that originally stood in the area.

Extensive documentary research and subsurface testing (a combination of machine-assisted excavation and hand testing) resulted in the location, identification, and assessment of structural features and deposits primarily associated with the Swift whaling industry-related occupation of the site between the late 1820s and early 1860s. The archaeological survey also recovered data relating to later maritime-oriented commercial land use by various owners and businesses.

The Swift Whaling site elements include subsurface structural remains of the former bake shop, and its southeast side and rear yard areas were identified and documented. The bake shop was built around 1836 during the Swift ownership and the three-and-a-half story wood-frame building rested on two courses of raised cut granite blocks placed on edge without mortar or concrete pointing. A course of dry-laid fieldstones was identified in this location and probably served as a shallow support for the raised granite foundation. A burned brick-and-mortar concentration to the northeast side of the foundation was probably associated with the demolition of the bake shop's chimney, which is depicted in photographs. The side yard area of the bake shop foundation also contained two probable footings, one of which likely supported the northeast corner of the one- and one-half story wood-frame paint shop in the village (Glover and Feighner 1991).

The subsurface cultural strata and associated artifact assemblage situated in the side yard area between the candle house and the former bake shop included historic ground surfaces, shallow fill deposit, and associated irregular fieldstones that were interpreted as the documented twenty-foot-wide right-of-way nineteenth-century accessway for the owners of the candle house lot. This space was not designed for a specific work activity but would have been regularly used by the workers, owners, and customers of the businesses it separated. The recovery of highly fragmented ceramics along with bottle glass, mammal and bird bone, and discarded clam shells suggest that laborers, managers, and possibly owners at both businesses took meals while they worked and discarded them in the public space, where they were trampled or possibly intentionally smoothed and covered with clean fill to maintain a tidy appearance. Clay smoking pipe fragments comprised a high percentage of the artifacts in this space, which is not surprising considering this was a well-traversed public space.

Another component of the Swift Whaling site was a series of deep fill deposits with a high density of cultural materials located along the original historic shoreline of Eel Pond. An 1832 plan made by Elijah Swift for his whaling complex depicts the shoreline in a location that corresponds to a stone retaining wall and builder's trench and top and bottom bank ground surface contours documented during the investigations. This area also contained an in situ wooden post, a wooden barrel, and a small brick support structure that may all be associated with a documented early to mid-nineteenth-century boat haul out. The large quantity of nails (including some copper examples) collected from the deepest fill deposits also suggests a related use for small boat repair/maintenance activities. The deepest cultural strata adjacent to the stone wall and brick structure may have formed the historic shoreline ground surface at or near the level of the Eel Pond high-water line. The dense organic soils found at this deepest level contained a concentration of predominantly second and third quarter nineteenth-century nonstructural artifact types and food refuse documenting a diet dominated by fish and mammals with lesser quantities bird, turtle, and shellfish including quahog, softshell clam, scallop, and whelk. This cultural strata was overlain by similar artifact concentrated organic fill deposits that also yielded predominantly mid-to-late-nineteenth-century nonstructural artifacts. This accumulation of fill deposits over what was probably the original ground surface suggests that episodes of food consumption-related trash dumping occurred simultaneously with shoreline whaling-related activities that may have included offloading spermaceti and transporting supplies and provisions onto outgoing vessels. The placement of the barrel either on what was probably the shoreline ground or beach surface or within fill deposits may have occurred during or after the whaling era. Most of the cultural materials contained within the barrel date from the second half of the nineteenth century.

A trash pit was partially excavated at the rear of the candle house and the cultural materials indicate it was utilized over a relatively short period of time in the third and fourth quarters of the nineteenth century for predominantly food/drink consumption-related and personal refuse disposal. Temporally diagnostic materials include tobacco pipes and fragments, ceramic vessel sherds including pearlware, ironstone, whiteware, porcelain, unglazed redware, and American stoneware, and glass bottles. An undocumented structure to the northeast side of the candle house was identified by a small stone structural footing. Historic accounts of the Swift whaling activities suggest that more than one small stone storage shed and/or carriage shed stored to the rear of the candle house during the Swift occupation (Glover and Feighner 1991).

The investigations also documented the remains of a small section of the circa 1836 try house foundation wall (where blubber would be boiled down to "try out" the oil), a possible wood-lined drainage system, and associated cultural material assemblage. The small artifact assemblage recovered from this section of the site area provided relatively little information concerning temporal affiliation or additional evidence of function. The exception may be the presence of two relatively thick window glass fragments that showed evidence of melting on one side. The former try house reportedly had a glass roof used in the bleaching process of whale oil (Glover and Feighner 1991).

The archaeological data collected from the Swift Whaling site contributes to an understanding of the important socioeconomic role of the whaling industry and other maritime-related activities that occurred in Falmouth from the early nineteenth century and into the present day. One of the most personal items to be collected at the site was a complete mid-nineteenth-century whale tooth (ivory) fid with decorative scrimshaw border. Fids were small handheld tools typically made of wood, bone, or ivory that tapered to a point at one end and were used by mariners to splice rope and work knots. This decorated fid was either made by its owner or perhaps exchanged through barter but was probably crafted by a whaleman on one of the yearslong transatlantic voyages that characterized the industry in that period. It was certainly a prized object both as an essential tool of the trade and as a highly visible personalized object and would have been missed by the individual who lost it in the yard next to the bakeshop. Objects like these stand out in the archaeological assemblage because they are so evocative and immediately conjure a mental image of the moment the item was dropped. They help to personalize the other often generic items that were handled and discarded at a busy commercial site used by many people over generations. Since it was recovered, the Swift site fid has been displayed at the nearby Woods Hole Museum as part of the interpretive exhibit documenting the village's whaling history.

Transportation Innovations and "Corridors of Movement"

In the seventeenth and eighteenth centuries, people and goods moved by road, river, and ocean. The development of steam- and coal-powered engines in the nineteenth century allowed the movement of raw materials and finished products at a scale, speed, and ease previously unknown. America's westward expansion opened up untapped supplies of wood, ore, and even water to replace those that had been exhausted in the east, but that required long-distance travel to get them to the industrial centers that needed them. Unlike coastal and ocean transport, Massachusetts's major inland waterways

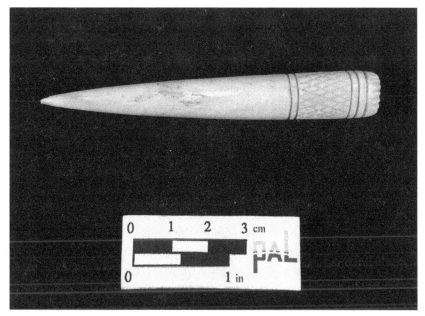

Figure 6.2. Worked ivory fid from the Swift Whaling site (Courtesy of The Public Archaeology Laboratory, Inc.).

had been dammed, impounded, and diverted, and the powerful natural falls that had provided an inexhaustible amount of power were an impediment to riverine transport. The hundreds of mills and other industries that had been built to harness these resources were located along these same waterways and needed faster forms of transportation to keep them running and profitable along what Fennell (2021) refers to as "corridors of movement."

Shipping

Maritime transport remained a reliable and heavily utilized form of transportation in the nineteenth century, even as railroads were introduced. In 2017, the deeply buried remains of a sixty-to-eighty-foot-long, two-masted wooden schooner were discovered under twenty feet of shoreline fill during the construction of an office building along Boston's Seaport district. After consultation with state and city officials, a plan was developed to fully expose and conduct in situ documentation of the undisturbed portions of the ship and limited excavation before the best-preserved portions of the vessel were removed to a storage facility (Banister 2017). Visible intact hull elements included exterior hull planking, heavy transverse rib timbers, ceiling planking, and floor planking. Debris observed within the shipwreck footprint included the forward portion of the keel, a knee timber for bracing/connecting beams to the frame, loose floor planking, and frame timbers. Excavation around the exterior of the ship determined that the hull had settled into the seabed clay after sinking. Analysis of the timbers indicated that the ship had been patched and was likely repurposed for use as a shipping schooner.

Hand and machine-assisted excavation were completed within and immediately surrounding the wreck and documented that the stern had been heavily burned and that many artifacts appeared to have remained in situ when the ship sank, including a stack of ironstone plates that indicate the vessel dates no earlier than the 1840s. Dozens of wooden barrels (most containing lime) were identified throughout the wreck, and portions of six full lime barrels and five partial barrels were found resting on their sides and oriented longitudinally to the ship. Most showed evidence of burning, more heavily on the barrels on the port side of the ship. A barrel lid found in the hull contained a partial stenciled label "ROCKLA" indicating that the ship and its cargo originated from Rockland, Maine, the leading lime producer in America during the mid- to late nineteenth century (Banister 2017).

Intact remains of the shipwreck included the majority of the bottom of the wooden hull above the mudline, and a visual inspection of the remains once they were removed from the project construction site also showed the intact keel and bottom hull planking. Remnants of numerous wooden barrels filled with lime were also present in situ within the ship's hull. Artifacts recovered from the wreck included ironstone and American stoneware ceramics; iron cutlery; a smoking pipe fragment; metal container fragments; machine-cut iron nails, sheathing spikes; fasteners and miscellaneous hardware; a broken whetstone; a flat piece of slate and an unidentified leather fragment. Samples collected for future analyses include barrel stave, lid, and hoop fragments; wooden plank and timber, oakum, iron and brass spikes, and wooden treenails from the ship itself; ballast stone; and lime, charcoal, and soil from directly under the hull (Banister 2017).

The highly combustible nature of lime made fire a fairly frequent occurrence on vessels like this one. The slightest leak could start a fire among the casks that could not be put out with water, and smothering the fire quickly was the only way to save the cargo and vessel. The ship would then head to the nearest harbor and anchor some distance from the wharves and other vessels. If the fire could not be smothered, the vessel was towed to a secluded

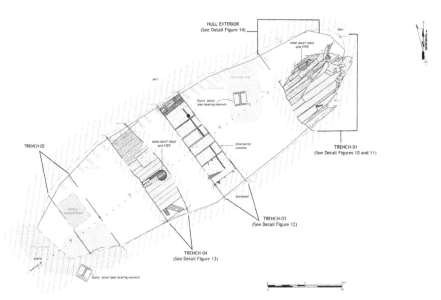

Figure 6.3. Overall plan showing the features of the Seaport Square ship and the location of machine-assisted trenches within the shipwreck (Courtesy of The Public Archaeology Laboratory, Inc.).

place, holes were cut in the hull, and the ship was scuttled. Heavy burning on the port side of the Seaport Square ship, including the lime barrels and the ceiling planking below, indicates the cause of the shipwreck. Fire damage evident in the mid-ship areas is more heavily concentrated toward the stern of the ship with very little evidence of burning on the bow or the starboard side. The orientation of the bow to the northeast, heading away from the wharves, indicates that the fire could not be smoldered and the vessel likely towed to the South Boston Flats, a safe distance away from the wharves and other vessels (Banister 2017).

The archaeological investigations and archived samples document a unique marine shipwreck completely buried under late nineteenth-century land-making deposits in Boston. Only a few examples of this type of site exist, most of which have been identified in New York City (e.g., Reiss 1987). Recordation of the Seaport Square ship's physical remains and cargo provides valuable information about construction techniques of nineteenth-century wooden vessels, mid- to late nineteenth-century coastal, mercantile shipping practices, and historical associations to the regional lime industry. Additional analysis and conservation of the artifacts and lime samples from the wood of the ship may help refine the data and provide more information about the age of the ship. The information gathered from the study was incorporated into an interpretive display and mobile app as part of the new building construction and is featured on the Boston City Archaeology Program website (https://www.boston.gov/departments/archaeology/seaport-shipwreck).

Railways

The Massachusetts Legislature commissioned a series of surveys in the 1820s to chart out an expanded system of canals and railroads across the state and granted rail charters to some companies as early as 1829. The first to be constructed and operated include the Boston and Lowell, Boston and Providence, and Boston and Worcester lines, all of which were operating by 1835. By 1840, there were 285 miles of operating track in Massachusetts, all of them located in the eastern half of the state and by 1850, that number had grown to 1,037 miles and included lines in western Massachusetts providing access to Springfield, Amherst, Pittsfield, and North Adams (Appleton 1871).

One of the most studied Massachusetts railroads is the Old Colony Line which began operation in 1845. Beginning in 1990, archaeological and historic architectural survey, evaluation, and specialized studies were completed along the Main, Middleborough, Greenbush, and Plymouth branches of the Old Colony Railroad in southeast Massachusetts as part of the Massachusetts Bay Transportation Authority's restoration of the lines for commuter rail use (Boire et al. 1994; Glover et al. 1993). The archaeological study areas included new stations, layover facilities, associated parking lots, and construction staging areas in twenty-five towns between Boston and Plymouth. The investigations included extensive research into the history and construction of the historic railroad right-of-way and testing and excavation in archaeologically sensitive areas. One of the archaeological resources investigated and documented as part of the project is the circa 1800s Whitman Roundhouse site. After its initial identification (Boire and Cherau 1995), the site was damaged during construction of the adjacent commuter station and as mitigation, the contractor agreed to pay for site restoration and the creation of an archaeological interpretive park (Cherau et al. 2000).

The investigations revealed the intact surface and below ground remains of the steam locomotive service facility that operated in the town of Whitman from the early 1880s to the late 1930s and includes the granite block structural remains of the four-stall roundhouse, turntable, water tank, ash pit, and bridge abutments. As part of the park creation, the archaeologi-

Figure 6.4. Photograph of the exposed Whitman Roundhouse site (Courtesy of The Public Archaeology Laboratory, Inc.).

cal team exposed the entire roundhouse foundation (exterior and interior walls and supports) and its four brick and granite inspection pits; the entire forty-five-foot-diameter turntable pit, sidewall, and pivot support; and the water tower supports. Additional site elements including a brick-lined ash pit, the boiler house foundation attached to the rear of the roundhouse, and a forge or furnace feature were exposed as part of the site clearing and grading activities. Artifacts collected during the site exposure work included whole and fragmentary bricks, railroad spikes, iron tie plates, wooden ties, cut metal, roof flashing, ceramic tile pipes, coal, and slag as well as several ball clay pipe fragments, molded bottle glass, metal railroad lantern parts, and a small number of ceramics.

The complete exposure of the site as part of the mitigation program helped to clarify the layout and function of the railroad servicing facility. The site originally contained a two-stall engine house that sat close to the Shumatus-cacant River, based on the center granite wall of the roundhouse foundation that likely formed an original outer wall to the earlier two-bay engine house, and supported by the construction technique, structural components, and variation in preservation of the inspection pits in the eastern and western halves of the structure. The railroad facility at this location in Whitman was constructed shortly after the Old Colony Railroad Company's land purchase in 1880. Over time, increased service on the line probably necessitated a larger and more modern engine house. The eastern half of the roundhouse, including a separate boiler house, was constructed in the area closest to the rail bed. The construction materials and technique used in these additions are similar to those used in the original (western) portion of the roundhouse. The roundhouse addition was present by 1906 when the town's tax records list a four-to-five-stall engine house at the site.

The boiler house was added to the structure to provide shelter for a small steam heating boiler and its fuel supply. Historic photographs of the Whitman roundhouse and similar Old Colony Railroad and regional roundhouses indicate that the boiler house was a small rectangular, wood-frame, one-story, shed-roofed addition projected from the rear of the roundhouse. The bulk of the interior was used for storing fuel, likely the same bituminous steam coal burned in the railroad's locomotives. This coal was probably stored in the earth fill section at the east end of the foundation. The boiler pad represents the base of a rectangular, hollow steam boiler housing that would have held a simple coal-fired steam boiler consisting of a horizontal steel tank set over a coal burning grate, with ports to manipulate the draft. A flue would have carried combustion gasses to the brick smokestack, the circular brick base of which is located at the northwest corner of the foundation. This short smokestack is visible in circa 1930s photographs of the roundhouse. The steam and hot water produced by the boiler were used for heating the building and cleaning purposes; and was routed through pipes in the inspection pits to melt accumulated ice and snow from the running gear of the locomotives during the winter.

The Whitman Roundhouse Park site was designed to be a passive archaeological and industrial landscape park, in which visitors or commuters can learn about the area's past within a historically appropriate setting. The placement of a permanent interpretive panel on the adjacent high-level commuter station platform provides a means for the general public to become informed about the site's history.

Archaeological mitigation was needed in East Boston in advance of a planned shoreline stabilization project there in response to the increased impacts of storm surges, storms, and sea level rise due to climate change. These surveys documented nineteenth-century marine railways that are components of the East Boston Dry Dock Company/Atlantic Works Yard, a National Register-eligible historic resource. Studies included a reconnaissance survey and extensive background research including site history, historic maps and photographs, and geotechnical studies around the shoreline that included three marine railways with two associated ship cradles, three piers, derrick foundation remains, and the footings of three buildings constructed and used by the Atlantic Works Company and its predecessor, the East Boston Dry Dock Company, between circa 1853 to circa 1950 (Cherau et al. 2008). The archaeological recordation provided important information concerning the design of the East Boston marine railways that may not be available in the written record (for example, original design and repair/reconditioning plans made by the Crandall Company).

Once project plans were finalized, archaeological investigations within a more limited portion of the site included total station mapping, measured drawings, and photography of the marine railway structures above the mean high-water line prior to construction, and archaeological documentation of their removal during construction (Banister et al. 2018). The intertidal and submerged portions of the railway were also documented as part of a separate project (Tuttle 2017).

The East Boston Dry Dock Company was established at the site in 1853 to design and build clipper ships, and, with the support businesses that grew around it, made East Boston the nationwide center for advanced ship design in the second half of the nineteenth century. The first marine railway was built circa 1854 by the Crandall Dry Dock Engineers (originally of Newport, Rhode Island, and later of East Boston and currently in Bourne, Massachusetts); it had one set of rails six hundred feet long with a 1,000-ton capacity at or near the location of Marine Railway No. 3. In 1892, the East Boston Dry Dock Company hired the Crandall Company again to construct a second, larger marine railway (2,000-ton capacity), with two sets of rails immediately north of the first, at the location of Marine Railway No. 2. The original (circa 1854) railway was rebuilt or extended inland, and a new railway head house was constructed for the winch engine and machinery about that time. The railways were in continuous use by the various owners of the East Boston shipyard until circa 1950.

The pre-construction and monitoring fieldwork recorded structural information for the railway's surface components and additional information about the interior cradle components and railway support system. Railway components for both structures consisted of two-track wood rail and sleeper systems, one of which had timber pile foundation supports; wrought-iron and steel bar yokes used as part of the hauling (chain) mechanisms. Wooden cradle remains consisted of transverse floor (deck) beams, longitudinal stringers, transverse keel blocks, and a few in situ vertical upright timbers. The archaeological record also included an associated stone crib that was likely related to a wood platform used to service the railways to either side.

The analysis of the recorded data confirms that the East Boston railways were of standard nineteenth-century composition for larger marine railways (over about 500 tons). The two railways, constructed two years apart, differed in size and tonnage capacity but were similar in design and materials used. A few notable differences pertain to their hauling mechanisms and rail system designs, both attributable to the size and tonnage of the vessels that each was designed to service in the late nineteenth and early to mid-twentieth centuries. The upland sections of the two railways were consistent with those documented underwater and extending seaward to the harbor channel (Tuttle 2017). Documentation of the East Boston marine railways provided an opportunity to analyze and interpret their design and construction in relation to other Crandall-built railways including the Burnham's Marine Railway Complex in Gloucester, Massachusetts, (Cherau et al. 2017) and Marine Railway No. 11 at the Charlestown Navy Yard in Boston (Carlson 2010), and other documented nineteenth- and early twentieth-century marine railways in southeastern Connecticut.

Because Marine Railway No. 2 in East Boston is one of the largest marine railways subject to formal archaeological study, the new data allow greater distinction to be made between rail and cradle designs for small and large capacity marine railways. Additionally, comparison of Marine Railway Nos. 2 and 3 in East Boston with those in southeastern Connecticut draws out regional differences in marine railway design. This combined new information contributes to a better understanding of these types of maritime resources in eastern Massachusetts specifically and in New England in general.

Conclusions

Massachusetts's industrial legacy figures prominently in current sociopolitical issues related to history, preservation, and environmental justice. In 2012, the Town of Ipswich in Essex County began debating the removal of the obsolete and deteriorating granite masonry Ipswich Mills Dam which was constructed in 1880 to help power the Ipswich Hosiery Mills. The historic dam is located at a site that has been used for water control since at least 1637, making it one of the earliest industrial sites on the Ipswich River to be developed by English settlers (Cherau and Banister 2024; Waters 1905,

1917). A noninvasive archaeological reconnaissance study completed as part of the federal and state funding partnership determined that two previously identified ancient sites and two seventeenth-century house foundations were located within the dam removal limit-of-work (MHC site files). The study also documented the potential for unrecorded archaeological sites within the work areas including a seventeenth-century footbridge of fording place, a 1729 sawmill, a 1764 English-built stone fish weir, a 1794 scythe mill, as well as evidence of the eighteenth- and nineteenth-century dams and mills that preceded the Ipswich Hosiery Mills: a gristmill, fulling mill, hemp mill, and lace factory (Cherau and Banister 2024). Like several other sites discussed above, the removal of the circa 1880 industrial dam may provide important new information about older industrial and archaeological resources that were covered or obscured when the historic dam was built.

Proponents of dam removal cited the benefits of returning tidal flow and natural fish passage to the river, which had been dammed for nearly four centuries. Those wishing to preserve the dam cited the ponded reservoir behind it that is a popular recreation area and the potential for sediment release that could contaminate shellfish beds downstream (Baker 2024a, 2024b). The Ipswich Historical Commission (IHC), which functions as an official local government body, reviewed the potential dam removal project, and offered a written opinion to the Town Select Board and Planner. The IHC said its review addressed a central question: "Is it essential to preserve the Ipswich Mills Dam to mark our recent industrial history, or should it be removed so that the river can run as it has for millennia?" (IHC 2024). They noted that while the dam was a historic resource, it had not been listed in the state's cultural resource inventory or in the National Register of Historic Places. They also noted that removal of the 1880 dam, if completed with archaeological monitoring, had the potential to expose and document earlier ancient and colonial archaeological resources that had been inundated by industrial development in the nineteenth century (see above discussion of Pelham Timber Dam). The IHC ultimately decided in favor of the historic dam removal, noting that they had considered "not just the last few hundred years of history along the Ipswich River, but also the many millennia that preceded it. . . . For 14,000 years, it has shaped the land, nourished flora and fauna, sustained the lives of Indigenous Peoples and European settlers, and was instrumental in the birth of our historic town. The IHC believes that we can best preserve the history of the Ipswich River by freeing it from unnecessary man-made encumbrance" (IHC 2024).

This case study and others in this chapter highlight many of the issues faced by American communities who are struggling to manage aging and obsolete industrial sites that often come with unsafe structures and equipment and contaminated soils and water. Many of these industrial developments helped to anchor and support the economies of the towns where they were built but are now a burden and potential liability to those charged with their maintenance. In Massachusetts and nationwide, concerns about social and environmental justice, climate change, sustainability, and affordable housing often coalesce around historic industrial sites and their treatment. Industrial and historic archaeologists are well-positioned to document and interpret the wide range and variety of industrial resources that make up part of our built environment prior to their remediation, rehabilitation, restoration, and/or removal.

Archaeologists can learn about technological innovations and improvements that were not part of original construction plans or company records; they can help answer questions about when and how technology altered the natural environment, and what materials may have contaminated an area; they can address capitalism's effects on power and resistance and its effects based on gender age, ethnicity, and social class; and they can provide information about the individuals who planned, built, owned, managed, labored at and often lived near the sites of industrial work. These stories are an important part of each community's history and a core component of American identity.

Work sites were not the only places where people were organized into a community. The increasingly stratified social, ethnic, and economic divisions created in part by the Industrial Revolution led to the formation of new groups within Massachusetts and across America. Some were voluntary and based on shared ideals and beliefs, others were involuntary and created to punish, reform, or aid. These communities may appear to have little in common, but they offer archaeologists the opportunity to compare the stated goals of these places to the lived experiences of their members.

7

The Archaeology of Community

The nineteenth-century industrialization of Massachusetts led to a decline in the agricultural economy and a population shift out of the small towns and rural communities that had characterized settlement for nearly two hundred years. This shift also corresponded to an influx of immigrants from European countries, who were eager to find employment in the region's factories and mills and in domestic service. As sites of labor became increasingly concentrated in urban areas, people from different ethnic and social backgrounds increasingly came into contact with one another. This pattern was seen across the country with more and more immigrant arrivals from the mid-nineteenth through early twentieth centuries.

At the same time, Massachusetts's Indigenous peoples were confronted with new challenges to their individual and collective tribal identities. After more than a century of government oversight within geographically isolated residential reservations, new laws ended communal land ownership and sought to break up Native groups. Massachusetts's Indian tribes responded by reinforcing their cultural bonds and even when the growing American mosaic created new divisions in society, where ethnicity and race, socioeconomic status, religion, and gender were increasingly used to categorize and separate people. Archaeological study of the places where groups of people lived, worked, worshipped, were confined, and died provides an opportunity to investigate individual and collective identity, expressions of power and control, and the methods and means of dominance and resistance.

This chapter explores how different communities were organized and maintained, how they were viewed in the past and are remembered today, and how the study of historical communities can inform modern-day sociopolitical discourse and government policy. Archaeologists have the ability to interrogate these concepts through the critical analyses of archives and material culture to help understand how communities (and the individuals within them) were defined by others and how they defined themselves.

Indigenous Identity and Heritage

The 1869 Massachusetts Indian Enfranchisement Act granted citizenship and voting rights to all "Indians and people of color, heretofore known and called Indians" within the Commonwealth. This legislation ended the reservation period and meant that Indigenous people were no longer considered wards of the state, conditions that had existed in one form or another since the creation of John Eliot's missionary villages in the 1600s (see Chapter 2). The Act was preceded by nearly two decades of study and debate including state-sponsored censuses to identify each Massachusetts Indian tribe and its members (Briggs 1849; Earle 1861), surveys of reservation lands, and their divisions into fee-simple lots owned by individual tribal members. This treatment of Massachusetts's Indigenous people dovetailed with federal Reconstruction-era policies that suppressed rights based on race and ethnicity (Plane and Button 1993).

The shift in Massachusetts's Indian policy was presented as a way to empower Indigenous people by removing the yoke of state oversight and, importantly, giving them the right, for the first time, to buy and sell land individually. For most Native groups, the Enfranchisement Act fractured community cohesion and wrested control from Indians of homelands that had been maintained communally for generations. The Act became another means for the government to attempt to strip Indians of their identity and impose non-Native systems of land tenure. This shift in Indian policy away from distinctive tribal recognition has also posed a significant obstacle for Massachusetts tribes seeking federal acknowledgment (Campisi 1993). The act of official "detribalization" meant that censuses and other government records no longer acknowledged Indigenous groups or individuals. This nineteenth-century legislation and Earle's own racist observations have been cited in denials of federal recognition for several Massachusetts Indian tribes (Thee 2006). The Office of Federal Acknowledgment has privileged these biased sources over ample evidence that Massachusetts tribes maintained social and political cohesion throughout the nineteenth and twentieth centuries.

Despite these external pressures, Indigenous groups maintained and strengthened their communities in the nineteenth century as they also incorporated new systems of government and an increasing focus on individual

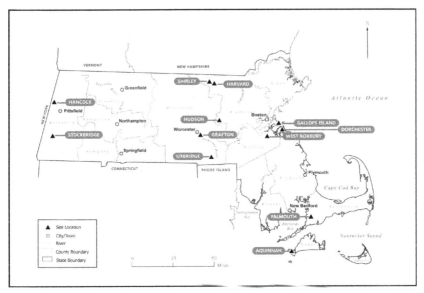

Map 7.1. Map of Massachusetts showing locations of sites discussed in Chapter /.

identity. Collaborative studies between Massachusetts tribes and archaeologists have focused on this period and the ways in which distinctly Native lifeways were maintained while they simultaneously evolved.

In the early 1990s, the federally recognized Wampanoag Tribe of Gay Head (Aquinnah) (WTGH/A) completed archaeological surveys across their more than 500 acres of tribal trust lands located on Martha's Vineyard (Glover and McBride 1991, 1992). Aquinnah is one of the few places in Massachusetts that remained an entirely Indigenous community into the early twentieth century. The studies were conducted by archaeologists in collaboration with tribal members, elders, historians, and ethnographic consultants, and documented more than forty home and farmstead sites dating from the mid-1700s to the late 1800s. The Wampanoag families that comprised the nineteenth-century Old South Road community relocated to the new main state road in the 1870s, leaving behind numerous well-preserved residential cellar holes, barns, outbuildings, animal pens, agricultural fields, and orchards, and cart paths that were documented as part of the tribal survey program (Glover and McBride 1991, 1992). The majority of these sites contain fieldstone foundations built into the south facing slope of a hill in an architectural style known as a "crofter cottage" that may have been adopted because of its similarity to traditional Indigenous building practices (Cherau 2001; McBride and Cherau 1996). The Aquinnah artifact deposits are rich in Euro-American domestic goods and building materials but also highly variable. The differences observed at these sites may reflect the occupation of the head of the family. Many Aquinnah Wampanoag men were employed in the whaling industry and away from the island for years at a time, while others maintained productive farmlands and pastures (Glover and McBride 1992; Glover et al. 1993).

Some of the nineteenth-century Wampanoag sites in Aquinnah contain chipped and ground stone tools that are typically associated with the pre-European period (Herbster and Cherau 2002, 2006). Studies at nineteenth-century Nipmuc homesteads in Worcester County have documented similar patterns of traditional tool use (Bagley et al. 2014) as well as procurement and consumption practices that demonstrate distinctively Native patterns (Allard 2014; Pezzarossi 2014).

Like the Aquinnah studies, decades of collaboration between the Nipmuc Nation and the University of Massachusetts Boston continues to document Native identity and cultural continuity in Grafton, the center of multigenerational tribal matriarchies (Gould et al. 2020). Archaeological investigations and analyses at the nineteenth-century homesteads of Sarah Boston and her descendants and Sarah Arnold Cisco and her descendants have led to the collection of thousands of belongings and identification of dozens of domestic and structural features. These homeplaces served as communal gathering spots where cultural identity was reinforced and strengthened at precisely the time when the government was trying to dilute it (Gould 2013, 2017; Law Pezzarossi 2014, 2019).

The Stockbridge-Munsee Community Band of Mohican Indians, through its Tribal Historic Preservation Office, has directed several cultural heritage and archaeological projects at important sites located in and around Stockbridge. The Tribe has conducted ground-penetrating radar to help identify and then mark Mohican ancestral graves in the town cemetery and hired cultural resource consultants to assist with archaeological survey at the circa 1739 meetinghouse site and the location of the 1783 Ox Roast Feast site. Both projects have utilized ground-penetrating radar and magnetometry to identify and document site components including possible structures without destructive excavation. The meetinghouse is central to the founding of "Indian Town"—present-day Stockbridge—and was a building where tribal members and colonists worshipped together and held communal advocacy meetings (Stockbridge-Munsee Community 2023). The Ox Roast Feast occurred at

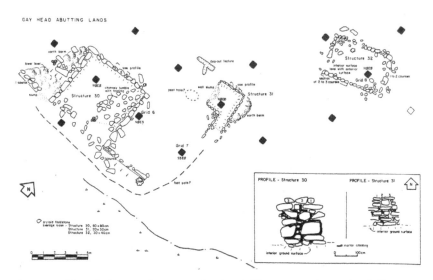

Figure 7.1. Plan of nineteenth century Aquinnah Wampanoag homestead site (Courtesy of The Public Archaeology Laboratory, Inc.).

the homesite of the Mohican leader Solomon Uhhaunaunauwaunmut, and is a well-documented event sponsored by General George Washington to thank Stockbridge-Munsee men who had served the colonial militia during the Revolutionary War (Campetti 2020). As of 2023, the documentation of both sites is ongoing. Archaeological study may provide material evidence of this historical event that can help tell a decolonized story of the feast and connect its location to generations of use by Stockbridge-Munsee ancestors. The Stockbridge-Munsee lived in present-day Stockbridge through the colonial period when they were displaced from their homelands and resettled in Wisconsin. For tribal members, the site of the Ox Roast Feast provides a physical connection to ancestors from whom they have been absent. Their active participation in the archaeological work is a means for the Stockbridge-Munsee to bring their own history forward and to reconnect them with the Stockbridge community (Abbott 2021).

Sites of Confinement

The nineteenth century saw the rise of formalized institutions that ranged from collective and utopian societies to places of confinement for sick, poor, and criminal residents of Massachusetts. They are places where people's daily lives were controlled either by choice or by force and where the goal, in one form or another, was to deprive people of liberty. Individuals were often denied material possessions, autonomy, family life, individual expression and even personal safety (Casella 2007). They are places where archaeology can address questions about gender, power, inequality, and social ideologies. They provide an opportunity to investigate how these places were organized and operated and connect individuals within their walls to the places where they came from and went before and after their institutional confinement.

Poor Farms and Almshouses

The Town of Falmouth adopted outdoor relief as the earliest form of support for the poor. In 1812, the town purchased a tavern to house the poor and hired the tavernkeeper to run the operation. The circa 1769 building had been moved from a rural area to the town center in 1814, and in the 1990s archival, architectural, and archaeological studies were undertaken prior to planned repairs and reuse (Strauss and Spencer-Wood 1999). The results were used to examine changing attitudes about how communities addressed poverty, and whether gender differences could be discerned (Spencer-Wood 2009; Spencer-Wood and Matthews 2011).

The documentary research tracked historic references and records to see how the institution was identified over time. Most maps label it the "Town Almshouse" and most town records refer to it as the "Almshouse" or "Poor House." A few sources refer to the "Town Farm" and in the early twentieth century it was labeled the "Town Infirmary" and alternatively as the "Work House." These shifting designations are typical of nineteenth-century town institutions and partially reflect outside perceptions of their purpose and occupants. They also provide clues about how the operations were run. In Falmouth's case, there is evidence that residents who were able tended a small farm on the property and possibly did domestic work like laundering and sewing. These tasks may or may not have been voluntary and residents were not paid for their labor but rather expected to help support themselves, with any surplus sold and profits taken by the Town.

Archaeological testing at the site was limited but identified mismatched ceramics dating from the 1780s to 1820s. This pattern documents the poor house's reliance on donations of old tablewares from residents, a practice encouraged by the Town. Fragments of labeled patent medicine bottled included one used to treat syphilis. Recovered liquor bottle fragments match supply records that indicate the medicinal use of alcohol rather than illicit drinking. The excavations also collected a variety of mixed types of buttons which suggest that the inmates did not wear standardized uniforms. Like the mismatched tablewares, the button varieties suggest that town officials were more concerned with the expense of supporting residents than with creating a homogeneous institutionalized setting.

The architectural review documented changes to the original tavern that included additions and the division of rooms into smaller segmented spaces. Initially, the tavern was unmodified, and the poor were housed in large communal areas. In 1823, the town's poor were classified as "partially supported . . . old and young in health . . . insane and nonCompos [*non compos mentis* is a Latin legal term translating literally to 'of unsound mind'] . . . [and] sick incurable past labor" (cited in Spencer-Wood 2009, 127). This description followed early nineteenth-century European ideologies about the care of the poor that had largely been adopted in America, where individuals were typically placed into two categories: the "worthy" poor who could not work because of age, illness or accidents, or mental ability and the "unworthy" poor who were considered able-bodied but lazy, immoral, criminals, or drunks. After 1824, modifications were made to the structure, including the creation of internal eight-foot square rooms, and it became much easier to segregate groups. Records indicate that first men, women, boys, and girls were separated into wings, and that a later division was made by floor, possibly segregating the insane to the attic and separating the disabled from the able-bodied. Divisions by age, gender, and health would have separated family members or kin from one another and contributed to the isolation and lack of autonomy for some residents.

Spencer-Wood (2009) found that in Falmouth, women were placed into both categories. Unwed pregnant women were considered "disabled" but also "unworthy" because of their immoral behavior. She attributed at least some of these classifications to the inherent patriarchy in these institutions. Men controlled the Town's government, wrote the state regulations, selected the locations and structures used, and appointed the keepers. These factors led to more women than men being confined in poorhouses. Unmarried or widowed women were less likely to be employed or make wages hence more likely to need assistance, and "disobedient" women were often institutionalized for not following the Victorian norms of domesticity expected in male-dominated families and marriage. Their sexual activity outside of marriage was classified as immoral or insane. Men were not accused of or institutionalized for the same behaviors. Over its existence, women comprised the majority of the Falmouth Poor Farm occupants except for a short period after the Civil War when injured veterans were the group, and a period during the 1870s depression when "tramps" (presumably men) worked in exchange for a night or two of lodging. Women were also less likely to be "put out" because they could not provide the level of labor that men did. Most were single women and, increasingly, women with children evidenced by receipts for small beds and other supplies for children. The historical stigma of homeless people as viewed by dominant members of society has been the subject of recent archaeological scholarship that finds parallels between the past and present treatment of the unhoused (Sayers 2023).

Most of the poor farm residents (often referred to in records as "inmates") were white, however ethnicity was only recorded after 1846, and records describe only three people of color and no Native Americans. Spencer-Wood speculated that given Falmouth's proximity to the nearby Mashpee Indian Reservation, the Indigenous community may have supported people of color in need of assistance. After 1866, records of payments by the Town indicate that people classified as "insane" were sent to the state institution in Taunton, coinciding with a shift from local to state-run institutions.

The care of the poor underwent a transformation across Massachusetts in the early nineteenth century after an 1821 legislative report recommended the creation of town almshouses as the most efficient, economic, and humane way to address the growing numbers of indigent residents in the state (Quincy 1821). The Quincy Report, as it was known, compiled information collected from each Massachusetts town to determine how much money was being spent annually on aid. The study determined that most towns primarily relied on "outdoor relief" which was the practice of paying town residents to board and care for indigent community members. The creation of town farms (alternately referred to as almshouses and poor farms) followed English reform ideologies and was seen as a way to consolidate resources, contain expenses, and provide a mechanism for able-bodied individuals to work or farm to help offset the cost of their care.

Town poor farms were established in most Massachusetts communities by the mid-nineteenth century, often on established farms with existing housing, barns, and outbuildings. The records for town farms are often incomplete and typically consist of yearly expense summaries at town meetings and occasional records of goods and supplies purchased for the residents. Individual names and dates of occupation do not often exist (if they were recorded at all). Archaeological investigations at two town farm cemeteries in Uxbridge and Hudson provided important information about these places that was not recorded elsewhere (Bell 1993; Cook 1991).

The Uxbridge Almshouse in Worcester County had been largely forgotten until the early 1980s when survey for a highway relocation project identified possible gravestones and an associated segment of a fieldstone wall. The almshouse was in operation between about 1831 and 1872, after which the town sold the property, and the abandoned buildings were demolished or removed. Town records indicated the size of the cemetery, and archaeologists used property maps and visible unmarked stones to identify, excavate, and relocate a total of thirty-one graves containing the remains of thirty-two individuals (Elia and Wesolowsky 1991). Records for the interments did not survive (if they existed at all), so researchers used the physical anthropology analyses and census records to try to identify the remains. Like many nineteenth-century institutions, the Uxbridge Almshouse residents were listed in federal and state censuses as a distinct "household," making these records one of the only ways to find individuals at town-supported facilities.

In the introduction to the osteological synthesis, Wesolowsky (1991, 230) noted that while the almshouse records contained minutiae about the costs of maintaining the residents, they contained virtually no information about the individuals themselves. While only one set of skeletal remains could be definitively linked to an individual whose name is known, the osteological analysis provided an opportunity to earn something of the people who died while at the poor farm. Nearly a third of the individuals who were buried in the cemetery were over the age of fifty and 20 percent were children under the age of two. While these percentages may be accounted for by health issues that would have afflicted the very young and the very old in the nineteenth century, the authors suggest that this follows the pattern of nineteenth-century support institutions, where able-bodied adults who were able to work were more likely to support themselves and therefore not need public aid. Within the twenty-to-forty-year age range, there were only two burials of men compared to seven of women.

This gender disparity was interpreted as possibly representative of men's relative freedom to travel away from their homes in search of work to support themselves, while women had less mobility and were also likely to stay close to their children or other family members (Wesolowsky 1991, 235). The analyses also determined that the interred individuals suffered from poor dental health with a large percentage of teeth lost in life, a possible indicator of scurvy or other nutritional deficiencies. There was also no evidence in any individual of any type of dental intervention in remaining teeth that showed signs of caries or other disease. While members of the non-indigent rural

Massachusetts population during this period may have also suffered from poor dental health, the skeletal analysis indicates that residents were not treated while they were there for what would have been extremely painful conditions (Wesolowsky 1991, 246).

One of the two adult males had been subjected to an autopsy (as evidenced by the removal of the top of his cranium), suggesting to the researchers that he may have suffered from some medical condition or mental state that prevented him from working. This individual may have been the involuntary subject of medical experimentation or training for a local doctor, who would have been able to use the body without consent from relatives (Wesolowsky 1991).

The burial and funerary treatment exhibited in the Uxbridge Almshouse artifact assemblage appeared to confirm that the town's desire was to care for the poor with as little expense as possible. Most individuals were buried in simple wooden coffins, the majority of which appeared to have been made by local carpenters with generic hardware that was locally available at mercantile stores (Bell 1991). A number of the graves contained remnants of decorative hinges, glass viewing plates, and possible coffin lining tacks. Several graves contained straight pins, textile fragments, and clothing fasteners (including a metal buckle and bone and mother-of-pearl buttons) that indicates individuals were dressed, possibly in their own clothing, when buried (Bell 1991). These materials document more than the minimal burial treatment, which would have consisted of a naked body wrapped in a shroud and would have been less costly than a coffin burial. This suggests that death and mortuary ritual held at least some importance to town officials or the overseers, and that they felt compelled to offer at least some dignity to the residents in death.

Government Institutions

By the mid-nineteenth century, Massachusetts, like many states, began transitioning to more formalized city and state-run institutions that were specifically designed as prisons and reformatory schools, infirmaries and sanatoriums, quarantine hospitals, training schools, and insane asylums (Casella 2007). The people who had formerly been housed collectively in local poor farms and almshouses were now categorized and placed in what was deemed to be the appropriate institution. These facilities were located across the state but typically near an urban center as well as on several of the Boston Harbor Islands, where physical isolation and proximity to Boston created ideal conditions for confinement and observation.

One of these sites in the Boston Harbor Islands is the Gallops Island Quarantine Hospital, opened in 1866 after the City of Boston took over an existing Civil War–era Army complex on the island. The timing coincided with a cholera outbreak that threatened to affect Boston, and the city felt that the location would be ideally suited with an existing wharf to receive patients and buildings ready to be occupied. In 1867, the city formally transferred Gallops Island to the Directors for Public Institutions to be used to care for infectious patients. This coincided with the arrival of great numbers of Irish immigrants who had fled the Great Famine beginning in the late 1840s. Between 1841 and 1861 nearly 170,000 Irish immigrants arrived in Boston by sea; 129,387 of them between 1846 and 1851. To place these numbers in perspective, in 1850 Boston's native-born population comprised 65 percent of the total population but Irish immigrants accounted for nearly 25 percent of the total and were far and away the largest immigrant group in the city (Handlin 1974, 242–3). Their transport to America on crowded and unsanitary "coffin ships," meant that many immigrants arrived in Boston with communicable diseases. The Irish were already stigmatized by Boston's Brahmin class for their Catholic religion and perceived lack of urban awareness and skills, so the potential to spread deadly disease only compounded political efforts to isolate them (Puleo 2010).

By 1870, Gallops Island had expanded into a complex of dormitories, a hospital, steam washing facilities, laboratories, and staff housing, although these were largely left over from the Civil War-era occupation of the island (George et al. 2021, 68). During an 1872–1873 smallpox outbreak, a total of 1,017 people died in Boston. Of these, 180 people died on Gallops Island, with 177 victims buried in the island cemetery. Records indicate that at least 238 people were interred in the island cemetery while it was in use (George et al. 2021).

Coastal erosion and damage to the existing seawall on Gallops Island led to the exposure of several graves and human remains prompting the Massachusetts Department of Conservation and Recreation, which owns and manages the island for the Commonwealth, to relocate threatened graves. Efforts included mapping of the visible cemetery, identifying burial shafts, coffins, and other features, and excavating and analyzing the recovered human remains, funerary material culture, and associated personal items prior to their reinterment.

The archaeological investigations were initially guided by a 1906 city engineer of Boston map of the Gallops Island Quarantine Cemetery that depicted eight parallel rows extending in an east to west direction and one row of burials in a north to south direction depicting at least 230 interments (City of Boston 1906). The 1906 map also recorded the location, number, name of the decedent, date of death, and age at death for each plotted grave, presumably recorded from the wooden markers that were placed at each grave beginning with its use during the 1872–1873 epidemic, had been replaced at least once, and were no longer present. Armed with this incredibly detailed information, the archaeological team assumed that it would be relatively easy to match each of the excavated remains with the map key and to in turn this information to assist with genealogical study to help identify living descendants (George et al. 2021, 92).

As soon as the excavations began, however, the archaeological team realized the map would not be a reliable resource. The locations of adults and children, as observed in the field by burial shaft size and through osteological examination, did not match the map records, and at least six earlier burials that were not documented on any available maps had been partially impacted by graves dug during the 1872–1873 epidemic. Fragments of coffin wood, nails, and unidentifiable rusted pieces of metal were identified in the grave shaft fill of several smallpox victim burials, evidence that the gravedigger had disturbed an older coffin burial as he prepared a new one. Additional research suggested that the unknown burials may have been individuals who died during short smallpox outbreak in 1867, and the archaeologists concluded that the 1906 mapmaker either relied on replacement markers that were not in their original locations and/or that record-keeping during the cemetery's period of use was not consistently accurate (George et al. 2021, 92).

In total, fifty-seven burials were excavated and forty-two individual sets of remains with varying degrees of preservation were identified. Though it was not possible to match patient hospital records with specific graves, the remains did allow for some demographic analysis. Young adults between the ages of fifteen and thirty-four made up slightly more than half of the excavated sample, followed by children and adolescents (birth to age fifteen) at 21 percent of the total. Individuals over fifty years of age were the smallest sample group, representing only 5 percent of the total. The analysis determined that many individuals suffered from chronic health conditions including dental caries, broken and healed bones, degenerative joint diseases, and dietary stress (George et al. 2021, 197–200).

Those who died on the island were buried in simple wooden coffins sealed with nails or wood screws, in stark contrast the "Beautification of Death" movement that was at its height during the 1870s and certainly because of the desire to quickly inter diseased corpses (Baugher and Veit 2014; Bell 1984). Relatively few personal items were found and mostly consisted of buttons and other clothing fasteners. Two crucifixes and rosary beads were the only religious items that survived (George et al. 2021). The fate of the remaining 150 known burials at the cemetery are tied to ongoing efforts to combat the effect of climate change on Gallops Island. If coastal stabilization efforts are not successful or if storms exacerbate shoreline erosion, the excavation of more threatened graves may be necessary.

The difficulties in identifying individuals at historic cemeteries is not unique to Gallops Island. As discussed above, individuals who died and were interred in institutional cemeteries at poor farms, orphanages, asylums, boarding schools, and prisons were often dehumanized in death as they had been in life (Baugher and Veit 2014; Bell 1994). Most died away from family and friends who would have overseen their funeral and burial, making sure the deceased was treated with care and buried with dignity. Even when relatives were notified of a death at an institution, they may not have had the financial means to pay for a coffin or burial plot or been able to afford to travel and retrieve the decedent. There are numerous examples of entire cemeteries in Massachusetts that have been lost over time, rediscovered only when modern development means they must be removed and relocated (Kelly 2023).

These examples are not unique to Massachusetts nor to the nineteenth century. Across the country, individual graves and entire cemeteries have been forgotten or destroyed due to intentional obfuscation; lax, lost, or nonexistent records; and faulty historical memory. Many of these locations contain the remains of people who were marginalized and often segregated while living because of their ethnicity, gender, socioeconomic status, physical or mental health, religion, or sexuality.

These burial places stand in stark contrast to the highly ordered and ornate Victorian cemeteries that were created during the same period, where the dead were permanently memorialized with elaborate markers and landscaped grounds. According to its website, Cambridge's Mount Auburn Cemetery is designed to "inspire all who visit, comfort the bereaved, and commemorate the dead in a landscape of exceptional beauty" (https://www.mountauburn.org/). Opened in 1831 as the first "garden cemetery" in America, it was designed to serve not only as a burial ground for some of Boston's most elite residents, some of whom, no doubt, influenced public policy regarding the institutions described above. Mount Auburn Cemetery is a National Historic

Landmark, a distinction that indicates its importance as an American historical resource. The individuals who were interred at nineteenth-century poor farms, prisons, schools, and hospitals are no less deserving of remembrance.

Training Institutions

Nineteenth-century confinement was not always involuntary. The Industrial School for Girls was founded in 1853 in Winchester, Massachusetts, by a group of wealthy primarily Bostonian women who wanted to ". . . remove from their miserable homes children whose circumstances surround them with temptation and whose education furnishes them with no means of resistance; to train them to good personal habits; to instruct them in household labor, and to exert a moral influence and discipline over them, which shall fit them to be faithful and efficient in domestic service, or in any probable mode of gaining their own livelihood" (Bagley et al. 2018b, 27; Industrial School for Girls 1860).

The Industrial School for Girls relocated to the Dorchester section of Boston in 1859 and operated there until 1890. Over its history, more than 180 girls, up to thirty at a time, lived there. Generally aged between nine and fifteen, girls as young as six appear in the records and a girl could stay until she turned eighteen, unless an exception was made for her to remain at the school for a longer period (Bagley et al. 2018b, 27). Students were sent to the school from disadvantaged homes to live there year-round and were given an education and taught the skills they would need to work in domestic service. Managers accepted girls into the school through an application process, and each girl was assigned a manager who was the point of contact with the family and responsible for the girl's progress while at the school.

The site was proposed for development in 2011, and while the original school building was to be left standing, new construction was planned in the areas surrounding the structure, so the Boston City Archaeology Program conducted testing at the rear of the property which identified the subsurface remains of a shed and a privy. The school records in 1860 noted, "We received . . . two liberal donations . . . appropriated to building a shed, with outhouses, which were emphatically required for health and convenience" (cited in Bagley et al. 2018b, 156). A second phase of fieldwork was completed under the direction of the City Archaeologist (and coauthor of this volume) Joseph Bagley and a team that included professional archaeologists, graduate students, members of the Boston Center for Youth and Family Youth Engagement and Employment "Dream Team" Program, and volunteer members of the public (Bagley et al. 2018b). Based on its length,

Figure 7.2. Excavated privy feature at the Dorchester Industrial School for Girls (Photo by the author from Bagley et al. 2018: 142).

the nearly five-meter-long brick and stone-lined privy that was described in the records probably had separate stalls with a series of doors to enter. The privy feature was fully excavated, and the homogeneity of the fill and number of cross-mended ceramics suggested it had been created as part of one discrete episode of use.

Background research conducted as part of the project identified a local archive that held student intake records, which provided family background and information about each student who attended the school. The archive also held monthly manager reports, which contained a wealth of detailed information about the school's day-to-day operations and were intended to be internal documents. Public annual reports produced by the school were also available in a number of libraries and provided researchers with information about the physical elements of the site, details about the behaviors of students and staff, and an opportunity to investigate differences between the public and private workings of the school.

The City Archaeology Program partnered with the University of Massachusetts Boston Public History Program to conduct additional research to help interpret and contextualize the archaeological data. Students in a graduate history seminar targeted their research on an 1860 Annual Report for the school and the listing in the federal census for that same year, which identified thirty-three women and girls at the school. Each graduate student in the seminar researched one adult staff person or officer and one student, utilizing the records from the school which are archived at Boston University, as well as any records or personal information they could locate. Their work, coupled with the archaeological data, revealed the stories of sixteen individuals and the intertwined stories of two distinctly different classes of females.

The research conducted for the project suggests that the female founders intended the industrial school to be distinct from the similar schools at the time that were primarily reform schools where children were sent as part of legal sentences. The school operated as a private, nonsectarian institution for its entire existence, but most of the women who ran the Industrial School for Girls were Protestant and the girls attended a Christian worship service on Sundays. The managers, teachers, and matrons of the school were all women, and while most of the managers were part of wealthy and prominent Boston families, their backgrounds were somewhat diverse (Bagley et al. 2018b, 29–44).

The intake records indicate that most girls came from large families who were unable to support all of their children, although daughters who had "disabled, young, poor, or temporarily insane mothers" were also accepted, as were some girls who were orphans, abused, runaways, or whose fathers were mariners who were abroad (Bagley et al. 2018b, 55). Siblings sometimes attended the school either at the same time or during different periods. Parents were encouraged to spend time with their daughters at the once monthly visiting day. While the school charged tuition, room, and board, the fees were reduced or waived if the family could not afford them.

Girls were taught skills that would help them to enter the working class in Victorian Boston. The school had a sewing and mending department to train the girls, and they were sometimes allowed to take in outside work if they had completed their assigned school tasks. Successful graduation from the school often meant placement in a home for service employment. Not every girl had a successful transition, though, and the records also indicate that many girls were sent home (either temporarily or permanently) for what they considered to be bad behavior (Bagley et al. 2018b). Were the behaviors really "bad" or were young girls simply behaving like children? Was a girl removed primarily because of her own actions, or because it was feared she would influence other students? The matrons considered attendance at the school a privilege, but they were also certainly aware that the threat of being sent back to a difficult home life without the skills needed to be employed must certainly have been a powerful form of control over the female students.

The excavations produced nearly 18,000 artifacts from the privy and an associated pit making it the one of the largest and most complete assemblages from a school site in New England (Bagley et al. 2018b). The site provides a unique opportunity for study because it was only in use for a specific period of time and because it was associated with a specific class, gender, and age of individuals. Sewing and textile arts-related artifacts dominated the assemblage and almost 900 nearly identical "all purpose" straight pins were collected at the site. These would have been appropriate for instruction as well as for general sewing and mending tasks. Related artifacts included nine thimbles in size ranges that would have fit a small girl to a woman with large hands; a complete tatting shuttle and several fragments used to make lace; and bone knitting needles used to make the socks and stockings described in school records (Bagley et al. 2018b, 207–216; Poulson 2018). The emphasis on sewing at a girl's educational trade school is illustrative of changes in women's labor across nineteenth-century America. Suzanne Spencer-Wood (1987, 7) has linked trade schools like this one as helping to "transform housework from private unremunerated labor into marketable professional wage labor" and the skills learned by the students at the Dorchester Industrial School may indeed have helped them improve their social and economic status as they moved into adulthood. This was certainly a goal that the school's white, wealthy, progressive female patrons and board members hoped to achieve, especially in response to the large numbers of unskilled immigrants who were arriving in large numbers in mid-nineteenth-century Boston (Poulson 2018, 1).

Girls at the school were taught to be virtuous and to adhere to female norms at the time which included morality, submissiveness, piety, and domesticity. One of the artifacts in the privy was a broken Parian ware (porcelain bisque) bust designed to look like marble but much cheaper to purchase. These were extremely popular in Victorian homes and were displayed to project education and worldliness. The recovered fragment is of a veiled girl with a tear running down her cheek. There is no way to know if this object depicted a religious figure, but it may have been in one of the women's rooms or in a public space. Such objects could have been placed where the girls would see them to familiarize them with the aesthetics of the homes that they would hopefully later work in, to expose them to culture, or simply because the matrons found them appealing. Was this object intentionally broken by an angry girl? Was it accidentally broken and discarded to hide the damage? (Bagley et al. 2018b, 180).

More than four hundred slate fragments and writing artifacts were collected in the privy fill, evidence of the educational mission of the Dorchester Industrial School. Slates were more efficient and cheaper than paper and ink, they could be cleaned and reused, and use of a slate eliminated the potential for spilled ink that could ruin clothing or school equipment. One of these objects was a piece of a writing slate with the name "Lilly" etched into it. This is one of the few artifacts that can be associated with a specific individual (or one of possibly two girls with this name who appear in school records) (Bagley et al. 2018b). It provides a connection through a utilitarian object that each girl would have used nearly every day during her time at the school. Given that this was the only personalized slate object found, did Lilly assert her autonomy by writing her name on an object that was meant for communal use?

More than 200 toys or fragments were collected at the site primarily in the privy fill, and the majority were either dolls or doll-sized dishes. The doll fragments represented a wide range of style and size, but a number of them were "Frozen Charlottes;" porcelain dolls that were a less expensive type and were often associated with the lower social classes. Mass-produced and popular in the mid-nineteenth through early twentieth centuries, these dolls were typically small, naked, and had no movable parts (hence the name) so a child would make their own coverings for the doll. The dolls may have been given out by the school or their use encouraged because it gave the girls an opportunity to practice their sewing and mending skills. While these dolls were usually left white and unpainted, fragments of one male "Frozen Charlie" doll were painted black; the only black doll artifact collected at the site (Johnson 2018). Was it owned by one of the few Black girls who attended the school, including two sisters who were there in the 1860s? Since most girls did not own many personal objects, was this doll used by the white students too?

The presence of a large number of doll fragments in the privy was initially considered unusual, since the students likely had few personal possessions and, if kept as personal objects, would have certainly been cherished. The archaeologists considered that dolls may actually have been distributed to each girl by the school and used as part of the curriculum for sewing and other life skills training, and that therefore there was less attachment to them as precious objects (Johnson 2018). Perhaps the dolls were communal property, passed around between the students and not carefully tracked, so the accidental breakage of one during play and subsequent disposal of the broken pieces along with other trash could have been a relatively common occurrence among young girls who were perhaps not always careful. There is also the possibility that some of the dolls deposited into the privy may represent the only act of defiance or rebellion identifiable in the archaeological data. An angry or unhappy girl could have taken her aggression out on one of the few objects she directly controlled, and then secretly thrown the doll into the privy (Johnson 2018).

Multiple porcelain toy tea set fragments may have been toys used by girls in their leisure time, but it also could have been part of a set used to teach the girls about the tea ritual, the components of a tea set, and how to properly serve it in a home where they might one day work. The small cup was probably either donated by a wealthy patron or one of the board members or bought by the school, because it was unlikely that the circumstances of the girls would have them arriving with toys. Given the degree to which the girls' daily lives were managed and overseen, the prevalence of the doll-sized tea sets suggests that while the girls may have considered them toys, the matrons also intended them as teaching tools that could be used to learn and practice the skills that many of the girls would need as they entered domestic service. Similarly, ceramic dolls needed clothing, and the girls would have practiced their sewing skills by making and mending items that fit their toys (Bagley et al. 2018b).

The project team created an online interactive exhibit that presents a history of the school; information on the archaeological study; the biographies of the fifteen students and nine women (including the president, a matron and assistant, a teacher, four managers, and a secretary), as well as resources for additional study. The website also includes what are described as "artifact biographies" that "demonstrate the wide variety of data, questions, and stories a single artifact can reveal about the past" (https://dorchesterindustrialschoolforgirls.wordpress.com/). The Dorchester Industrial School project exemplifies the contributions archaeology can make to the study of institutional life. The project team's extensive records research provided tangible links between the girls and women who spent time at the school and the objects they used and discarded. Connecting the materiality of the site to the individuals who spent time there allows a partial understanding of the day-to-day world the students experienced and a fuller accounting of life within the walls. The archaeological deposits suggest that while life at the school was rigidly structured and designed for instruction, the girls experienced moments of self-expression as they played with their dolls or acted out against another student or a matron. The work at this site demonstrates the potential for comprehensive historic and archaeological research at places of confinement to shed light on individual stories.

Intentional and Utopian Communities

While many collective groups were formed involuntarily due to circumstance or force, some communities were formed voluntarily by groups of like-minded people who intentionally separated from nineteenth-century society to live together in a common location. These groups usually followed principles of behavior, belief, and action that were distinctive to the group. Archaeologists have studied experimental collectives as places of dissent on one hand and consent on the other (Kozakavich 2017). The people who formed and joined nineteenth-century "ideal societies" were generally dissatisfied with religious and/or secular culture and societal norms and attempted to consciously live a more egalitarian or simple life. Because they were consciously trying to be different in all aspects of life, many of the ideals that characterized these groups were grounded in the material world: What should a house look like? How should people dress? When should they work? What should they eat? These ideals were often written down to help ensure consistency. Archaeological investigation at these sites can be used to document the materialization of these ideals, investigate public versus private space, and help determine whether the residents of communal spaces were totally committed to the rules they agreed to follow (Kozakavich 2017; Tarlow 2002).

The Shakers

The Shaker movement emerged from Quakers in the Manchester, England, area in the mid-eighteenth century who were drawn to a belief in mystical experiences, visions and voices from heaven, and lights in the sky. They were originally known as "Shaking Quakers" because they chanted, danced, and shook during worship (Andrews 1963). "Mother" Ann Lee experienced visions as a young girl and grew up in the early movement and became the spiritual leader of the group around 1770 after she was sent to an asylum for her ecstatic behavior during services. Mother Lee soon had a vision that took her and a small group of followers to New York, where their first communal village was established near Albany. During their first years in America, the community isolated themselves and developed the major tenets of their faith, including equality between the sexes, celibacy, confession of sins, and communal ownership of earthly goods. They also valued order, cleanliness, simplicity, nonviolence, care in workmanship, and the rejection of individual or material wealth. The Shakers embraced spiritual family over blood relations, further isolating many followers from their biological families and the outside community (Savulis 2003).

In 1781, Mother Ann Lee embarked on a missionary tour through Massachusetts and Connecticut, staying in homes along the way and proselytizing to attract new members. The Shaker commitment to celibacy meant that active recruitment was essential to maintaining the religion. Small Shaker congregations were established in Harvard, Shirley, Hancock, and Tyringham, Massachusetts, as well as in Connecticut, New Hampshire, and Maine. After Mother Ann Lee died, Father Joseph Meacham formalized the organizational structure of Shaker society into "families" who pooled their resources into common stock (Morse 1980). These families formed villages centered around a meetinghouse. Each family had its own house or dormitory, shops, and kitchen gardens usually ordered in straight lines and at right angles along a central avenue or lane aligned with the meetinghouse. Common agricultural lands and outbuildings were located outside of and surrounding the central village. The regimented and orderly physical appearance of buildings, roadways, and even the fields was critical for the Shakers (Andrews and Andrews 1984).

Shaker communities sought to live independently and their focus on cooperative labor and craftsmanship led to the development of industries including tanneries, fulling mills, weaving workshops, clothing and chair factories, and by 1789, a commercial-scale garden seed industry. While there was gender equality, strict divisions of labor by age and sex were enforced. Alcohol, drugs, and sex were strictly forbidden. Each family was expected to specialize in some form of production whose products could be shared and exchanged with other Shaker families with surplus sold outside the communities. Detailed records were kept for all aspects of Shaker life from garden layouts to construction specifications to business records, providing archaeologists with a trove of archival material that has been used to help locate and interpret Shaker sites (Andrews 1933). The records also indicate that buildings were often demolished, moved, and/or repurposed, activities that were not as well documented and that could be better understood through archaeological study.

The success of the independent Shaker communities began to decline after the Civil War. Their artisanal products could not compete with the cheaper mass-produced goods from New England mills and international factories, it became more difficult to attract new members, and some of the larger agricultural landholdings failed. By 1950, only three Shaker communities remained, and the Hancock village was the only one still operating in Massachusetts. In the 1960s, several former Shaker villages were turned into museums and living history centers, and today the Sabbathday Lake Shaker Village community in Maine is the only active Shaker congregation in the world (Andrews and Andrews 1984; Brewer 1986; https://www .maineshakers.com/).

The Hancock Shaker Village was established in 1780 in the southeastern section of Hancock extending into Pittsfield. Between 1820 and 1830, nearly 300 Shaker families lived in the community (Burns 1993; Ott 1976). Today numerous structures that formed the historic village, including a circa 1826 unique round stone barn, are preserved as part of an open-air museum and visitor center and the site is a designated National Historic Landmark. Numerous archaeological investigations have been completed within the museum grounds and surrounding former fields, including a series of surveys completed in the 1990s as part of access and infrastructure improvements for the museum (Donta et al. 2000). Collected artifacts included scatters of domestic refuse and architectural materials that provide information about daily Shaker life. The food refuse indicates nineteenth-century Shakers were eating the same foods as their neighbors (cow, pig, sheep, chicken, turkey, clams,

Figure 7.3. Photograph of remnant building at former Harvard Shaker Village (Photo by the author).

plums). All of the recovered creamware and pearlware ceramic fragments were plain, undecorated types and utilitarian wares (whiteware, redware, stoneware) comprised more than 80 percent of the assemblage, with only a few pieces of finer or expensive wares like porcelain present. Archaeological studies at the nearby Canterbury Shaker Village in New Hampshire suggest that the Shakers may have been more focused on efficiency (including utilizing technology) and order (indoors and out) than with simplicity or austerity (Starbuck 1998; Tarlow 2002). Another survey documented the subsurface remains of an industrial lime kiln in a remnant agricultural field (Cherau and Banister 2006). The site was used for processing limestone quarried from nearby sources, and the ground lime would have been used as fertilizer and to make whitewash and mortar. The production of lime is not well documented in Hancock's records so additional investigations at this site could provide valuable information about the technology and products.

While Shaker society was egalitarian, men and women were segregated for much of the day working at different tasks in different areas, and families (defined as individuals who lived together) often worked as a unit within the larger communal village. Archaeological study has contributed to a better understanding of how space was used by distinctive groups of people.

Communal cooking and eating areas were documented by the presence of large pots and serving dishes, and by a large fireplace footing at one of the Hancock Village dwellings where food for the thirty-to-forty church members who lived there would have been prepared (Vaillancourt 1983; Spencer-Wood 2006).

The Hancock Trustees' Office and Store was built in 1813, enlarged and reoriented in 1852, and enlarged again in 1859. The building served several important public functions including being the place where Shakers met with non-Shakers to conduct business; where visitors and guests ate and lodged; and where community Trustees lived and managed the community affairs and property. It was also a recreation center for the community. Testing around the foundation of the Trustees' building was completed as part of a utility upgrade project (Harper and Clouette 2011). Despite the fact that people lived, lodged, and ate there, very little domestic debris and very little kitchen or food-related artifacts were identified, and no middens or trash pits were located. The absence of these deposits was attributed to the Shaker emphasis on appearance and order, and to the likelihood that the community wanted to provide a clean, orderly place for visitors and organized space for themselves. The lack of food remains suggests that meals were prepared and serving ware stored elsewhere, and that waste was taken away for disposal in a less public space.

The study documented the building construction techniques and changes that occurred when it was expanded and moved. The areas around the building were entirely made land, carefully landscaped to create an even sloped space between the building and nearby Shaker Brook. The structure sits on massive cut stone blocks that are similar to other Shaker sites and would have required large draft animals, ramps, deep excavation cuts, and a tremendous amount of soil movement to install. The Office did not, however, have corbelled foundation stones like other buildings of similar size and age and a technique that added strength and helped move rainwater away from the foundation and cellar. At the Hancock Shaker site, the walls are vertical and straight with careful cut and fitted stones that made the foundation watertight and may have been more economical. The re-exposure of the foundation walls confirmed that they had been built to last for generations—a hallmark of Shaker construction (Harper and Clouette 2011).

The Shirley Shaker village was formed like many others when a group of neighboring converts pooled their individual farms into a jointly held property, expanding to nearly 2,000 acres at the peak of membership. By

1790, approximately sixty people were living communally, and by 1792, the meetinghouse had been built (moved a few miles east to Harvard when the community closed) and a cemetery established. Throughout the nineteenth century, the Shirley community supported itself primarily by farming and selling cattle, produce, and seeds. It also operated a broom shop, blacksmith, and herb preparation shop. In 1904, the village was closed and the land and buildings sold to the Commonwealth of Massachusetts who repurposed the residences, shops, and buildings for use as a boys' industrial school and later a correctional facility. Archaeological investigations completed as part of construction projects documented structural remains and yard areas from one of the original Shaker dormitories that helped to document Shaker building techniques (Cherau and Boire 1999). Testing in and around the historic village and surrounding agricultural fields identified discrete trash middens as well as thin scatterings of domestic and structural debris in the kitchen gardens closest to the village but virtually no materials in the outlying agricultural fields. This sharp demarcation is not typical of contemporary non-Shaker farmsteads where sheet refuse scatters are common and has been interpreted as archaeological evidence of the Shaker insistence on order and cleanliness (Beaudry 1984; Cherau and Boire 1999). Soils were carefully prepared and cultivated for planting, and fields were often fenced or enclosed to separate them from each other and the outside world. The disposal of refuse into designated spaces was not only designed to keep the community visually "clean" but to maintain the purity of the soil used to grow crops.

Shaker village sites, perhaps more than any other collective society, have been preserved and/or recreated as living history museums, research centers, and historical societies at locations across the eastern United States (https://www.shakerworkshops.com/shaker-museums.html). The Sabbathday Lake Shaker Village in New Gloucester, Maine, established in 1783, is the only remaining active Shaker community and its grounds include original buildings and landscapes, a museum, and a cultural center (https://www.maineshakers.com/). These sites are actively interpreting eighteenth-, nineteenth-, and even early twentieth-century Shaker societies for a public that is interested in the bucolic setting of these places. Many visitors see the Shaker ideals of simplicity, equality, and cooperative harmony physically represented at these sites by neat and ordered landscapes and spare and simple rooms. Like other living history museums across the United States, these places present a carefully crafted image of the past that is often frozen in a specific historic moment in time. The archaeological analysis of these sites can provide a critical perspective that is often missing from interpretive displays and tours. Archaeology can illuminate diversity, resistance, dissent, and other individual actions that are largely absent from homogeneous presentations of Shaker life and that can provide a more complex and nuanced history of this and other utopian societies.

Brook Farm Institute

The Brook Farm Institute for Agriculture and Education (the Institute) was organized by disillusioned Unitarian minister George Ripley and fellow members of the Transcendental Club (including Nathaniel Hawthorne, who fictionalized his time in the community in his 1852 novel *The Blithedale Romance*) as a utopian community removed from the materialistic urban society where members could reside for periods of time to connect with nature, attend lectures, and engage in liberal and intellectual thought. The Institute was also intended as a place to educate and prepare young adults to become part of a more liberal and intelligent society (Rose 1981). Brook Farm is today a 180-acre National Historic Landmark in West Roxbury, just outside Boston. The property has been occupied for thousands of years and served many purposes but is best known for being the site of a utopian community founded in 1841.

The Institute established a dairy and agricultural farm that produced only enough food for the members, who were paid one dollar per day for their labor and worked only when they wanted to. Housing, food, and clothing were provided and members lived in the farmhouse which became known as "the Hive." The compound expanded to include a classroom (the "Nest"), more dormitory-style housing, a workshop, greenhouse, barns, and terraced gardens. The community rebranded in 1844 as the Brook Farm Phalanx after members adopted an alternate social philosophy known as Fourierism and began to operate industrial ventures including a print shop and pewter and shoe shops. By 1847 that enterprise had failed, and the farm and school ceased operations (Bradford 1890; Codman 1894).

The property and its structures continued to be used for institutional purposes, serving as a city almshouse and hospital in 1849; a Civil War Army camp in 1861; a Lutheran-run orphanage and cemetery in 1872; and a residential treatment center and school for children with behavioral problems in 1948 (Lutheran Works of Mercy 1971; Richardson 1994). By the time the state purchased the property in 1987 to preserve it as a historic and recreational site, none of the buildings associated with the original utopian community were still standing (Cavanaugh et al. 1990; Pendery and Preucel 1992).

The first archaeological studies at Brook Farm were completed in 1988, just after the state's purchase, and included a detailed land use history and archival research to identify the many historical maps, plans, photos, and even paintings depicting the property over time (Schultz 1998a, 1998b). The information was used to create interpretive materials and to guide future infrastructure improvements. Subsurface testing across the areas of former buildings was completed in 1990 and identified the foundation of the Hive, the orphanage, a workshop and several other Brook Farm buildings, as well as a trash midden and concentrations of early nineteenth-century structural debris. These investigations produced large amounts of charcoal, melted glass, and architectural debris that helped to document the destruction of several buildings by fire (Pendery 1991).

Between 1990 and 1994, Harvard University operated a seasonal field school at Brook Farm that included students as well as community volunteers (Pendery and Preucel 1992, 2017). These investigations covered the majority of the property and resulted in the collection of almost 100,000 artifacts (Kelly and Olson 2022). In the past decade, student projects have focused on reanalyzing some of the collections and creating updated exhibit content that better reflects the varied continuous land use over thousands of years. In 2019, the Boston City Archaeology Program received grant funding to catalog and/or digitize several important Boston archaeological collections, including those from Brook Farm (City of Boston 2022). An online digital exhibit for Brook Farm is also hosted by the Commonwealth Museum with content created by the City Archaeology Program (Kelly and Olson 2022).

Collections reviews and student research projects have been used to connect specific artifact and structural deposits with different periods of site use, which has helped to better understand how space was used over time (e.g., Laskowski 2013; Savory 2015). One project compared ceramics from the Brook Farm site with those found at an urban site from the same period and noted the same preference for plain utilitarian wares found at many Massachusetts Shaker sites (Cherau and Boire 1999; Harper and Clouette 2011; Timms et al. 2006; see above).

Despite a plethora of writings and artistic representations, there are no extant plans of the Brook Farm community, none of the original buildings remain, and the locations of many of the original structures are unknown. The extensive archaeological investigations identified all of the utopian-era building sites that allowed researchers to produce the first accurate map of the complex. This included the vernacular structure known as the Phalanstery, which has been described in historical texts (Codman 1894) and paintings but not physically documented on the landscape. The archaeology and collections research helped to differentiate and better understand the different occupations of the site, and to clarify the historical relationships between the Hive, the almshouse, and the orphanage that were not well understood from the documentary record (Preucel and Pendery 2006, 7). The physical space and landscape at Brook Farm were very intentionally ordered to suit the philosophical and ideological goals of its residents. Archaeological study provides a means to identify and interpret the organization of Brook Farm (and other intentional community settlements) and to compare the aspirational ideals recorded in documents and remembered history versus the actual lived experiences of residents.

Conclusions

Community takes many different forms across time and within different sets of circumstances. As demonstrated by the case studies presented in this chapter, there is tremendous variation in the historical communities of Massachusetts ranging from voluntary elite white enclaves to institutions where the poor lived and died. These disparate groups are tied together because they were all distinguished by themselves or others, intentionally or by force, as somehow separate.

Some nineteenth-century communities like Shakers and followers of transcendentalism formed by consensus when like-minded individuals chose to remove themselves from what they viewed as an increasingly capitalistic and materialistic world to live in intentionally designed enclaves. These Massachusetts groups share common characteristics with other American social and religious communities including the Latter-Day Saints, Harmonists, and Moravians. The physical sites created by these well-studied groups are sometimes memorialized as living history museums or open-air historic landscapes where the stated idealism of the residents is sometimes presented in a nostalgic way. The archaeological study of utopian and intentional communities provides opportunities to investigate the perceived versus lived experiences at these places, which were designed to present a specific image to the outside world (Kozakavich 2017).

Community also serves as a means to retain and reinforce cultural heritage. Beginning in the seventeenth century, Massachusetts's Native American populations were encouraged and sometimes forced to live in geographically bounded "praying towns" and then reservations that were physically separate from white colonial settlements (see Chapter 2 and Chapter 5) where they were encouraged to shed their identity and adopt the religion and customs of the dominant society. This pattern of cultural isolation to promote acculturation is common to the experience of America's Indian tribes, experienced at reservations and boarding schools across the country. In the nineteenth and twentieth centuries, Black and Indigenous communities fought to maintain their distinct identities against public institutions that worked to obscure them. As discussed in Chapter 4, Massachusetts's people of color formed social and physical communities in bondage and in freedom. Black and Indigenous homesteads were places where community members were free to express their cultural heritage and where traditions and history could be passed from one generation to the next. These places contain unique material culture and landscapes that document cultural persistence long after the dominant white culture declared it was gone and continue to be places of heritage today.

Community was not always formed voluntarily. Almshouses, asylums, reform schools, and even cemeteries brought people together by circumstance or by the will of others. These places of collective residence, work, and care were often in operation for long periods of time and the residents temporary or transitory, so without detailed documentary records it can be difficult to identify individuals by name or identify cultural materials and features from a specific period of occupation. Despite these impediments, archaeologists are sometimes able to make these connections through diligent research and can illuminate individual or collective actions of opposition or resistance (Casella 2007).

Archaeologists who study historic communities can make important contributions to national discourse about the major social issues that confront the United States today. America incarcerates more people than any other democratic nation and the incarceration rate of each state in the nation is higher, per capita, than that of most countries (https://www.prisonpolicy.org/global/2024.html). We face a growing crisis in homelessness with more than 653,000 Americans unhoused in 2023 and nearly 327,000 living in emergency or transitional housing as of 2024 (US Department of Housing and Urban Development 2023; https://www.census.gov/library/stories/2024/02/living-in-shelters.html). The Department of the Interior's Federal Indian Boarding School Initiative has issued two reports outlining the intergenerational trauma caused to Native American tribes, families, and individuals at Indian Boarding Schools across the country (Newland 2022, 2024). The archaeological investigation of historic places of confinement and public assistance document the impacts of institutional agencies on the lives of individuals and offer lessons that can inform public policy in the future. They offer powerful examples of the ways in which groups of people have been historically marginalized, coerced, punished and/or mistreated that can and should be part of conversations about how groups are treated today.

8

Archaeology Bends Toward Social Justice

Historical archaeology has undergone significant fundamental changes in its relatively short existence. With notable exceptions already discussed, the earliest interest in Massachusetts historical archaeology were the flagship colonial and Revolutionary War sites of popular commemoration. As the methodological and interpretative foundations of historical archaeology grew, researchers were able to begin to narrow research questions and untangle complex intersectional histories. From this foundation, Massachusetts's historical archaeologists were able to pursue interest in the experiences of children, women, Indigenous, Black, immigrant, poor, and other peoples in Massachusetts.

Changes in archaeological interest and consideration is easily traced in the Boston "Big Dig" project reports. The Parker-Harris Pottery site in Charlestown was excavated in 1986 but reported in 1992 (Gallagher et al. 1992). The Parkers were the primary component of the site discussed throughout the report; however, their two enslaved people, a man named Jack and a boy named Acton, who were likely potters themselves, are not mentioned in the report.

The report for excavations at the Three Cranes Tavern (Gallagher et al. 1994) was not completed until the mid-1990s, but the survey's design and excavation happened in late 1985. In this report, the archaeologists acknowledge that the mid-eighteenth-century tavern owner Nathaniel Brown enslaved a woman named Zipporah who was married to another enslaved person named Cesar in 1757 (Gallagher et al. 1994). They state that enslaved people and others "also affected the site's archaeological record" (Gallagher et al. 1994, 175). They excavated over 200 square meters recording 193 features and recovering 108,669 artifacts (Gallagher et al. 1994: 72, 151) including five intact privies and a tavern site owned by a woman for decades. While the analysis of the food and culture of taverns was robust throughout the report (see Chapter 3), they concluded after a page of analysis that "study of gender's relationship to the structure of the archaeological record is problematic" and "the documented presence of slaves, servants, tenants, and dependent children is apparently only poorly reflected archaeologically" (Gallagher et al. 1994, 188).

By the mid-1990s, the Paddy's Alley and Cross Street Back Lots data recovery investigations (Cook and Balicki 1996), which examined the Katherine Nanny Naylor privy and John Carnes pewterer site among others, included research questions specifically addressing the presence of five enslaved people recorded in probates of the owners of the project area and several pages of detailed analysis on the potential material culture of these enslaved people.

Historical archaeology is an inherently iterative process, and while it provides great opportunities for collections-based reanalysis of previously excavated sites, it is frustrating today to read reports where opportunities for significant analysis were missed. It is also doubtless that the lack of acknowledgment of the presence of enslaved people on these sites meant that there was no effort made to design a survey methodology that could best record and recover data associated with these people, likely obscuring, destroying, or missing some of the information that may have been present. Archaeological interpretations are inherently influenced by present norms (Conkey and Spector 1984), and the reality that biases and ignorance designed into a scientific process like archaeology results in missing data or analysis. In other words, "you can not find what you are not looking for."

This is changing over the past decades with the influence of queer, feminist, Indigenous, Black, Black feminist, anticolonial, and critical race theory (and others), which expose and critique the heteronormative, masculine, Eurocentric, exclusionary, and complicit bias that has become structural within archaeology by the very nature of its origins as a predominantly white, male, heterosexual, elite, colonial pursuit that has created ongoing negative impacts on archaeology and archaeologists alike (Arnett 2024; Battle-Baptiste 2011; Dowson 2000; Eperson 2004; Voss 2000). This chapter will focus on how the influence of these theoretical ideas can and has made historical archaeology in Massachusetts culturally relevant to a broader and more diverse community and placed it at the front lines of the social justice movement. We demonstrate this relevance through examples of community historical archaeology at sites of "hard histories" (Bagley et al. 2024). These sites present opportunities for present-day communities to feel they are recognized parts of the collective American experience, that their presence today is valid, and their opinions and voices welcome when discussing history and the stories of their own past.

Gender and Sexuality

Brothels and other locations used for illegal, unregulated, or socially discouraged activities have been a focus of archaeologists for some time because they can be difficult to document from written records alone (Yamin and Seifert 2019). The contents of an excavated privy feature behind a building in Boston's North End provided an opportunity to study the private worlds of the women who operated and worked at a mid-nineteenth-century brothel (Luiz 2023). The use of the building on Endicott Street as a site of sex work was initially suggested by one piece of evidence: an 1866 tax record that listed the occupation of a woman who lived there as "prostitute." Additional research identified a pattern between 1853 and 1867 of changing female occupants at the address and at surrounding properties, many of whom did not list their occupations. Census records for the period showed that the majority of the women who worked in the brothel under three female owners were New England-born, despite the fact that Boston's North End was a primarily immigrant neighborhood during the period. The analyses of the archaeological materials provided a way to understand how the commercial aspects of prostitution intersect with the private worlds of the women who made their livings as sex workers. The organization of the brothel's work spaces and the appearance and personal items of the women who worked there were driven by economic factors, but as a residence, the private lives of the occupants are also reflected in the material culture.

The site provides an opportunity to explore theoretical issues associated with the archaeology of gender, sexuality, ethnicity, the senses, family life, feminism, and violence (Luiz 2023). A comprehensive study of the Endicott Street brothel included a reconstruction of its physical and cultural environments, including the contextualization of the artifacts found in the privy; the collection of demographic information on the identifiable sex workers and patrons; a discussion of the evolving social politics of prostitution in nineteenth-century Massachusetts; and an examination of the labor choices made by the three women who ran the brothel and the women they employed. The nearly 8,000 artifacts collected from the privy were interpreted within these research contexts and considered as a corporate "household" assemblage deposited primarily by the women who lived there, similar to the Boott Mill boardinghouse deposits created by individuals living in communal housing. A few of the materials were those found at other brothel sites, including vaginal syringes used for douching, perfume and astringent bottles, jewelry, and alcohol and drinking glassware, however taken out of context the assemblage as a whole would be difficult to differentiate from a typical nineteenth-century middle-class home.

In her dissertation, Jade Luiz examined the brothel site assemblage looking to see how the women at the site negotiated the carefully crafted commercial aspects of the brothel and their own identities. The material world of the brothel represented contributions to the fantasy of the space while brothel madams strived to create a sense of respectability. This was represented through personal adornment such as crosses, the use of middle-class genteel practices like serving tea to clients, a distinct attention to bodily cleanliness in the form of tooth powders and vaginal syringes, and the creation of a thoroughly domestic-feeling space. This worked to provide clients and workers a sense of anonymity within the streetscape of other businesses and homes, while also avoiding the attention of police (Luiz 2018).

The archaeology of sexuality in Massachusetts has represented an overall movement within the field of historical archaeology toward a willingness to approach taboo topics as pragmatic experiences of everyday life. This openness to the topics explored through archaeology has helped create a more open environment for archaeologists with diverse backgrounds and identities to enter into the field and bring with them their unique viewpoints and analytical insights into people's lives. One of the most significant shifts in recent years toward inclusivity and the benefits it brings to the practice of historical archaeology has been the increased inclusion of non-archaeologists in the work of archaeologists.

Community Archaeology Defined

There is little consensus on the definition of community archaeology (Thomas 2017), though the general concept of community archaeology, public archaeology, engaged archaeology and various other similar terms is the genuine empowerment of community partners, a commitment to an exchange of information, and an accountability toward partners (Nassaney 2020, 2021; Thomas 2017). This goes beyond allowing visitors to a site where they can watch a dig and interact with the archaeologists and instead attempts to elevate non-archaeological stakeholders in an archaeological project to the status of decision-making in project design, direct involvement in excavations, and active and valuable participants in interpretation of archaeological materials and data (Atalay 2006, 2012; Colwell-Chanthaphonh and Ferguson 2007).

In recent years, the City Archaeology Program in Boston, directed by a coauthor of this book, has committed to community archaeology practice, going so far as to rebrand its facility as a community archaeology center (Laskowski 2023). A recent criticism of community archaeology is its ability to be used relatively easily as a term when the practice itself is remarkably difficult and rare to achieve. Michael Nassaney (2020, 2021) has deployed the term "authentic collaboration" in recognition of the wide gaps between goals and actions in community archaeology and the inherent risk of real harm that is possible when done superficially or without commitment to long-term support, trust, and exchange. In the Boston program, we have encountered many of the same challenges and needs Nassaney discusses including the reality that when done well, collaboration is messy, time consuming, and requires an abandonment of rigidity (Nassaney 2021). In fact, when working collaboratively with the Massachusett Tribe at Ponkapoag, we routinely call each other out when processes are going too smoothly as likely needing to be reexamined to see if the process has been done collaboratively.

Native Community Archaeology in Massachusetts

Indigenous archaeology (Atalay 2006) and the involvement of more Native people in Massachusetts historical archaeology has been long-overdue and much needed. The exemplary collaborative work between the Nipmuc and historical archaeologists at UMass Boston, and collaborative projects on Martha's Vineyard with the Wampanoag Tribe of Gay Head/Aquinnah and in western Massachusetts with the Stockbridge-Munsee Community Band of Mohican Indians are examples that have been highlighted in other sections of this book. One exciting aspect of this ongoing collaborative work is the decision by Nipmuc tribal members and other Massachusetts Indigenous individuals to pursue graduate-level education in Native studies with an emphasis on archaeology at UMass Boston. This new generation of Native archaeologists has already been instrumental in Massachusetts's historical archaeology projects, including ongoing work on the Boston Harbor Islands.

Throughout the 2010s, leadership from the Massachusett Tribe, City Archaeology Program and regional National Park Service office that includes the Boston Harbor Islands National Recreational Area were routinely attending the same meetings about plans and operations of the Harbor Islands. These twenty-one islands are within the NPS system, but individually owned by a tapestry of local, state, and private organizations and individuals. While archaeological mitigation was always included in discussions of planned infrastructure, development, and programming projects that risked damaging archaeological sites, the biggest threat to the sites on the islands—erosion—was not a trigger for archaeological action unless it impacted cemeteries.

Discussions between the three groups recognized this flaw and the need for action but lacked the ability to finance the work when there was no entity to charge. This changed with the 2016 passage of the Community Preservation Act (CPA) in Boston. CPA is state law that allows individual towns to vote to add a 1 to 3 percent local property tax surcharge. These funds are then matched by a statewide CPA trust fund and become a dedicated fund to use exclusively toward grants for historic preservation, outdoor spaces, and low-income housing. Each town gets to decide on the surcharge and distribution of funds across the three funding themes. In 2024 alone, CPA awarded over $10 million to historic preservation projects just in Boston and has funded millions of dollars in archaeological work across Massachusetts.

Since 2020, the City Archaeology Program has received $350,000 for a project called the Boston Harbor Islands Archaeology Program. The co-principal investigators include the coauthors of this book and Elizabeth Solomon, an elder of the Massachusett Tribe with an archaeological background. The goal of this project is to create a harbor-wide plan to mitigate the effects of erosion on the archaeological sites most at risk of erosion due to climate change (COB 2024). There are more than one hundred documented archaeological sites in the Boston Harbor Islands though many remain unsurveyed. These sites on the Harbor Islands are nearly evenly divided between ancient Native and historical archaeological sites, including two islands that were the locations of seventeenth-century internment camps of Massachusett and Nipmuc people following King Philip's War (see Chapter 5). The project began in earnest in the fall of 2023, with a re-cataloging and re-examination of a massive ancient Native assemblage of objects and creations from the Harbor Islands excavated by archaeologist Barbara Luedtke during the 1970s, '80s, and '90s (see Luedtke 1975). Collections work has included a project team of archaeologists and tribal members from the Massachusett Tribe at Ponkapoag and Nipmuc Nation with some members representing both groups. These projects include both training of Native people in archaeological methods while actively engaging in critique of the terminology and methods resulting in real-time changes to standard procedures that will become new best practices. For example, when Native collaborators raised concern about the processing workspaces not reflecting the significance and reverence of the rehousing and cataloging activities, the team commissioned handmade quilted red fabric mats. The deployment of these mats allows for the contemplation of the work about to be done, the creation of a reverential space, and a protective pad to ensure creations are safe. Terminology such as the word "creation" instead of the archaeological standard "artifact" have been incorporated. There are many other best-practice aspects of this project that may become public, but we have not yet confirmed with our Native collaborators that these are ready for public consumption at this time. We have built trust with our Native collaborators over two decades by ensuring collaborative decision-making and avoiding assumptions, and this trust is critically important to maintain as it is slow to develop and easy to lose.

Native collaborators are compensated for their work on this project at the current rate of $100/hour reflecting the rarity and demand for their knowledge and time, and also the hardship of Native people having to confront the products of colonization and then work to help mitigate them. At the city level, the City Archaeologist is promoting the need to allow significant time for Native collaboration due to the demand of Native people's assistance by others as well as the reality of these collaborators usually also having other jobs. We are also using the $100/hour compensation rate internally for all projects involving Native consultation and collaboration regardless of archaeological aspects as compensation rates are a highly effective means to communicate importance when working with people who rarely or never work with Native collaborators.

The key aspects of this project that make it different from previous projects is the recognition of tribal authority in decision-making and day-to-day aspects of this work, which includes constant interaction with ancestral creations and decision-making on how best to mitigate loss of ancestral spaces on the islands. The results of this project are still very much a work in progress but have already been transformative. Prior to work beginning, the project team met multiple times to discuss mindsets, schedule challenges (all tribal members had at least one other job), and terminology. Cataloging metadata terms were permanently altered to replace functional terminology with descriptive terminology (for example, "net weight/plummet" became "notched stone") because at no point were Native people consulted in the early decision-making of tool functions by non-Native archaeologists. While this chapter is being written, the project team is actively discussing methods to decolonize the structure and format of the Archaeological Climate Action Plan. We are also ensuring that the Massachusett have decision-making on determining significance and mitigation strategies. In the past, Native flake scatters and fire pit features with few diagnostic creations have not been considered significant by archaeologists on the Harbor Islands allowing for these sites to be developed. This has triggered a discussion of equality versus equity. CRM archaeologists and the State Historic Preservation Office (SHPO) have treated Native cultural spaces that are relatively commonplace throughout Massachusetts equally when these same places are encountered in the urbanized Boston region. The Massachusett argue that their ancestral spaces have experienced far greater loss than other tribal areas and that what is commonplace elsewhere is rare and of critical importance to their community. Therefore, our project will be making recommendations to the SHPO for a more equitable evaluation of site significance that is inclusive of both overall cultural landscape integrity and living tribal concerns. Emphasizing the "need to allow no," the project team's mitigation response to erosion has already included the viability of a potential recommendation by the Tribe (this has not been formally made yet pending tribal council consideration) that erosion is preferred over archaeological mitigation in some or possibly all Native spaces on the islands. We have emphasized both within this project and with others in archaeological and non-archaeological spaces that collaborative work which does not include equal ability by all involved to say "no," and be listened to, is not actually a collaboration but a sign-off request. These practices, methods, terminology, and other significant outcomes of this project will be promoted as a new set of best practices for archaeological work in Native spaces in Boston and in the Harbor, with intentions that these practices be adopted as widely as possible.

Where capacity issues have made Indigenous archaeology at its purest (archaeological investigations on Native spaces run by Native archaeologists) difficult in Massachusetts, we are working to build capacity through collaborative training of Native people in archaeological skills, demonstrating the value of Native collaboration toward the goal of adequate compensation, and building in a broader timeline to allow for adequate collaboration. This is of course in addition to the presumed inclusion of Native people in projects where tribal members are directly impacted, which is very fortunately becoming de facto practice in many communities in Massachusetts.

Transformative Archaeology of the Recent Past

A particularly helpful aspect of being located in Massachusetts while doing historical archaeology is the fact that one needs to expend very little energy fundamentally convincing the public that history is either present or important. Despite this, there appears to be a presumption among the public that archaeology in any given area of Massachusetts is likely being done on ancient Native sites or a place related to colonial or Revolutionary War sites—the oldest places in Massachusetts. There still exists a public assumption that either archaeology is not a consideration for twentieth-century history, or that these things simply are not archaeological because we have so many other ways of knowing (Barth 1995) the more recent past. This is further complicated within the goals of community archaeology of urban spaces, where the idea of community can be complex and layered. In its most perfect form, community archaeology is initiated by the community, not archaeologists (Atalay 2006, 2012). But what happens when the community does not consider archaeology an option? In these cases, it is the archaeologists' responsibility to alert communities of potential archaeology, develop archaeological literacy among communities, and new relationships of trust. The following are two examples of urban archaeological projects in Boston that provided challenges and opportunities that illustrate the complexity of urban community archaeology.

In 2014, Rodnell Collins submitted a proposed plan to repair the foundations of his house to the Boston Landmarks Commission. Collins is the nephew of Malcolm X, and lives in the landmark-designated Malcolm X-Ella Little-Collins House, where Malcolm actively lived with his sister, Ella, from 1941–1943, listed as his home address during his incarceration, and used as a meeting place while Malcolm recruited for the Nation of Islam (Bagley et al. 2018a). Ella Little-Collins, Rodnell's mother, was a mother figure for Malcolm. She demanded he make use of his time during his incarceration to gain an education. She was an early leader in the Nation of Islam, she funded Malcolm's Hajj, and she took over the leadership of the Organization of Afro-American Unity (an African American human rights organization) following Malcolm's assassination. Concerned about the potential archaeological impacts of this work, City Archaeologist Joseph Bagley flagged the project for archaeological review and reached out to Collins to discuss potential archaeology on the property (Bagley et al. 2018a).

The "Malcolm X House," as it is known, is located in the center of the neighborhood of Roxbury in Boston. Roxbury is one of the four neighborhoods in Boston where Black residents outnumber white (Boston Planning and Development Agency 2021). This is a twentieth-century phenomenon though. In the nineteenth century, this neighborhood was primarily occupied by immigrant laborers from multiple European countries following the jobs and housing associated with the many industries arising along the streams and rivers of Roxbury (Boston Landmarks Commission 2022). During the seventeenth and eighteenth centuries, Roxbury was farmland with many rural estates of wealthy Bostonians with second homes downtown (Bagley 2021a, 2021b) and before that, it was Massachusett land.

Collins, who had participated in archaeological work in Africa, was enthusiastic about the idea of archaeological investigations prior to the foundation work and opened his property to a public community CRM dig with the City Archaeology Program. All aspects of the survey method were discussed prior to agreeing to conduct the dig, and Collins was directly involved with the daily excavations, public education for numerous groups of visiting school children, and engagement with the near-constant press presence (Bagley et al. 2018a). Following the dig, Collins washed the artifacts from his house with City of Boston staff, cataloged them, and continues to be a presence at archaeological investigations.

There are key components of this project that represent successes of community archaeology both for this project in particular as well as the broader scope of social justice and reparative archaeology. The visibility of the project and the clear connection the current population of Roxbury had with the story of Malcolm X helped Collins's goals of reconnecting the house back to the story of his family and the history of the property prior to the 1940s (Bagley et al. 2018a). The family vacated the home following Malcolm's assassination in 1965 (Collins 1998). In the 1970s, while Rodnell's mother, Ella, was ill, a group of construction workers working on the road in front of the house who knew of the house's history maliciously broke into the house, destroyed the interior contents, and threw as much as they could out of the windows into the yard (Bagley et al. 2018a; 2024). Though Rodnell cleaned up, numerous fragments of his life remained in the yard and became significant parts of the archaeological assemblage. Rodnell saw this vandalism as a deliberate and racist attempt to destroy the legacy of his uncle and his mother (Bagley et al. 2018a; 2024). He was moved by the project's ability to rediscover objects from his family home and reconnect them to his personal stories (Bagley et al. 2018a; 2024). In order to record these stories, the City Archaeology team decided to go beyond a traditional artifact catalog for the surface collection at the site. Rodnell came to the Archaeology Lab where he sat down with the archaeological team, and they recorded an "oral history catalog" of the artifacts. These stories included his mother's peach cobbler bowl, perfume, and glasses (Bagley et al. 2018a; 2024). In addition to the twentieth-century component of the site, the archaeological team uncovered a late nineteenth century brick feature, possibly a privy, containing food and medicinal artifacts relating to the first Irish and English occupants of the mid-nineteenth-century house, a remarkably dense early eighteenth-century artifact scatter likely associated with the nearby Abijah Seaver mansion, and several stone flakes from the earlier Massachusett use (Bagley et al. 2018a). Seaver was a wealthy gentleman who descended from one of the first English settlers of Roxbury and had a grandson who would become mayor of Boston in 1852 (Bagley et al. 2018a). Historical research on the home prior to this survey had never included the Seaver estate connection due to the main house being formerly located multiple house lots away (Bagley et al. 2018a). This particular deposit helped to document the evolution of Roxbury as a neighborhood and its identity changing from that of wealthy rural estates of gentlemen farmers to immigrant housing, to the majority-minority economically disadvantaged community of the present (Bagley et al. 2018a). The reality of the neighborhood once being large wealthy farm estates of some of the richest people in Boston appeared to be surprising to nearly all visitors to the site.

A key revelation of this project to the archaeological team was the visibility of Ella Little-Collins in the material record. Though Malcolm's presence is what brings name recognition and intrigue to the property's history, there were no artifacts, except possibly a pair of glasses, that could be definitively connected to Malcolm, yet Ella was likely the individual who purchased and curated nearly every item recovered. She was the presence that had the greatest impact on the archaeological record, just as she had the greatest impact of any person on Malcolm's early life. Beyond the immediate history of the site, this project had additional goals. It was an attempt to state clearly that the history of Boston included twentieth-century Black history. It was a conscious challenge to demonstrate the potential for archaeology on mid-twentieth-century sites, regardless of affiliation, and it was a conscious attempt by the City Archaeologist to test the openness of the city toward archaeology of the more recent past and archaeology of controversial historical figures. With the exceptions of rare criticisms including a since-deleted online news comment that the excavations supported terrorism (presumably due to Malcom X's controversial comments regarding race and violence, or his association with Islam), the overall positive reception both in the press, social media, and at the city level (Bagley et al. 2024) demonstrated an overall willingness of city leadership to support potentially controversial archaeological subjects, the public to see this work as archaeologically relevant, and a general acceptance that Malcolm X and his property in Boston was an important place deserving of celebration.

The work of the City Archaeology Program in Chinatown had a more complicated outcome. Boston Chinatown historian, Tunney Lee, approached the City Archaeologist following a public lecture at Boston University. Bagley had commented that he wished to do a project someday in Chinatown and Lee had a place that may work. Soon after, Tunney provided Bagley with a tour of historic spaces in Chinatown concluding at 6 Hudson Street, a small vacant lot that was formerly the site of a brick 1830s row house and a twentieth-century well-known Chinese restaurant owned by Ruby Foo called Ruby Foo's Den (Bagley 2019). The project site was also part of the historic heart of Boston's Syriatown, an ethnic neighborhood that preceded Chinatown by several decades (Bagley 2019). The current owner of the property, a prominent neighborhood figure and cofounder of the Chinese American Heritage Foundation, intended to develop the property in the coming years, but there was no imminent threat of development. Still, this potential development was sufficient justification for the preemptive CRM-style dig, and it also meant there was not the typical "ticking clock" of standard CRM excavations.

Both Lee and Bagley had shared goals with this project, the first archaeological excavations in Boston's Chinatown: to highlight the historic nature of Boston's Chinatown and to feature the story of Chinese Bostonians as contributors to Boston's history (Bagley 2019). Beyond these broader goals, the project research questions revolved around recovery of an artifact assemblage that reflected the four main occupation periods of the home's two-century history: Chinese American and immigrant residents and Ruby Foo's Den, early twentieth-century Syrian immigrant laborers, nineteenth-century Irish immigrant borders, and mid-twentieth-century working-class families (Bagley 2019).

Early community archaeology components of the project included numerous meetings and presentations with community leaders, organizations, and neighborhood organizations (Bagley 2019). These presentations and conversations included Jocelyn Lee, an experienced Chinese diaspora archaeologist, digital presentation in both English and Chinese, a professional interpreter at talks, and bilingual news coverage in the local newspaper (Bagley 2019). Reception of the project was positive with questions and concerns primarily involving the potential impacts of the project on the area's limited parking, with a commitment that the entire archaeology team take public transportation to the site each day except for equipment loaded in and out at the beginning and end of the project. The opening of the dig saw over one hundred community members gather for a very literal groundbreaking ceremony that included property owners, elected officials, neighborhood leaders, local archaeologists, and local residents. In many ways, the overarching project goals of community visibility, highlighting of the historic nature of the Chinese community in Boston, and public engagement in the narratives of displacement were achieved before the excavations got underway. The reality of community archaeology is that the public impacts and significance of the project are often weighted more toward the preliminary work and the excavation itself, regardless of what is found during the dig, than other types of excavations where "success" and significance are more dependent on the information gathered from the excavations and subsequent analysis.

Though much of the early phases of the work at 6 Hudson Street appeared to be both positive and have community support, there were considerable issues with community engagement during and soon after the dig. While volunteer positions were left open specifically for neighborhood residents and notice of their availability was circulated widely through local neighborhood associations and the local Chinese historical society, no volunteers from the community signed up to join the dig. There were many visitors from the neighborhood, especially given the proximity of the dig site abutting a popular community park, but none came to join the excavations. At the park-side of the project, the team found that engagement with viewers tended to cause them to leave. As many were watching in groups and talking among themselves, the team kept engagement beyond smiles and waves to a minimum to encourage viewers to stay longer and have opportunities to engage in the archaeological work.

It was clear from this lack of engagement during the fieldwork that while the project had received community support, it did not achieve authentic collaboration. The work done before the excavations did not help develop a trusting relationship with members of the community that could result in the active sharing of data and open lines of communication. This issue came to a head following the dig. The owner of the property asked that the excavation hole be left open as the property would likely be developed soon. The team complied with the request, leaving the hole open throughout the winter of 2019–2020. By February 2020, COVID-19 had become an established threat, but with positive cases in the US numbering less than two dozen, Chinatowns including Boston's experienced a sudden drop in restaurant-goers due to misinformation, fear, and racism (Doyle 2020). Bagley received calls from the local city council's office after hearing that locals were complaining that the three-by-twelve-meter open trench was attracting rats and local residents feared that the trench was contributing to the lack of restaurant visitors and the resulting local economic crisis (Bagley et al. 2024). There was further misinformation among community members that the dig ended because it ran out of money (Bagley et al. 2024). In fact, the dig ended because it reached the water table at six feet of excavation, and the bulk of the project area was disturbed by an unrecorded building addition (Bagley 2019). Much of the immediate concern was quelled by the effective closing of Boston in mid-March 2020, but the hole would remain open until it was filled with the support of the Boston Parks Department in July 2020.

It seems apparent that the project at 6 Hudson Street helped elevate the need for consideration of places like Boston's Chinatown by the SHPO. While there have been multiple projects in Boston's Chinatown before 2019 that likely had state or federal triggers for SHPO review, no previous project was flagged by the SHPO for survey of potential Chinatown- or Syriatown-related history before the work at 6 Hudson. Several weeks after the completion of the 6 Hudson project, the SHPO reached out to the City Archaeologist about an expansion of the Tai Tung Village, a low-income housing development, at 288 Harrison Ave in Chinatown, confirming its archaeological sensitivity and triggering the need for a CRM archaeological survey. Unfortunately, when no twentieth-century deposits related to Chinese or Syrian immigrants were found, the State Archaeologist cited the lack of these deposits as the reason against having a data recovery (phase 3) survey on the project area. This was in spite of the team's uncovering of a large late nineteenth-century deposit from the communities who pre-dated the Chinese immigration history of the site, the willingness of the owners to continue surveys, and recommendations for additional survey by the CRM team and City Archaeologist. A private development and CRM project, this survey included visits by the City Archaeologist but was otherwise not public. The resulting development will be eighty-five much-needed affordable housing units within the expanded Chinese Consolidated Benevolent Society of New England's Tai Tung Village residences (City of Boston Planning Department 2022).

Conclusions

These two examples illustrate the complex nature of community urban archaeology. At the Malcolm X House, the "community" was both a singular individual, Malcolm X's nephew, Rodnell Collins, and a complex global community of individuals who connected to Malcolm X through their participation in the Civil Rights Movement, their direct relationship with Malcolm through personal or familial ties, their interest or involvement in Black nationalism or the Nation of Islam, and many who have a deep personal connection to Malcolm X through their interaction with his work long after his assassination. In Chinatown, the "community" included Chinese Americans in Boston, the property owner, Chinatown residents, the regional Syrian descendant community, and the general public of Boston. In both of these projects, it was fundamentally impossible to create authentic collaborative archaeological excavations that were inclusive of all of these communities. Some were inaccessible within the scope of the project team's abilities, some were too amorphous to engage authentically, some were not ready to engage, and some were unwilling. The solution, or at least an avenue toward improvement, is time.

Leadership of the Boston Landmarks Commission asked the City Archaeologist how they can be more engaged with the Massachusett people. He responded, "start ten years ago." Authentic relationships do not happen instantly. Collaboration between the City Archaeologist and the Massachusett Tribe began with his undergraduate project in 2002. For two decades, this collaborative relationship "moved at the speed of trust," meaning progress has been based on the development of trust, not innately on time itself. An indication of the strength of this relationship was when the City of Boston's administrative offices were finally able to process the contract with a Massachusett tribal consultant so they could be paid for their upcoming services several months later. During the following meeting City Archaeologist Joe Bagley remarked to the Massachusett Tribal Collaborator that they can start submitting invoices "now that they're on the dole." The facial reactions and audible alarm of the members of the meeting made it clear that he had made a terrible mistake. After clarifying that he had incorrectly believed "on the dole" meant "on the accounting books" and not the derogatory euphemism for receiving government handouts, everyone had a genuine laugh, and the meeting continued. This outcome would have been unlikely without the trust developed between the team members over a decade.

Outside of Boston, community archaeology is making headways in CRM and academic endeavors. Laura Heath-Stout is engaging in a new project at the Belchertown State School focusing on community archaeology and the reckoning of "hard histories" like eugenics and the impact of disabilities on people of the past and present (Heath-Stout 2024). Still in its development stage, Heath-Stout's is working to build a "community-driven disability-justice-oriented universally designed archaeology project at the Belcher-town State School in Belchertown" (Heath-Stout 2024). This work includes outreach and engagement with Belchertown survivors, survivors of other institutions, and the broader disabled community to have this community develop research questions for the project that are meaningful and relevant (Heath-Stout 2024). Heath-Stout identifies as disabled further aligning with the community archaeology ideals presented by Atalay (2006, 2012). An exciting aspect of the project is Heath-Stout's cofounding (with Kate Kinkopf) of the Disabled-Archaeologist Network, whose goals include making archaeology more accessible to disabled people, and the project goals of making the fieldwork at Belchertown accessible to disabled survivor-collaborators.

A significant hindrance to community archaeology is the public-private barrier that still exists within the CRM industry. Like the examples in Chinatown, the municipal-led project at 6 Hudson was far more capable of community archaeology than the more "traditional" CRM-style excavations at the Tai Tung Village project. The dominance of CRM in the archaeological landscape of Massachusetts means the increase in community archaeology in CRM will only happen if clients are willing to accept the added time and costs of slower projects with longer project development timelines, allow public presence on projects that may be controversial or increase liability issues, and are willing to fundamentally allow community voices to directly influence and guide both the archaeological work and ultimate development. As all of these are likely to negatively impact the profitability or costs of development; community archaeology is likely to significantly lag in Massachusetts without expanded inclusion of community archaeology principals in state-level regulations and better communication with clients about the potential benefits of engaging with a public interested in archaeology.

Academic community archaeology has stronger prospects in Massachusetts but still faces significant challenges. At present, the archaeology program at UMass Amherst is under significant pressure, having lost its CRM role. At UMass Boston, the historical archaeology work of the department remains strong and there are excellent recently completed and ongoing community archaeology projects within Massachusetts and New York (Silliman 2008; 2018). The pace and longevity of academic archaeological projects, including field schools, is inherently better suited to authentic community collaboration than CRM projects. Successes at Plymouth and Hassanamesit Woods with Native community archaeology and Indigenous archaeology have already been highlighted in this book. The likelihood for expansion of academic community archaeology is strong, but this will require a redirection of current and new community archaeology projects into Massachusetts.

Social justice archaeology does not require community archaeology (see Shackel 2013 and earlier discussions of sex and mill workers in previous chapters), but its emphasis on the needs of a community and the empowerment of community decision-making are inherently components of social justice. Barbara Little (2023) identifies the destabilization of violence and the creation of peace as significant goals of social justice and cites community archaeology as a means to achieve them. Social justice is a collaborative action, disruptive to injustice, and reflective of past and present histories of power, all of which are inherent aspects of community historical archaeology (Little 2023). Community archaeology is also an iterative process. Early community archaeology may not be authentic collaboration at its beginning, but these relationships grow with trust, and future projects with a more informed, more prepared, more archaeologically literate, more familiar, and more trusting community will be better for it. In urban places like Boston where there are dozens of "communities," these relationships are naturally going to be at multiple places on the trust relationship scale, but that does not mean that engaging with new communities should be avoided or that failure to be the most authentically collaborative right out of the gate are not important building blocks upon which to develop better community archaeology.

With a high cost of living (Rothstein 2024; Zumper 2024), the threats of climate change (Massachusetts 2023), and significant racial inequality (Lipkin 2024), Massachusetts has significant social justice issues. As Little (2023) states, these social justice issues have a past. Community historical archaeology connects social justice issues between the past and present and provides opportunities for meaningful and potentially transformative change. As the Tai Tung CRM survey project demonstrates, even the more static aspects of historical archaeology are responding to the work of community archaeology. It appears that the future of historical archaeology in Massachusetts will be more diverse, equitable, and inclusive.

9

Massachusetts Historical Archaeology as an American Experience

Massachusetts's residents of the past and present embody the quintessential American experience. Since the arrival of some of the earliest European explorers and settlers in America, Massachusetts has made significant contributions to the diverse histories of America. Historical archaeologists have flocked to Massachusetts to study these histories, and today, the Commonwealth is one of the leading producers of historical archaeological data and the professionals who uncover it. This book has explored the historical archaeology of Massachusetts to reveal how these practices, sites, and archaeologists have contributed to a better understanding of the American experience.

The geography of Massachusetts greatly influenced the trajectory of its history. Located on the East Coast, it received some of the earliest European colonists. From the coast, Euro-Americans expanded westward. In many ways, the geography of Massachusetts reflected the overall geography of the United States, with highlands on either end of the state and a low-lying river valley that was ideal for crop development and north–south trade. These geographical features had similar effects on expansion and economic narratives of the broader country, making Massachusetts history a microcosm of the American experience.

It was the early colonial settlements that first attracted historical archaeologists to Massachusetts. Here, archaeological pioneers like James Deetz, Roland Robbins, and Ripley Bullen developed many of the survey and analytical techniques that would shape the field not only in Massachusetts but throughout the nation. These early historical archaeologists recognized that adding material culture to historical narratives provided additional information that was simply not recorded by other means. Beyond the details and nuance of the lives of well-documented peoples, historical archaeologists recognized right away that this scientific practice had the ability to add fundamental knowledge to people who remained under recorded in history including women, Black people, Indigenous people, the working class, children, and others. Without historical archaeology, the story of the American experience is incomplete.

Colonists arrived on a complicated cultural landscape in Massachusetts. For millennia, tribes had maintained and fought over the diverse territories of the Commonwealth. Early explorers brought European diseases that decimated New England's coastal Native populations; settlers who claimed Indigenous lands pushed Native people into increasingly smaller and more marginalized spaces. The survivors of these early years fought to maintain their identities despite active endeavors to eradicate Native language, culture, and people. Historical archaeologists have explored the sites of early encounters between Native people and Massachusetts colonists finding complex interrelationships and bi-directional exchange of materials and ideas. Collaborative and public archaeology work like Project 400 (Beranek et. al 2015, 2016, 2019) proved that while Europeans became a dominant culture in Indigenous space, the impacts of the cultural collision were far from unilateral.

Historical archaeologists and Native communities have fully recognized the cultural continuity of Native people and the need for true archaeological collaboration to be fully inclusive of Indigenous research interests, knowledge, and participation. Transformative projects such as that between the Nipmuc Nation and the Fiske Center at the University of Massachusetts Boston have revealed the shared benefits to archaeologists, Native people, and Indigenous archaeologists working together to better reveal meaning and significance in the complex experience of colonialism.

As cities, towns, farms, and mills were developed, Massachusetts became a vibrant part of global trade. Early colonial domestic sites in Boston occupied by James Garrett (Pendery 1999) and Katherine Nanny Naylor (Cook 1998) indicate that a wide range of international goods were brought into Massachusetts. These are represented archaeologically in the remains of homes, outhouses, and businesses, and experienced at the time in the dishes on tables, the animals at the butcher, the weeds growing in yards, and the pests invading the pantry.

This international presence included the arrival of ideas. With the rise in wealth among Massachusetts residents, the people of the Commonwealth wished to partake in the evolving cultural norms they saw being adopted by their wealthy and more privileged counterparts abroad. The gentrification of colonial Massachusetts is abundant in the historical archaeological record from Yankee stoicism of the Spencer-Pierce-Little House in coastal Newburyport (Beaudry 1995) to the Williams family's aspirational landscape of gentility in far-western Deerfield (Reinke and Paynter 1984).

Many of those who gained wealth and power through the exploding Massachusetts economy used their elevated positions to oppress people of color through enslavement. The legal ownership of Black and Native people as chattel slaves in Massachusetts was one of the first laws encoded in the colony. Historical archaeologists have not always been adept at recognizing the presence of enslavement on archaeological sites or doing the work necessary to fully account for this presence in analytical study. Fortunately, that trend is changing, with the active investigations of sites of enslavement, sites of free Black and Indigenous people, and analytical work that prioritizes the agency and resistance of oppressed people in Massachusetts. There were those who fortunately recognized this important story in the early years of archaeology including the excavations at the Lucy Foster site in Andover in the 1940s (Bullen and Bullen 1945). A free woman of color, the analysis of Foster's possessions had paralleled decades of archaeological practice and theory from early establishment of cultural material identifications to Black feminist theory (Battle-Baptiste 2011).

The history of Massachusetts has unfortunately resulted in ample opportunities to study the effects of oppression and the resistance it creates. The earliest interactions between colonists and Native people in Massachusetts included the invasion of Native bodies by disease. Conflict that arose from colonial practices of land-taking, enslavement, and outright genocide resulted in the late seventeenth-century King Philip's War, one of the bloodiest wars in American history. The archaeological signatures of this battle are visible not just in the fortifications and ruined foundations that remain visible on the landscape of Massachusetts, but in the material culture of Native people like Sarah Boston, a Grafton Nipmuc woman, who lived in her home under supervision of English overseers as a direct result of the war over 150 years prior (Gould et al. 2020).

Despite their enslavement and oppression of Black and Native peoples, the colonists of Massachusetts rebelled against what they saw as the British Crown violating their rights as English subjects. In what would help define not only the American experience but the concept of America itself, the people of Massachusetts instigated what would become a war of independence. The archaeological signature of what may be the most pivotal event in American history is ironically diminished by its relative brevity on the timeline of the nation. Still, the fortifications, encampments, sea battles, and cultural upheaval that occurred during the Revolution have inspired some of the most innovative archaeological methods of documenting these events including ground-penetrating radar, metal detector studies, digital viewshed analysis, and new collaborative projects (Heitert 2009; Mastone et al. 2011; Beranek et al. 2019).

The people of Massachusetts are known not only for drinking Dunkin Donuts coffee, having strange accents, and driving aggressively, but also for their industrious nature. Boston is regularly ranked one of the hardest-working cities (WHDH 2018) and is accepted as a "traditional" tech hub (Davenport 2024) in the United States. This labor has deep roots. Massachusetts was all but forced to invest in its own manufacturing of goods after blockades of the War of 1812 devastated its merchant and trade economy. The resulting industrial boom is still visible across the Commonwealth in the form of entire towns, massive mill complexes, thousands of immigrant laborer descendants, and the disappearance of old English families from political leadership. Historical archaeologists have sought these industrial sites for the ability to document the development of industry and technology, but also because they contain many of the spaces where immigrant laborers lived and worked. These people are particularly underrepresented in written records beyond the basics of their identity and their cumulative production statistics. The excavations at the Boott Mills in Lowell, a town that did not exist until the Industrial Revolution, revealed the complex relationship between the laborers living in worker housing and their supervisors (Mrozowski et al. 1996). These workers maintained their Irish heritage and resisted the rules meant to keep them under control. The parallels between these workers and the Native people in Grafton, both dating to similar time periods, demonstrate the universality of the American experience of resistance in the face of oppression.

Some in Massachusetts made the decision to create entirely new societies when they felt oppressed or misaligned with cultural norms. These places have created fascinating opportunities for historical archaeologists to study the many deliberate choices made by these constructed cultural utopian communities like Brook Farm (City of Boston Archaeology 2022) and the Hancock Shaker Village (Donta et al. 2000). These not only document the alternative experience of these communities but also reflect the normative culture they rebel against. While these were both intended to be utopic, the nature of people to act with agency resulted in inevitable fragility and eventual collapse.

Massachusetts is today known for its educational institutions, but its broader institutional history is problematic. Many of the Commonwealth's institutions originate from genuine desire to help those in need, but these ideals are rarely achieved. Some of Massachusetts's poorest and most vulnerable people, including the residents of the Falmouth Poorhouse (Spencer-Wood 2009) and Dorchester Industrial School for Girls (Bagley et al. 2018b), experienced a created living space fundamentally limited by the resources of its overseers and the practices of its managers. The resistance of girls in Dorchester to the forced complicity of even the most basic individual agencies of clothing and toys, despite what may be one of the more idyllic institutional living conditions studied by archaeologists (Bagley et al. 2018b), shows that even under relatively good conditions, institutionalization will inevitably lead to rebellion.

The theme of resistance and agency lies at the heart of the American experience and historical archaeology in Massachusetts. As historical archaeologists grapple with the existential crisis of a political and economic landscape that makes the profession of historical archaeology ever more impractical, we are also faced with a crisis of relevance. Many have turned toward the practices of community and collaborative archaeology for its dual nature of supporting the needs and social justice of communities today while continuing to follow passions in historical archaeology, excavations, and analysis. These mutually beneficial projects include the spotlighting of displacement of Chinese Americans in Boston through the archaeology of a 1960s Chinese food restaurant site (Bagley 2019) and the multigenerational Nipmuc archaeologists working to study their ancestors while reshaping how archaeology is done and who it is done by (Gould et al. 2020).

This book has reviewed the incredible work of historical archaeologists in Massachusetts. These efforts have spanned decades of archaeology and thousands of projects, produced tens of thousands of pages of reports and publications, and documented millions of artifacts. Still, there is much to do. Historical archaeologists must continue returning to these older sites and collections to reexamine them with new ideas and revive their collections standards. Others will continue to expand historical archaeology to new sites, new stories, and new opportunities to make historical archaeology in Massachusetts relevant and meaningful in a changing world. The historical archaeology of Massachusetts is the story of the American experience: the growth, resistance, agency, ambition, labor, and curiosity of past people and those who study them now. The community of historical archaeology is embracing growth in diversity and inclusion of both its members and the sites studied, which will only improve it as a discipline. Massachusetts's past has a bright future.

BIBLIOGRAPHY

Abbott, Kate. 2021. "Mohican Families Connect in the Land—Across Time." *BTW Berkshires,* October 13. https://btwberkshires.com/regions/mohican.

Adams, William Hampton. 1993. "Historical Archaeology Strove for Maturity in the Mid-1980s." *Historical Archaeology* 27, no. 1: 23–31.

———. 2003. "Dating Historical Sites: The Importance of Understanding Time Lag in the Acquisition, Curation, Use, and Disposal of Artifacts." *Historical Archaeology* 37: 38.

Allard, Amélie. 2014. "Foodways, Animal Husbandry and Nipmuc Identity: Faunal Analysis from Sarah Boston's Farmstead, Grafton, MA, 1790–1840." *International Journal of Historical Archaeology* 19: 208–231.

Alston, Paris, and Gal Tziperman Lotan. 2024. "How Liquor License Legislation Could Make Boston's Restaurant Scene More Equitable." *WGBH News,* July 17. https://www.wgbh.org/news/local/2024-07-17/how-liquor-license-legislation-could-make-bostons-restaurant-scene-more-equitable.

Alterman, Michael, and Richard M. Affleck. 1999. *Archaeological Investigations at the Former Town Dock and Faneuil Hall, Boston National Historic Park, Boston, Massachusetts.* Report to the Massachusetts Historical Commission, Boston, from the Cultural Resource Group, Louis Berger & Associates, East Orange, NJ.

Anderson, Virginia DeJohn. 1991. *New England's Generation: The Great Migration and the Formation of Society and Culture in the Seventeenth Century.* Cambridge, UK: Cambridge University Press.

Andrews, Edward Deming. 1933. *The Community Industries of the Shakers.* Albany: University of the State of New York.

———. 1963. *The People Called Shakers: A Search for the Perfect Society.* New York: Dover Publications Inc.

Andrews, Edward Deming, and Faith Andrews. 1984. *Work and Worship Among the Shakers: Their Craftsmanship and Economic Order.* New York: Dover Publications, Inc.

Anthony, David. 1978. *The Archaeology of Worcester County: An Information Survey.* Report to the Massachusetts Historical Commission, Boston, from the Institute for Conservation Archaeology. Cambridge, MA: Harvard.

Apaydin, Veysel. 2020. "Heritage, Memory and Social Justice: Reclaiming Space and Identity." In *Critical Perspectives on Cultural Memory and Heritage: Construction, Transformation and Destruction,* edited by Veysel Apaydin, 84–97. London, UK: UCL Press.

Appleton, Edward. 1871. "History of the Railways of Massachusetts by Hon. Edward Appleton, Massachusetts Railway Commissioner." In *Official Topographical Atlas of Massachusetts from Astronomical, Trigonometrical and Various Local Survey,* compiled and corrected by H. F. Walling and O. W. Gray. Boston, MA: Stedman, Brown, and Lyon.

Archer, Gabriel. 1843. "The Relation of Captain Gosnold's Voyage." *Collections of the Massachusetts Historical Society,* third series, vol. 8: 72–81.

Arnett, Chris. 2024. "Origin Stories of the Central Salish Archipelago." In *Salish Archipelago: Environment and Society in the Islands Within and Adjacent to the Salish Sea,* edited by Moshe Rapaport, 107–22. Canberra, AU: ANU Press.

Atalay, Sonya. 2012. *Community-Based Archaeology: Research With, By, and for Indigenous and Local Communities.* Berkeley: University of California Press.

———. 2010. "Indigenous Archaeology as Decolonizing Practice." In *Indigenous Archaeologies: A Reader on Decolonization,* edited by Margaret Bruchac, Siobhan Hart, and H. Martin Wobst, 79–85.

Bagley, Joseph. 2013. *Intensive Archaeological Survey Training Field/Winthrop Square Park. City Archaeology Program for the Boston Parks and Recreation Department.* Report on file at the Massachusetts Historical Commission.

———. 2016. *A History of Boston in 50 Artifacts.* Hanover, NH: University Press of New England.

———. 2019. *Report for Intensive Location and Site Examination Archaeological Survey at 6 Hudson Street, Boston (Chinatown), Massachusetts City Archaeology Program for the Boston Landmarks Commission.* Report on file at the Massachusetts Historical Commission.

———. 2021a. *A History of Boston in 50 Artifacts.* Waltham, MA: Brandeis University Press.

———. 2021b. *Boston's Oldest Buildings and Where to Find Them.* Waltham, MA: Brandeis University Press.

Bagley, Joseph M., Andrew Glyman, and Sarah Johnson. 2018a. *Report for Intensive (Locational) Archaeological Survey at the Malcolm X / Ella Little-Collins House 72 Dale Street, Boston (Roxbury), Massachusetts.* City Archaeology Program for the Boston Landmarks Commission. Report on file at the Massachusetts Historical Commission.

Bagley, Joseph M. et al. 2018b. *Report for Archaeological Intensive (Locational) and Site Examination Survey at the Industrial School for Girls, 232 Centre St., Dorchester, Massachusetts.* City Archaeology Program for Epiphany School. Report on file at the Massachusetts Historical Commission.

Bagley, Joseph M. et al. 2024. "Dirt in the Wounds: Confronting Hard Histories through Public Community Archaeology in Boston." *Historical Archaeology* 58: 282–306. https://doi.org/10.1007/s41636-024-00513-8.

Bagley, Joseph M. et al. 2014. "Continuity of Lithic Practice from the Eighteenth to the Nineteenth Centuries at the Nipmuc Homestead of Sarah Boston, Grafton, Massachusetts." *Northeast Historical Archaeology* 43, no. 1: 172–188.

Bailey, George E. 1871. *Improvement in Bakers' Ovens.* Specification forming part of Letters Patent No. 121,573, dated December 5, 1871. Washington, DC: United States Patent Office.

———. 1872. *Improvement in Bakers' Ovens.* Specification forming part of Letters Patent No. 129,080, dated July 16, 1872. Washington, DC: United States Patent Office.

Bailyn, Bernard. 1955. *The New England Merchants in the Seventeenth Century.* Cambridge, MA: Harvard University Press.

Bain, Allison. 1998. "A Seventeenth-Century Beetle Fauna from Colonial Boston." *Historical Archaeology* 32, no. 3: 38–48.

Baker, Billy. 2024a. "In Ipswich, a Big Dam Fight." *Boston Globe,* May 6. https://www .bostonglobe.com/2024/05/06/metro/ipswich-mills-dam-removal-vote/.

———. 2024b. "After Contentious Debate, Ipswich Voters Support Removal of Controversial Dam." *Boston Globe,* May 22. https://www.bostonglobe.com/2024/05/22/ metro/ipswich-mills-dam-ballot-question/.

Baker, Brenda J. 1994. "Pilgrim's Progress and Praying Indians: The Biocultural Consequences of Contact in Southern New England." In *In the Wake of Contact: Biological Responses to Conquest,* edited by Clark Spencer Larsen and George R. Milner, 35–45. New York: Wiley-Liss.

Baker, James W. 1997. *Plimoth Plantation: Fifty Years of Living History.* Plymouth, MA: Plimoth Plantation Inc.

Baker, Vernon G. 1980. "Archaeological Visibility of Afro-American Culture: An Example from Black Lucy's Garden, Andover, Massachusetts." In *Archaeological Perspectives on Ethnicity in America,* edited by Robert L. Schuyler, 29–37. Farmingdale, NY: Baywood.

Banister, Jennifer. 2017. *Seaport Shipwreck Remains, Boston, Massachusetts.* Report to Skanska USA Commercial Development Inc., from The Public Archaeology Laboratory, Inc., Pawtucket, RI.

Banister, Jennifer, Suzanne Cherau, and John Daly. 2018. *Archaeological Data Recovery and Monitoring, Marine Railways No. 2 and No. 3, East Boston Dry Dock Company/ Atlantic Works Yard (MHC #BOS.ZH), 105 Border Street–DPA Parcel, East Boston, Massachusetts.* Report to Trinity Border Street Sitework Inc., Boston, MA, from The Public Archaeology Laboratory Inc., Pawtucket, RI.

Banister, Jennifer, John Daly, and Suzanne Cherau. 2016. *Historic/Archaeological Assessment and Evaluation and Archaeological Monitoring and Recordation Timber Dam, Amethyst Brook. Pelham, Massachusetts.* Report to Stantec Consulting Services Inc., Northampton, MA, from The Public Archaeology Laboratory Inc., Pawtucket, RI.

Banks, Charles E. 1911. *The History of Martha's Vineyard.* Edgartown, MA: Dukes County Historical Society.

Barth, Fredrik. 1995. "Other Knowledge and Other Ways of Knowing." *Journal of Anthropological Research,* 51, no. 1: 65–68.

Bates, Frank A. 1898. *The Ancient Iron Works at Braintree, Mass.* South Braintree, MA: F. A. Bates.

Bates, Ralph S. 1986. "In Memoriam: Henry Hornblower II (1917–1985)." *Bulletin of the Massachusetts Archaeological Society* 47, no. 2: 81.

Battle-Baptiste, Whitney. 2011. *Black Feminist Archaeology*. Walnut Creek, CA: Left Coast Press.

Baugher, Sherene, and Terry Klein, eds. 2003. "Historic Preservation and the Archaeology of Nineteenth-Century Farmsteads in the Northeast." *Northeast Historical Archaeology*, 2001–2002 issue, 30–31.

Baugher, Sherene, and Richard Veit. 2014. *The Archaeology of American Cemeteries and Gravemarkers*. Gainesville: University Press of Florida.

Beaudry, Mary C. 1984. "Archaeology and the Historic Household." *Man in the Northeast* 28: 27–38.

———. 1993. "Public Aesthetics Versus Personal Experience: Worker Health and Well-Being in 19th-Century Lowell, Massachusetts." *Historical Archaeology* 27, no. 2: 90–105.

———. 1995. "Scratching the Surface: Seven Seasons at the Spencer-Pierce-Little Farm, Newbury, Massachusetts." *Historical Archaeology* 24, no. 4: 19–49.

———. 1998. "Farm Journal: First Person, Four Voices." *Historical Archaeology* 32, no. 1: 20–33.

———. 2003. "James Deetz (1930–2000)." *American Anthropologist* 105, no. 1: 231–233.

Beaudry, Mary C., and Ellen Berkland. 2007. "Archaeology of the African Meeting House on Nantucket." In *Archaeology of Atlantic Africa and African Diaspora*, edited by Akinwumi Ogundiran and Toyin Folala, 395–412. Bloomington: Indiana University Press.

Beaudry, Mary, Loren Cook, and Stephen Mrozowski. 1991. "Artifacts and Active Voices: Material Culture as Social Discourse." In *The Archaeology of Inequality*, edited by R. McGuire and R. Paynter, 150–91. Oxford, UK: Basil Blackwell.

Beaudry, Mary C., and Stephen A. Mrozowski. 1988. "The Archaeology of Work and Home Life in Lowell, Massachusetts: An Interdisciplinary Study of the Boott Cotton Mills Corporation." *The Journal for the Society for Industrial Archaeology* 14, no. 2: 1–22.

———., eds. 1987a. *Interdisciplinary Investigations at the Boott Mills Lowell, Massachusetts, Volume I: Life at the Boarding Houses*. Report for National Park Service, Boston, MA. Boston, Center for Archaeological Studies, Boston University.

———., eds. 1987b. *Interdisciplinary Investigations at the Boott Mills Lowell, Massachusetts, Volume II: The Kirk Street Agents' House*. Report for National Park Service, Boston, MA, from Center for Archaeological Studies, Boston University.

———., eds. 1989. *Interdisciplinary Investigations at the Boott Mills Lowell, Massachusetts, Volume III: The Boarding House System as a Way of Life*. Report for National Park Service, Boston, MA, from Center for Archaeological Studies, Boston University, Boston, MA.

Beisaw, April, and James Gibbs, eds. 2009. *The Archaeology of Institutional Life*. Tuscaloosa: University of Alabama Press.

Bell, Edward L. 1991. "Artifacts from the Almshouse Burial Ground." In *Archaeological Investigations at the Uxbridge Almshouse Burial Ground in Uxbridge, Massachusetts,* edited by Ricardo J. Elia and Al B. Wesolowsky, 254–283. British Archaeological Reports International, Series No. 564. Oxford: Tempus Repartum.

———. 1993. "Historical Archaeology at the Hudson Poor Farm Cemetery, Hudson, Massachusetts." In *Occasional Publications in Archaeology and History,* no. 5. Boston: Massachusetts Historical Commission.

———. 1994. *Vestiges of Mortality and Remembrance: A Bibliography on the Historical Archaeology of Cemeteries.* Metuchen, NJ: The Scarecrow Press Inc.

Bendremer, Jeffrey C., and Elaine L. Thomas. 2008. "The Tribe and the Trowel: An Indigenous Archaeology and the Mohegan Archaeological Field School." In *Collaborating at the Trowel's Edge: Teaching and Learning in Indigenous Archaeology,* edited by Stephen W. Silliman, 50–66. Tucson: University of Arizona Press.

Beranek, Christa M. 2007. *Merchants, Gentry, Farmers, and Brokers: Archaeology of the Complex Identities of the Tyng Family of Dunstable, Massachusetts, in the Eighteenth Century.* PhD diss., Boston University Department of Archaeology.

Beranek, Christa et al. 2014. *Spring Street Archaeological Survey, Plymouth, Massachusetts, Cultural Resource Study No. 65.* Report to the Massachusetts Historical Commission, Boston, MA, from the University of Massachusetts, Boston Andrew Fiske Memorial Center for Archaeological Research, Boston, MA.

Beranek, Christa M., and Katie L. Kosack. 2009. *Collections Inventory of the Roland Robbins Archaeological Collection from the Hancock-Clarke House, Lexington, Massachusetts.* Report to Lexington Historical Society, Lexington, from Fiske Center for Archaeological Research, University of Massachusetts Boston.

Beranek, Christa, and David Landon. 2023. "Re-Imaging the Early Plymouth Colony: The View from Burial Hill." 2023. Paper presented at the 2023 Conference for New England Historical Archaeology, Plymouth, MA.

Beranek Christa M. et al., eds., 2016. *Project 400: The Plymouth Colony Archaeological Survey, Public Summary Report on the 2015 Field Season, Burial Hill, Plymouth, Massachusetts, Cultural Resource Study No.75a.* University of Massachusetts Boston, Andrew Fiske Memorial Center for Archaeological Research.

Beranek, Christa M. et al. 2019. *Project 400: The Plymouth Colony Archaeological Survey, Report on the 2018 Field Season, Brewster Gardens and Burial Hill, Plymouth, Massachusetts, Cultural Resource Study No. 83.* University of Massachusetts Boston, Andrew Fiske Memorial Center for Archaeological Research.

Beranek, Christa M. et al. 2015. *Project 400: The Plymouth Colony Archaeological Survey, Report on the 2014 Field Season, Burial Hill, Plymouth, Massachusetts, Cultural Resource Study No. 70.* University of Massachusetts Boston, Andrew Fiske Memorial Center for Archaeological Research.

Berkland, Ellen Patricia. 1999. *The Centering of an African-American Community: An Archaeological Study of the African Baptist Society Meeting House, Nantucket, Massachusetts.* Report on file, Massachusetts Historical Commission, Boston, MA.

Bigelow, Paul. 1993. *Wrights and Privileges, The Mills and Shops of Pelham, Massachusetts, from 1740 to 1937*. Athol, MA: Haley's Publishing.

Binzen, Timothy L. 2001. *Archaeological Reconnaissance and Intensive (Locational) Survey for the Proposed Powder Mill Square Development, Andover, Massachusetts.* Report on file, Massachusetts Historical Commission, Boston.

Boire, Kerrylynn, and Suzanne G. Cherau. 1995. *Archaeological Site Examination, Old Colony Railroad Roundhouse (WHI-HA-2) Whitman Station Project Area, Old Colony Railroad Rehabilitation Project, Whitman, Massachusetts.* Report to Sverdrup Civil Inc., Boston, MA from The Public Archaeology Laboratory Inc., Pawtucket, RI.

Boire, Kerrylynn, Suzanne G. Cherau, and William Begley. 1994. *Archaeological Reconnaissance Survey for the Greenbush Line of the Old Colony Railroad Rehabilitation Project, Cohasset, Hingham, Hull, Scituate, and Weymouth, Massachusetts.* Report to Sverdrup Civil Inc., Boston, MA from The Public Archaeology Laboratory Inc., Pawtucket, RI.

Boisvert, Richard. 2007. "Paleoindian Sites and Finds in the Lower Merrimack River Drainage." *Bulletin of the Massachusetts Archaeological Society* 68, no. 1: 12–21.

Bonauto, Mary. 2005. "Goodridge in Context." *Harvard Civil Rights-Civil Liberties Law Review* 40: 2–69.

Boston Landmarks Commission. 2022. *Highland Park Architectural Conservation District, Boston Landmarks Commission Study Report.* Boston, MA.

Boston Post. 1902. "Historical Gosnold Island Settlement of Buzzards Bay." June 8, p. 28.

Boston University. 1987. *Central Artery (I-93)/Third Harbor Tunnel (I-90) Project Archaeology Program Progress Report No. 2, June 1987.* Boston University for the Massachusetts Department of Transportation. On File at the Massachusetts Historical Commission.

Boston University Archaeology. 2021. "History of the Program." http://www.bu.edu/ archaeology/about-us/greetings-from-the-director/history/.

Bosworth, Janet, ed. 1993. *Cuttyhunk and the Elizabeth Islands From 1602.* Cuttyhunk, MA: Cuttyhunk Historical Society.

Bower, Beth Ann. 1978. *Report on the Archaeological Excavations at the Doggett and Cunningham Houses, Roxbury, Massachusetts.* Boston, MA: Museum of Afro American History.

———.1990. *The African Meeting House Boston Massachusetts: Summary Report of Archaeological Excavations 1975–1986.* Final Report. Boston, MA: Museum of Afro American History.

———. 1991. "Material Culture in Boston: The Black Experience." In *The Archaeology of Inequality,* edited by R. McGuire and R. Paynter, pp. 55–63. Oxford, UK: Basil Blackwell.

———. 1984. "Social Systems and Material Culture: Afro-Americans in Nineteenth-Century Boston." *Man in the Northeast* 27: 67–78.

Bower, Beth, and Byron Rushing. 1980. "The African Meeting House: The Center for the 19th Century Afro-American Community in Boston." In *Archaeological Perspective on Ethnicity in America: Afro-American and Asian American Culture History*, edited by R. L. Schuyler, 69–75. Farmingdale, NY: Baywood.

Bower, Beth Anne, Claire Dempsey, and Stephen Mrozowski. 1983. *Long Wharf: Archaeological Testing at Parcel D-l0, Boston, Massachusetts*. Report to the Massachusetts Historical Commission, Boston, from the Museum of Afro American History, Boston.

Bower, Beth Anne, Constance Crosby, and Byron Rushing. 1984. *Report on the Phase II Archaeological Subsurface Testing of the Southwest Corridor Project Area, Roxbury, Massachusetts*. Report on file at the Massachusetts Historical Commission.

Bower, Beth Ann, John Cheney and Byron Rushing. 1984. *Report on the Archaeological Testing Program in the African Meeting House Basement, October 1984*. Museum of Afro American History Inc. Roxbury, Massachusetts.

Bower, Beth Ann, and Sheila Charles. 1986. *Summary of the Laboratory Processing and Analysis for the 1985 African Meeting House Excavations*. Museum of Afro American History, Boston. Report on file, Massachusetts Historical Commission, Boston, MA.

———. 1988. *The Highland Foundry Site, Roxbury, Massachusetts, Report on Phase III Archaeological Data Recovery*. Report on file, Massachusetts Historical Commission, Boston, MA.

Bowden, Henry W., and James P. Ronda, eds. 1980. *John Eliot's Indian Dialogues: A Study in Cultural Interaction*. Westport, CT: Greenwood Press.

Bradford, George P. 1890. "Reminiscences of Brook Farm." *The Century* 45, no. 1: 141–148.

Bradford, William. 1952 [1590–1657]. *Bradford's History of Plymouth Plantation, 1606–1646*. New York: Barnes and Noble.

Bradley, James W., and Jeff Boudreau. 2006. "Re-Assessing Wapanucket: PaleoIndians in Southeast Massachusetts." *Bulletin of the Massachusetts Archaeological Society* 67, no. 2: 59–72.

Bragdon, Kathleen J. 1981. "Occupational Differences Reflected in Material Culture." *Northeast Historical Archaeology* 10, no. 10: 27–39.

———. 1996. *Native Peoples of Southern New England, 1500–1650*. Norman: University of Oklahoma Press.

Brenner, Elise M. 1978. "To Pray or to Be Prey: That is the Question: Strategies for Cultural Autonomy of Massachusetts Praying Indian Towns." *Ethnohistory* 27, no. 2: 135–152.

———. 1984. *Strategies for Autonomy: An Analysis of Ethnic Mobilization in Seventeenth Century Southern New England*. Ph.D. diss., University of Massachusetts Amherst.

———. 1986. "Archaeological Investigations at a Massachusetts Praying Town." *Bulletin of the Massachusetts Archaeological Society* 47, no. 2: 69–77.

Brewer, Priscilla J. 1986. *Shaker Communities, Shaker Lives*. Hanover, NH: University Press of New England.

Briggs, George N. 1849. *Report of the Commissioners Relating to the Condition of the Indians in Massachusetts.* House of Representatives, No. 46, Boston, MA.

Brooke, John L., and Douglas J. Norton. 1976. *A Preliminary Archaeological Survey of the West, Upper North, and South Families, Hancock Shakers.* Report on file, Massachusetts Historical Commission, Boston, MA.

Brooks, Lisa. 2008. *The Common Pot: The Recovery of Native Space in the Northeast.* Minneapolis: University of Minnesota Press.

———. 2018. *Our Beloved Kin: A New History of King Philip's War.* New Haven, CT: Yale University Press.

Browman, David L., and Stephen Williams. 2013. *Anthropology at Harvard: A Biographical History, 1790–1940.* Cambridge, MA: Peabody Museum Press, Harvard University.

Brown, Gregory J., and Joanne Bowen. 1998. "Animal Bones from the Cross Street Back Lot Privy." *Historical Archaeology* 32, no. 3: 72–80.

Brown, Marley R. III. 1978. "A Survey of Historical Archaeology in New England." In *New England Historical Archaeology. The Dublin Seminar for New England Folklife: Annual Proceedings,* edited by Peter Benes, 4–15. Boston, MA: Boston University.

Brown, Marley R. III, and Edward A. Chappell. 2004. "Archaeological Authenticity and Reconstruction at Colonial Williamsburg." In *The Reconstructed Past: Reconstructions in the Public Interpretation of Archaeology and History,* edited by John H. Jameson Jr., 47–64. Lanham, MD: AltaMira Press.

Brown, Marley R., III, and Harold D. Juli. 1974. *Archaeological Excavations at the Fairbanks Homestead, Dedham, Massachusetts, 1973–1974.* Report to the Fairbanks Family in America Inc., Dedham, MA.

Bruchac, Margaret M. 2005. "Earthshapers and Placemakers: Algonkian Indian Stories and the Landscape." *In Indigenous Archaeologies Decolonizing Theory and Practice,* edited by C. Smith and M. Wobst, 57–80. New York: Routledge.

Bruchac, Margaret M., and Siobhan M. Hart. 2012. "Materiality and Autonomy in the Pocumtuck Homeland." *Archaeologies* 8, no. 3: 293–312.

Bruchac, Margaret M., Siobhan Hart, and H. Martin Wobst, eds. 2010. *Indigenous Archaeologies: A Reader on Decolonization.* Walnut Creek, CA: Left Coast Press.

Bulger, Teresa Dujnic. 2015. "'The Character of a Woman': Womanhood and Race in Nineteenth-Century Nantucket." In *The Archaeology of Race in the Northeast,* edited by Christopher N. Matthews and Allison Manfra McGovern, 98–117. Gainesville: University Press of Florida.

Bullen, Adelaide K., and Ripley P. Bullen. 1945. "Black Lucy's Garden." *Bulletin of the Massachusetts Archaeological Society* 6, no. 2: 17–28.

Burnett, Jeffrey J. 2022. "Seeking Radical Solidarity in Heritage Studies: Exploring the Intersection of Black Feminist Archaeologies and Geographies in Oak Bluffs, MA." *International Journal of Historical Archaeology* 26: 53–78.

Burns, D. E. 1993. *Shaker Cities of Peace, Love, and Union: A History of the Hancock Bishopric.* University of New England, Hanover, NH.

Cacchione, Victoria A. 2019. "Public Face and Private Life: Identity through Ceramics at the Boston-Higginbotham House on Nantucket." *Journal of African Diaspora Archaeology and Heritage* 8, no. 1–2: 57–77.

Campetti, Casey. 2020. *Phase I Intensive (Locational) Archaeological Survey, Preserving Our Place on Stockbridge Main Street: Ox Roast Investigations, Stockbridge, Massachusetts.* Report to Stockbridge Munsee Community Tribal Historic Preservation, Stockbridge, MA, from AECOM, Chelmsford, MA.

Campisi, Jack. 1993. *The Mashpee Indians: Tribe on Trial.* Syracuse, NY: Syracuse University Press.

Carlson, Catherine. 1986. *Archival and Archaeological Research Report on the Configuration of the Seven Original Seventeenth Century Praying Indian Towns of the Massachusetts Bay Colony.* Amherst: University of Massachusetts Archaeological Services.

Carlson, Stephen P. 1973. *Saugus Iron works National Historical Site, Historical Sketch.* Washington: National Park Service.

———. 2010. *Charlestown Navy Yard Historic Resource Study.* Produced by the Division of Cultural Resources, Boston National Historical Park, National Park Service, US Department of the Interior, Boston, MA.

Carpenter, Dolores Bird. 1994. *Early Encounters: Native Americans and Europeans in New England.* East Lansing: Michigan State University Press.

Carpenter and Morehouse. 1896. *The History of the Town of Amherst, Massachusetts.* Amherst, MA: Carpenter & Morehouse.

Carson, Cary. 1994. "The Consumer Revolution in Colonial British North America: Why Demand?" In *Of Consuming Interests: The Style of Life in the Eighteenth Century,* edited by Cary Carson, Richard Hoffman, and Peter J. Albert, 483–697. Charlottesville: University Press of Virginia.

Cassedy, Daniel et al. 2013. *Archeological Investigations in Support of the Transportation and Information Hub Project, Faneuil Hall, Boston, Massachusetts.* Report to the Massachusetts Historical Commission, Boston, from URS, Burlington, NJ.

Casella, Eleanor Conlin. 2007. *The Archaeology of Institutional Confinement.* Gainesville: University Press of Florida.

Cavanaugh, Jean, Mary Dewart, and Judith Stoessel. 1990. *A Pastoral Vision Reclaimed: A Preliminary Master Plan for Brook Farm Historic Site, an MDC Reservation, West Roxbury, Massachusetts.* On file, Massachusetts Department of Conservation and Recreation, Boston, MA.

Ceci, Lynn. 1975. "Fish Fertilizer: A Native North American Practice." *Science* 168: 26–30.

———. 1990. "Radiocarbon Dating Village Sites in Coastal New York: Settlement Pattern Change in the Middle to Late Woodland." *Man in the Northeast* 39: 1–28.

Chan, Alexandra A. 2007. *Slavery in the Age of Reason: Archaeology at a New England Farm.* Knoxville: University of Tennessee Press.

Chandler, Jim. 2001. "On the Shore of a Pleistocene Lake: The Wamsuttta Site (19-NF-70)." *Bulletin of the Massachusetts Archaeological Society* 62, no. 2: 52–62.

Cherau, Suzanne Glover. 2001. "Native Building Traditions in Southern New England: A Study of the Aquinnah Wampanoag Community, Martha's Vineyard." Paper presented at the Annual Meeting and Conference, Vernacular Architecture Forum, Mashantucket Pequot Museum and Research Center, Mashantucket, CT.

Cherau, Suzanne G., and Jennifer B. Banister. 2006. *Intensive (Locational) Archaeological Survey for the Proposed Carriage Way Extension Project in Hancock Shaker Village, Hancock and Pittsfield, Massachusetts.* Report to Massachusetts Highway Department, Boston, MA, from The Public Archaeology Laboratory Inc., Pawtucket, RI.

———. 2024. *Archaeological Reconnaissance Survey, Ipswich Mills Dam Removal, Ipswich, Massachusetts.* Report to Ipswich River Watershed Association, Ipswich, MA, from The Public Archaeology Laboratory Inc., Pawtucket, RI.

Cherau, Suzanne G., and Kerrylynn Boire. 1999. *Intensive (Locational) Archaeological Survey, Conference Center Parking Lot and Archaeological Site Examination, NR-7 Shaker Building Conference Center, MCI Shirley Correctional Facility, Shirley, Massachusetts.* Report to The Preservation Partnership, Weare, NH, and Division of Capital Assets Management, Boston, MA, from The Public Archaeology Laboratory Inc., Pawtucket, RI.

Cherau, Suzanne, John Daly, and David S. Robinson. 2008. *Cultural Resources Reconnaissance Survey, Boston East Development Project, East Boston, Massachusetts.* Report to Fort Point Associates Inc., Boston, MA, from The Public Archaeology Laboratory Inc., Pawtucket, RI.

Cherau, Suzanne G., Matthew A. Kierstead, and Sarah B. Chase. 2000. *Site Repair/Restoration and Creation of Archaeological Interpretive Park Old Colony Railroad Roundhouse Site (WHI-HA-2), Whitman, Massachusetts.* Report to Massachusetts Bay Transportation Authority, Boston, MA, and J. F. White Contracting Co., Boston, MA, from The Public Archaeology Laboratory Inc., Pawtucket, RI.

Cherau, Suzanne, David S. Robinson, and John Daly. 2017. *Archaeological Data Recovery Program, Granite Seawalls and Burnham's Marine Railway (MHC #GLO.939), Former Gloucester Gas Light Company Manufactured Gas Plant, Massachusetts Contingency Plan Remediation Project, Gloucester, Massachusetts.* The Public Archaeology Laboratory Inc. Report No. 2778.03., to Anchor QEA, LLC, Beverly, MA, from The Public Archaeology Laboratory Inc., Pawtucket, RI.

Chilton, Elizabeth S. 2002. "'Towns They Have None': Diverse Subsistence and Settlement Strategies in Native New England." In *Northeast Subsistence and Settlement Change: A.D. 700–1300,* edited by John P. Hart and Christina B. Reith, 289–300. Albany: New York State Museum.

———. 2010. "The Origin and Spread of Maize (Zea Mays) in New England." In *Nantucket and Other Native Places,* edited by Elizabeth S. Chilton and Mary Lynne Rainey, 159–180. Albany: State University of New York Press.

Chilton, Elizabeth S., Tonya B. Largy, and Kathryn G. Curran. 2000. "Evidence for Prehistoric Maize Horticulture at the Pine Hill Site, Deerfield, Massachusetts." *Northeast Anthropology* 59: 23–46.

Chilton, Elizabeth, Thomas Ulrich, and Niels Rinehart. 2005. "A Re-Examination of the Deerfield Industrial Park Survey." *Bulletin of the Massachusetts Archaeological Society* 66, no. 2: 58–66.

Chireau, Yvonne. 1997. "Conjure and Christianity in the Nineteenth Century: Religious Elements of African American Magic." *Religion and American Culture* 7, no. 2: 225–46.

Cipolla, Craig N., James Quinn, and Jay Levy. 2019. "Theory in Collaborative Indigenous Archaeology: Insights from Mohegan." *American Antiquity* 84, no. 1: 127–142.

City of Boston. 1906. *City of Boston, Gallops Island, Boston Harbor, May 23, 1906, Plan Showing Cemetery Gallops Island Boston Harbor.* Boston, MA: City Engineering Department.

City of Boston Archaeology. 2022. "Brook Farm Archaeological Site." https://www .boston.gov/departments/archaeology/brook-farm-archaeological-site.

———. 2023. "Boston Harbor Islands Archaeological Climate Action Plan." https:// www.boston.gov/departments/archaeology/boston-harbor-islands-archaeological -climate-action-plan.

City of Boston Planning Department. 2022. "288 Harrison Avenue." https://www .bostonplans.org/projects/development-projects/288-harrison-avenue.

Clements, Joyce M. 1993. "The Cultural Creation of the Feminine Gender: An Example from 19th-Century Military Households at Fort Independence, Boston." *Historical Archaeology* 27, no. 4: 39–64.

———. 2002. "Moving Beyond Irrelevant Relativism: Reflections on the Women from Ponkapoag Praying Town, Massachusetts." *Bulletin of the Massachusetts Archaeological Society* 63, no. 1–2: 44–50.

Codman, John Thomas. 1894. *Brook Farm: Historic and Personal Memoirs.* Boston, MA: Arena Publishing Co.

Cogley, Richard W. 1999. *John Eliot's Mission to the Indians Before King Philip's War.* Cambridge, MA: Harvard University Press.

Colwell-Chanthaphonh, Chip, and T. J. Ferguson. 2007. *Collaboration in Archaeological Practice: Engaging Descendant Communities.* Lanham, MD: AltaMira Press.

Conkey, Margaret W., and Janet D. Spector. 1984. "Archaeology and the Study of Gender." *Advances in Archaeological Method and Theory* 7: 1–38.

Cook, Lauren J. 1991. "The Uxbridge Poor Farm in the Documentary Record." In *Archaeological Investigations at the Uxbridge Almshouse Burial Ground in Uxbridge, Massachusetts,* edited by Ricardo J. Elia and Al B. Wesolowsky, 40–81. British Archaeological Reports International Series No. 564. Oxford: Tempus Repartum.

———. 1998. "Katherine Nanny, Alias Naylor: A Life in Puritan Boston." *Historical Archaeology* 32, no. 3: 15–19.

Cook, Lauren J., and Joseph Balicki. 1998. *Archaeological Data Recovery: The Paddy's Alley and Cross Street Back Lot Sites (BOSHA-12/13), Boston, Massachusetts.* Report to the Massachusetts Historical Commission, Boston, from John Milner Associates, Inc, Danbury, CT.

Cook, S. F. 1976. *The Indian Population of New England in the Seventeenth Century.* Berkeley: University of California Press.

Cooke, Edward S. Jr. 2019. *Inventing Boston: Design, Production, and Consumption 1680–1720.* New Haven, CT: Yale University Press.

Coombs, Linda. 2002. "Holistic History: Including the Wampanoag." *Plimoth Life* 1, no. 2: 12–15.

Cooper, Carolyn C. 1988. "'A Whole Battalion of Stackers': Thomas Blanchard's Production Line and Hand Labor at Springfield Armory." *The Journal of the Society for Industrial Archaeology* 14, no. 1: 36–58.

Copeland, Jennie F. 1936. *Every Day but Sunday: The Romantic Age of New England Industry.* Brattleboro, VT: Stephen Daye Press.

Copley, John Singleton. 1772. *Eleazer Tyng.* Accession Number 1965.6.1 Washington, DC: National Gallery of Art.

Copplestone, J. Tremayne. 1998. *John Eliot and the Indians, 1604–1690.* Privately printed.

Cotter, John L. 1993. "Historical Archaeology Before 1967." *Historical Archaeology* 27, no. 1: 4–9.

Cummings, Abbott Lowell. 1964. *Rural Household Inventories, Establishing the Names, Uses, and Furnishings of Rooms in the Colonial New England Home, 1675-1725.* Boston, MA: Society for the Preservation of New England Antiquities.

———. 1979. *The Framed Houses of Massachusetts Bay, 1625–1725.* Cambridge, MA: Belknap Press of Harvard University.

Curran, Mary Lou, and Dena F. Dincauze. 2006. "Paleoindians and Paleo-Lakes: New Data from the Connecticut Drainage." *Annals of the New York Academy of Sciences* 288, no. 1: 333–348.

Currie, Douglas R. 1994. "Micromorphology of a Native American Cornfield." *Archaeology of Eastern North America* 22 (Fall 1994):63–72.

Daly, Aoife, Fred Hocker, and Calvin Mires. 2022. "Dating the Timbers from the 'Sparrow-Hawk,' a Shipwreck from Cape Cod, USA." *Journal of Archaeological Science* 42: 103374.

Daum, Randy C. 2008. *Discovery and Investigation of a late Seventeenth-Century Colonial Village Site: The Hatfield Old Farms Settlement.* Report to University of Massachusetts Amherst Anthropology Department.

———. 2014. *Investigations of the Hatfield Old Farms Settlement Site 2009–212.* Report to University of Massachusetts Amherst Anthropology Department.

Davenport, Paul. 2024. "Where Are the Fastest-Growing Startup Cities in the United States?" *BOAST.* https://boast.ai/blog/where-are-the-fastest-growing-startup-cities -in-the-united-states/.

Deetz, Hartman. 2023. "United Through History and Experience: Wampanoag-Bermuda Connections." *Cultural Survival,* September 8. https://www .culturalsurvival.org/news/united-through-history-and-experience-wampanoag -bermuda-connections.

Deetz, James. 1968. "Late Man in North America: Archaeology of European Americans." In *Anthropological Archaeology in the Americas,* edited by Betty J. Meggers, 121–130. Washington, DC: Anthropological Society of Washington.

———. 1977. *In Small Things Forgotten.* Garden City, NY: Anchor Books.

———. 1995. *In Small Things Forgotten: An Archaeology of Early American Life.* Farden City, NY: Anchor Books.

Deetz, James, and Patricia E. Scott Deetz. 2000. *The Times of the Their Lives: Life, Love, and Death in Plymouth Colony.* New York: W.H. Freeman.

DeLucia, Christine. 2019. *Memory Lands: King Philip's War and the Place of Violence in the Northeast.* New Haven, CT: Yale University Press.

———. 2020. "Recovering Material Archives in the Native Northeast: Converging Approaches to Traces, Indigeneity, and Settler Colonialism." *Early American Literature* 55, no. 2: 355–394.

DeLucia, Christine, and Meghan Howey. 2022. "Spectacles of Settler Colonial Memory: Archaeological Findings from an Early Twentieth Century 'First' Settlement Pageant and Other Commemorative Terrain in New England." *International Journal of Historical Archaeology* 26: 974–1007.

Demos, John. 1970. *A Little Commonwealth: Family Life in Plymouth Colony.* New York: Oxford University Press.

Dempsey, Claire. 1988. *Massachusetts Historical Commission Area Form A–Pioneer Village, Salem, MA (SAL.GM).* On file, Massachusetts Historical Commission, Boston.

Dermer, Thomas. 1905 [1625]. "To his worshipfull friend M. Samvel Pvrchas, preacher of the Word, at the Church a little within Ludgate, London." In *Sailors Narratives of Voyages along the New England Coast 1524–1624,* edited by GP Winship, 251–258. Boston, MA: Houghton, Mifflin and Co.

Dincauze, D. F. et al. 1981. *Retrospective Assessment of Archeological Survey Contracts in Massachusetts 1970–1979,* 3 vols. Report prepared for Massachusetts Historical Commission, Boston.

Dimmick, Frederica R. 2006. *Archaeological Investigations at the Bog House, Truro, Massachusetts.* Report prepared for Massachusetts Historical Commission, Boston.

Dobyns, H. F. 1983. *Their Number Become Thinned: Native American Population Dynamics in Eastern North America.* Knoxville: University of Tennessee Press.

Donta, Christopher L., Ellen-Rose Savulis, and Thomas L. Arcuti. 2000. *Archaeological Intensive (Locational) Surveys for Proposed Improvement Projects at Hancock Shaker Village, Hancock, Massachusetts.* Report on file, Massachusetts Historical Commission, Boston.

Donta, Christopher L., and Jennifer Wendt. 2002. *Archaeological Intensive (Locational) Survey for the Proposed Williams Street Bridge Replacement Project, Mansfield, Massachusetts.* Report on file at the Massachusetts Historical Commission, Boston.

Doucette, Dianna L. 2015. *Sanderson Tannery Site (PET-HA-2), 2010 Archaeological Field School, Harvard Forest, Petersham, Massachusetts.* Report on file at the Massachusetts Historical Commission, Boston.

Douyard, Christopher M. 2014. "Property, Capital, and Race: Rural Capitalism and Racialized Landscapes in Nineteenth-Century Massachusetts." *Journal of African Diaspora Archaeology and Heritage* 3, no. 2: 175–196.

Dow, George Francis. 1925. *Whale Ships and Whaling: A Pictorial History of Whaling During Three Centuries with an Account of the Whale Fishery in Colonial New England.* Salem, MA: Marine Research Society.

———. 1935. *Every Day Life in Massachusetts Bay Colony.* Boston, MA: The Society for the Preservation of New England Antiquities.

Dowson, Thomas A. 2000. "Why Queer Archaeology? An Introduction." *World Archaeology* 32, no. 2: 161–65.

Doyle, Terrance. 2020. "Go Eat in Boston's Chinatown." *Eater Boston,* February 20. https://boston.eater.com/2020/2/20/21143865/chinatown-boston-coronavirus -financial-losses.

Dublin, Thomas. 1992. *Lowell: The Story of an Industrial City: A Guide to Lowell National Historical Park and Lowell Heritage State Park, Lowell, Massachusetts.* Washington, DC: Division of Publications, National Park Service, US Department of the Interior.

Dudek, Martin G., Lawrence Kaplan, and Marie Mansfield King. 1998. "Botanical Remains from a Seventeenth-Century Privy at the Cross Street Back Lot Site." *Historical Archaeology* 32, no. 3: 63–71.

Dujnic, Teresa. 2005. *Intentions of Independence: Medicinal Practice and Community Identity at Boston's African Meeting House.* Master's thesis, University of Massachusetts Boston.

Earle, John Milton. 1861. *Report to the Governor and Council Concerning the Indians of the Commonwealth (Including Chappaquiddick) Under the Act of April 6, 1859.* Boston, MA: William White, printer to the state.

Elia, Ricardo J. 1984. *Proposal for Phase III Data Recovery Operations at eleven Historical Sites in the Central Artery, North Area, Charlestown, Massachusetts.* Report on file at the City of Boston Archaeology Laboratory.

———. 1989. *Archaeological Excavations at the East Ell of the Golden Ball Tavern in Weston, Massachusetts.* Report to the Massachusetts Historical Commission, Boston, from the Office of Public Archaeology, Boston University.

———. 1990. "Reflections on Contract Archaeology in the 1980s." *Bulletin of the Massachusetts Archaeological Society* 51, no. 2: 86–89.

———. 1992. "The Ethics of Collaboration: Archaeologists and the Whydah Project." *Historical Archaeology* 26, no. 4: 105–17.

Ellis, James H. 2009. *A Ruinous and Unhappy War: New England and the War of 1812.* New York: Algora Publishing.

Englund, John. 1982. *Sawmills of Worcester County.* On file, Old Sturbridge Village, Sturbridge, MA.

Evans, Oliver. 1850 [1795]. *The Young Mill-Wright and Miller's Guide,* thirteenth edition. Lea & Philadelphia, PA: Blanchard.

Fennell, Christopher C. 2021. *The Archaeology of Craft and Industry.* Gainesville: University Press of Florida.

Fermino, Jessie Little Doe. 2001. "You Are a Dead People." *Cultural Survival Quarterly* 25, no. 2 (Endangered Languages, Endangered Lives) https://www.culturalsurvival .org/publications/cultural-survival-quarterly/you-are-dead-people

Fiske Center for Archaeological Research. 2010. "Brochure." http://www.fiskecenter .umb.edu/Pdfs/Fiske%20Center%20brochure.pdf.

Fitts, Robert K. 1996. Landscapes of Northern Bondage. *Historical Archaeology* 30, no. 2: 54–73.

——. 1999. "Archaelogy of Middle-Class Domesticity and Gentility in Victorian Brooklyn." *Historical Archaeology* 33, no. 1: 39–62.

Flewellen, Ayana Omilade et al. 2021. "'The Future of Archaeology Is Antiracist': Archaeology in the Time of Black Lives Matter." *American Antiquity* 86, no. 2: 224–43.

Foss, A. E. and Co. 1887. *Resident and Business Directory of Mansfield, Massachusetts for 1887*. Needham, MA: Chronicle Steam Press.

Frizell, Joseph P. 1901. *Water-Power*. New York: John Wiley & Sons.

Fuhrer, Mary. 2004. *Sowing the Seed of Liberty: Lexington and the American Revolution*. Exhibition Files, MNH004, Scottish Rite Masonic Museum and Library, d.b.a. National Heritage Museum. n.d. The Battle for Freehold Farms: Lexington, 1735–1800. Unpublished. Lexington, MA.

Gallagher, Joan, and Patricia E. Rubertone. 1982. *Final Report of the Interstate Highway 495 Archaeological Data Recovery Program, Volume IV, Part I, Patterns of Rural Migration: Evidence from the Historic Sites and Part II, Site Summaries,* edited by Patricia E. Rubertone. Report to the Massachusetts Historical Commission, Boston, from PAL Inc., Pawtucket, RI.

Gallagher, Joan et al. 1992. *The Parker-Harris Pottery Site, Central Artery North Reconstruction Project, Archaeological Data Recovery, Charlestown, Massachusetts, Volume III*. Report to the Massachusetts Historical Commission, Boston, from PAL Inc., Pawtucket, RI.

——. 1994a. *The Town Dock Wharves/Dry Dock Site, Town Dock Pottery Site, Central Artery North Reconstruction Project, Archaeological Date Recovery, Charlestown, Massachusetts, Volume IVA*. Report to the Massachusetts Historical Commission, Boston, from PAL Inc., Pawtucket, RI.

Gallagher, Joan et al. 1994b. *Archaeological Data Recovery, City Square Archaeological District, Central Artery North Reconstruction Project, Charlestown, Massachusetts, Volume VII*. Report to the Massachusetts Historical Commission, Boston, from PAL Inc., Pawtucket, RI.

Gallivan, Martin. 2021. "Deep Histories in the Archaeology of Colonialism." In *The Routledge Handbook of the Archaeology of Indigenous-Colonial Interaction on the Americas,* edited by Lee M. Panich and Sara L. Ginzalex, 14–29.

Galvin, William Francis. 2024. *Bibliography of Archaeological Survey & Mitigation Reports: Massachusetts, 2024 Supplement*. Massachusetts Historical Commission, Boston.

Garman, James C. 1996. *Intensive (Locational) Archaeological Survey, United Shoe Manufacturing Corporation Redevelopment*. Report on file at the Massachusetts Historical Commission.

Garman, James C., and Paul Russo. 1999. "The Town Farm and Class Realignment in Nineteenth-century Rural New England." *Historical Archaeology* 33, no. 1: 118–35.

Garman, James C., Paul A. Russo, and Lauren J. Cook. 1998a. *Archaeological Site Examination of the Osborn-Read-Paige Pottery, AHEPA/Penelope 120 Assisted Living*

Project, Peabody, Massachusetts. Report to Krapf Associates, Boston, MA, from The Public Archaeology Laboratory Inc., Pawtucket, RI.

Garman, James C. et al. 1998b. *Archaeological Investigation at Derby and Central Wharves, Salem Maritime National Historic Site, Salem, Massachusetts.* Report to the Massachusetts Historical Commission, Boston, from UMass Archaeological Services, Amherst.

Garvin, James L. 2001. *A Building History of Northern New England.* Lebanon, NH: The University Press of New England.

Gary, Jack, and Kirstin Randall. 2006. *Archaeological Investigation of the Northeast Lawn of the Golden Ball Tavern, Weston, Massachusetts.* Report to the Massachusetts Historical Commission, Boston, from the Fiske Center for Archaeological Research at UMass Boston.

George, David, and Jeffrey Bendremer. 1995. "Late Woodland Subsistence and the Origins of Maize Horticulture in New England." Paper presented at 60th Annual Meeting of the Society for Historical Archaeology, Minneapolis, MN.

George, David R. et al. 2021. *Archaeological Burial Recovery and Site Stabilization, Gallops Island Quarantine Cemetery (BOS-HA-82), Boston, Massachusetts.* Two volumes. Report on file, Massachusetts Historical Commission, Boston, MA.

Gibb, James. 2000. "Imaginary, but by No Means Unimaginable: Storytelling, Science, and Historical Archaeology." *Historical Archaeology* 34, no. 2: 1–6.

Gibb, J., and April Beisaw. 2000. "Learning Cast Up from the Mire: Archaeological Investigations of Schoolhouses in the Northeastern United States." *Northeastern Historical Archaeology* 29: 107–29.

Gibson, Susan G., ed. 1980. *Burr's Hill, A 17th-Century Wampanoag Burial Ground in Warren, Rhode Island.* Providence, RI: Eastern Press Inc.

Glover, Suzanne, and Edna Feighner. 1991. *Intensive (Locational) Archaeological Survey and Site Examinations, Marine Resources Center, Woods Hole, Falmouth, Massachusetts.* Report to Marine Biological Laboratory, Falmouth, MA, from The Public Archaeology Laboratory Inc., Pawtucket, RI.

Glover, Suzanne, Kerrylynn Boire, and Kevin McBride. 1993. *Intensive (Locational) Archaeological Survey, Individual Lots Abutting Parcels I, IIA, IIB, III-Tribal Trust Lands, Gay Head, Massachusetts.* Report to the Wampanoag Tribe of Gay Head (Aquinnah), Gay Head, MA, from The Public Archaeology Laboratory Inc., Pawtucket, RI.

Glover, Suzanne, and Kevin A. McBride. 1991. *Intensive (Locational) Archaeological Survey, Parcel I, Tribal Trust Lands, Gay Head, Massachusetts.* Report to the Wampanoag Tribe of Gay Head (Aquinnah), Gay Head, MA, from The Public Archaeology Laboratory Inc., Pawtucket, RI.

———. 1992. *Intensive (Locational) Archaeological Survey and Additional Testing, Parcels I, IIA, IIB, and III—Tribal Trust Lands, Gay Head, Massachusetts.* Report to the Wampanoag Tribe of Gay Head (Aquinnah), Gay Head, MA, from The Public Archaeology Laboratory Inc., Pawtucket, RI.

Glover, Suzanne, William Begley, and Virginia H. Adams. 1993. *Intensive (Locational) Archaeological Survey of the Old Colony Railroad Rehabilitation Project: Main,*

Middleborough, and Plymouth Lines, Plymouth and Norfolk Counties, Massachusetts. Report to Sverdrup Corporation, Boston, MA, from The Public Archaeology Laboratory Inc., Pawtucket, RI.

Goodby, Robert. 2021. *A Deep Presence:13,000 Years of Native American History.* Portsmouth, NH: Peter E. Randall Publisher.

Goodman, Davis. 1975. *Report on Excavations at Fort Washington 1974–1975.* Peabody Museum of Archaeology. Report on file at the Massachusetts Historical Commission.

Gookin, Daniel. 1970 [1792]. *Historical Collections of the Indians in New England; of Their Several Nations, Numbers, Customs, Manners, Religion and Government, Before the English Planted There.* Boston, MA: Towtaid Press.

Goodwin, Lorinda B. R. 1999. *An Archaeology of Manners: The Polite World of the Merchant Elite of Colonial Massachusetts.* New York: Kluwer Academic/Plenum Publishers.

Gookin, Warner F. 1950. "The Pilgrims as Archaeologists." *Bulletin of the Massachusetts Archaeological Society* 11, no. 2: 19–21.

Gordon, Robert, and Patrick Malone. 1994. *The Texture of Industry: An Archaeological View of Industrialization in North America.* New York: Oxford University Press.

Gould, Donna Rae. 2013. "Cultural Practice and Authenticity: The Search for Real Indians in New England in the 'Historical Period.'" In *The Death of Prehistory,* edited by Peter Schmidt and Stephen A. Mrozowski, 241–266. Oxford, UK: Oxford University Press.

———. 2017. "NAGPRA, CUI and Institutional Will." In *The Routledge Companion to Cultural Property,* edited by Jane Anderson and Haidy Geismar, 134–151. London, UK: Routledge.

Gould, D. Rae et al. 2020. *Historical Archaeology and Indigenous Collaboration: Discovering Histories That Have Futures.* Gainesville: University Press of Florida.

Grant-Costa, Paul, and Tobias Glaza. 2017. "Access to the Past: A New Trial-Friendly Approach Explains Old Archives." *American Indian* (Magazine of the Smithsonian's National Museum of the American Indian), 18, no. 2: 1–8.

Green, Mason A. 1886. *Springfield, 1636–1886: History of Town and City: Including an Account of the Quarter-Millennial Celebration at Springfield, Mass., May 25 and 26, 1886.* Springfield, MA: C. A. Nichols & Co.

Griswold, William A. 2011a. "Preface." In *Saugus Iron Works: The Roland W. Robbins Excavations, 1948–1953,* edited by William A. Griswold and Donald W. Linebaugh, i-x. Saugus, MA: National Park Service, Saugus Iron Works National Historic Site.

———. 2011b. "Excavating the Blast Furnace." In *Saugus Iron Works: The Roland W. Robbins Excavations, 1948–1953,* edited by William A. Griswold and Donald W. Linebaugh119–134. Saugus, MA: National Park Service, Saugus Iron Works National Historic Site.

Griswold, William A., and Donald W. Linebaugh, eds. 2011. *Saugus Iron Works: The Roland W. Robbins Excavations, 1948–1953.* Saugus, MA: National Park Service, Saugus Iron Works National Historic Site.

Gross, Laurence. 1988. "Building on Success: Lowell Mill Construction and Its Results." *The Journal of the Society for Industrial Archaeology* 14: 29–30.

Hamilton, Christopher E. 2006. "From the Pirate Ship Whydah." In *X Marks the Spot: The Archaeology of Piracy,* edited by Russell K. Skowronek and Charles R. Ewen, 131–59. Tallahassee: Florida A&M University.

Hamilton, Christopher E., James R. Reedy Jr., and Kenneth J. Kinkor. 1988. The Final Report of Archeological Testing- The *Whydah* Shipwreck: Site WLF-HA-1, Cape Cod, Massachusetts. Report to U. S. Army Corps of Engineers, New England Division, Waltham, MA from Maritime Explorations Inc., South Chatham, MA.

———.1990. The 1988 Report of Archeological Data Recovery. The *Whydah* Shipwreck: Site WLF-HA-1, Cape Cod, Massachusetts. Report to U. S. Army Corps of Engineers, New England Division, Waltham, MA from Whydah Joint Venture Laboratory, South Chatham, MA.

Hamilton, Christopher E., James R. Reedy Jr., Kenneth J. Kinkor, and D. A. Muncher. 1989. The 1988 Annual Report of Archeological Data Recovery- The *Whydah* Shipwreck: Site WLF-HA-1, Cape Cod, Massachusetts. Report to U. S. Army Corps of Engineers, New England Division, Waltham, MA from Maritime Explorations Inc., South Chatham, MA.

Handler, Jerome S. 1997. "An African-Type Healer/Diviner and His Grave Goods: A Burial from a Plantation Slave Cemetery in Barbados, West Indies." *International Journal of Historical Archaeology* 1, no. 2: 91–127.

Handlin, Oscar. 1974. *Boston's Immigrants.* New York: Atheneum.

Handsman, Russell G., Kathryn Mullins, and Donald Warrin. 2021. *New Bedford Communities of Whaling: People of Wampanoag, African, and Portuguese Island Descent, 1825–1925.* New Bedford Whaling National Historical Park Special Ethnographic Report. Northeast Region Ethnography Program, National Park Service, Boston, MA.

Hardesty, Jared Ross. 2018. *Unfreedom: Slavery and Dependence in Eighteenth-Century Boston.* New York: New York University Press.

———. 2019. *Black Lives, Native Lands, White Worlds: A History of Slavery in New England.* Amherst, MA: Bright Leaf.

Harper, Ross K., and Bruce Clouette. 2011. *Site Examination Survey, Hancock Shaker Village Trustees' Office and Store, Pittsfield, Massachusetts.* Report on file, Massachusetts Historical Commission, Boston.

Harper, Ross K. 2021. "The Ca. 1638 Waterman Site, Marshfield, Massachusetts: Anatomy of a Pilgrim House." *Historical Archaeology* 55, no. 2: 188–218.

Harrington, Faith. 1994. "'We Took Great Store of Cod-fish': Fishing Ships and First Settlements on the Coast of New England, 1600–1630." In *American Beginnings: Exploration, Culture, and Cartography in the Land of Norumbega,* edited by Kenneth Baker, 191–216. Lincoln: University of Nebraska Press.

Harrison, Samuel. 1876. *"Shall a Nation Be Born at Once?"—A Centennial Sermon Delivered in the Chapel of the Methodist Episcopal Church.* Pittsfield, MA: Chickering & Axtell, Steam Book and Job Printers.

———. 1877. *An Appeal of a Colored Man, To His Fellow-Citizens of a Fairer Hue, in the United States.* Pittsfield, MA: Chickering and Axtell.

———. 1899. *Rev. Samuel Harrison: His Life Story, as Told by Himself.* Pittsfield, MA: Eagle Publishing Co.

Hart, Siobhan M. 2004. "Mixed Assemblages and Indigenous Agents: Decolonizing Pine Hill." *Northeast Anthropology* 68: 57–71.

Hart, Sioban M., and Katherine Dillon. 2019. "Entangled Things and Deposits in Early Colonial Native New England." *Historical Archaeology* 53, no. 2: 265–279.

Hartley, E. N. 1957. *Ironworks of the Saugus: The Lynn and Braintree Ventures of the Company of Undertakers of the Ironworks in New England.* Norman: University of Oklahoma Press.

Hasenstab, R. J. 1999. "Fishing, Farming, and Finding the Village Site: Centering Late Woodland New England Algonquians." In *The Archaeological Northeast,* edited by M. A. Levine, K. E. Sassaman, M. S. Nassaney, 139–153. Westport, CT: Bergin and Garvey.

Harvard Crimson. 1983. "ICA Nears Extinction." *Harvard Crimson,* 28 September.

Hayes, Charles F. III. 1971. "Review of Pilgrim John Alden's Progress: Archaeological Excavations in Duxbury." *Historical Archaeology* 5: 115.

Haynes, George H. 1901. "The Tale of Tantiusque: An Early Mining Venture in Massachusetts." American Antiquarian Society, *Proceedings,* n.s., xiv (1900–1901): 471–497.

Heitert, Kristen. 2009. *Archaeological Overview and Assessment, Bunker Hill Monument, Charlestown, Massachusetts.* Report to the Northeast Region Archeology Program, National Park Service, by The Public Archaeology Laboratory Inc., Pawtucket, RI.

Heitert, Kristen, Stephen Mrozowski, and O. Don Hermes. 2002. *Archaeological Data Recovery Program, Osborn-Read-Paige Pottery, Peabody, Massachusetts.* Report to Krapf Associates, Boston, MA from The Public Archaeology Laboratory Inc., Pawtucket, RI.

Herbster, Holly, and Suzanne G. Cherau. 2001. *2001 Technical Report, Archaeological Site Examination, Lot 11 Site (19-DK-143), Lot 11 Building Envelope, Squibnocket Ridge, Chilmark, Massachusetts.* Report to Parker Montgomery c/o Wallace and Co., Edgartown, MA, from The Public Archaeology Laboratory Inc., Pawtucket, RI.

———. 2002. *Technical Report, Archaeological Reconnaissance Survey, Town of Aquinnah, Martha's Vineyard Massachusetts.* Report to the Town of Aquinnah, Aquinnah, MA, from The Public Archaeology Laboratory Inc., Pawtucket RI.

———. 2006. "The Past is Present: CRM Archaeology on Martha's Vineyard." In *Cross-Cultural Collaboration: Native Peoples and Archaeology in the Northeastern United States,* edited by Jordan E. Kerber, 165–182. Lincoln: University of Nebraska Press.

Herbster, Holly, Suzanne G. Cherau, and Virginia Adams. 1995. *Intensive (Locational) Archaeological Survey, Walmart Project, Plymouth, Massachusetts.* Report to Walmart Stores Inc. c/o Sumner Schein Architects and Engineers Inc., Cambridge, MA, from The Public Archaeology Laboratory Inc., Pawtucket RI.

Herbster, Holly, Nichole Gillis, and Dianna Doucette. 2014. *Archaeological Data Recovery Program and Supplemental Testing, Lot 5/6 Site (19-DK-138), Lot 5, Assessor's*

Map 35, Parcel 1.5, Squibnocket Ridge, Chilmark, Massachusetts. PAL report no. 2026.02. Report to Steven Robbins c/o Colonial Reproductions, Edgartown, MA, from The Public Archaeology Laboratory Inc., Pawtucket RI.

Herbster, Holly, and Kristen Heitert. 2007. *Archeological Overview and Assessment, Boston African American National Historical Site, Boston, Massachusetts.* Report to Northeast Regional Archeology Program, National Park Service, Lowell, MA, from The Public Archaeology Laboratory Inc., Pawtucket, RI.

Hodge, Christina. 2013. "'A Small Brick Pile for the Indians': The 1655 Harvard Indian College as Setting." In *Archaeologies of Mobility and Movement,* edited by Mary C. Beaudry and Travis Parno, 217–236. New York: Springer.

Hodge, Christina J., Diana DiPaulo Loren, and Patricia Capone. 2015. "Materializations of Puritan Ideology at Seventeenth-Century Harvard College." In *Rethinking Colonialism: Comparative Archaeological Approaches,* edited by Craig N. Cipolla and Katherine Howlett Hayes, 142–160. Gainesville: University Press of Florida.

Hohman, Elmo Paul. 1928. *The American Whaleman, A Study of Life and Labor in the Whaling Industry.* New York: Longmans, Green and Co.

hooks, bell. 1990. *Yearning: Race, Gender, and Cultural Politics.* Boston, MA: South End Press.

Holmes, Richard D., Carolyn D. Hertz, and Mitchell T. Mulholland. 1994. Archaeological Site Locational Survey of the Bayview Corporate Park, Quincy, Norfolk County, Massachusetts. Report to the Massachusetts Historical Commission, Boston, MA, from UMass Archaeological Services, Amherst.

Hounshell, David A. 1984. *From the American System to Mass Production, 1800–1932: The Development of Manufacturing Technology in the United States.* Baltimore MD: Johns Hopkins University Press.

Huey, Paul R. 1986. "The Council for Northeast Historical Archaeology: The Early Years." *Northeast Historical Archaeology* 15: 2–15.

Hornblower, Henry II. 1943. "The Status of Colonial Archaeology in Massachusetts in 1941." *Bulletin of the Massachusetts Archaeological Society* 4, no. 3: 41.

Hosmer, Charles B. 1965. *Presence of the Past: A History of the Preservation Movement in the United States Before Williamsburg.* New York: G. P. Putnam's Sons.

Hurd, D. Hamilton. 1883. *History of Bristol County, Massachusetts with Biographical Sketches of many of its Pioneers and Prominent Men.* Philadelphia, PA: J. W. Lewis & Co.

Hutchins, Karen Anne. 2013. *In Pursuit of Full Freedom: An Archaeological and Historical Study of the Free African American Community at Parting Ways, Massachusetts, 1779–1900.* Report on file, Massachusetts Historical Commission, Boston.

Hutchins-Keim, Karen A. 2015. "Parting Ways Revisited: Archaeology at a Nineteenth-Century African-American Community in Plymouth, Massachusetts." *Journal of African Diaspora Archaeology and Heritage* 4, no. 2: 115–142.

———. 2018. "The Plurality of Parting Ways: Landscapes of Dependence and Independence and the Making of a Free African American Community in Massachusetts." *Historical Archaeology* 52: 85–99.

Industrial School for Girls. 1860. *Annual Report of the Board of Managers of the Industrial School for Girls, in Dorchester.* Boston: Massachusetts State Archives.

Innes, Stephen. 1983. *Labor in a New Land: Economy and Society in Seventeenth Century New England.* Princeton, NJ: Princeton University Press.

———. 1995. *Creating the Commonwealth: The Economic Culture of Puritan New England.* New York: W. W. Norton and Company.

Ipswich Historical Commission (IHC). 2024. Position of the Ipswich Historical Commission on Removal of the Ipswich Mills Dam. Letter to the Town of Ipswich Select Board, January 9. https://ipswichmillsdam.com/wp-content/uploads/2024/03/IHC -Dam-Position-Memo-1-9-24.pdf

James Leffel & Co. 1874. *The Construction of Mill Dams.* Springfield, OH: James Leffel & Co.

Jameson, John. 2004. *The Reconstructed Past: Reconstructions in the Public Interpretation of Archaeology and History.* Lanham, MD: AltaMira Press.

John Milner Associates (JMA). 1978 *Archaeological Investigations at Saugus Ironworks National Historic Site, 1976.* Report prepared for National Park Service, Denver Service Center, Denver, CO. On file at the Northeast Region Archeology Program, Lowell, MA.

Johnson, Eric S. 1997. *Archeological Overview and Assessment of the Saugus Iron Works National Historic Site, Saugus, Massachusetts.* Report to the National Park Service, Lowell, MA.

———. 2000. "The Politics of Pottery: Material Culture and Political Process among Algonquians of Seventeenth-Century Southern New England." In *Interpretations of Native North American Life: Material Contributions to Ethnohistory,* edited by Michael S. Nassaney and Eric S. Johnson, 118–145. Gainesville: University Press of Florida.

———. 2012. *Roads, Rails, and Trails: Transportation-Related Archaeology in Massachusetts.* Boston: Massachusetts Historical Commission.

Johnson, Sarah. 2018. "'The True Spirit of Service': Toys as Tools of Ideology at the Dorchester Industrial School for Girls." Unpublished master's thesis, historical archaeology, University of Massachusetts Boston.

Jones, Donald G., and Nancy S. Seasholes. 1992. *Phase II Site Examination of a Shaker Village Foundation in Segment 2X of Tennessee Gas Pipeline Company's Northeast Settlement Expansion Project in Tyringham, Massachusetts.* Report on file, Massachusetts Historical Commission, Boston.

Karr, Ronald Dale. 1999. *Indian New England 1524–1675: A Compendium of Eyewitness Accounts of Native American Life.* Pepperell, MA: Branch Line Press.

Kelly, John M. 2023. "Examining Nineteenth-Century Urban-Cemetery Relocations: Two Cemetery Sites from the Roxbury Section of Boston, Massachusetts." *Historical Archaeology* 57: 727–742.

———. 2024. *Intensive (Locational) Archaeological Survey, Route 80 Cemetery Project, Plymouth, Massachusetts.* Report to Ray Dunetz Landscape Architecture Inc., from The Public Archaeology Laboratory Inc., Pawtucket, RI.

Kelly, John M., and Kevin A. McBride. 2016. "Gunflint Production and Lithic Tool Use at the Monhantic Fort Site, a Mashantucket Pequot Fortified Village (1675–1677)." *Historical Archaeology* 50, no. 4: 115–129.

Kelly, John M., and Heather L. Olson. 2022. *Archaeological Overview and Planning Assessment, Brook Farm Historic Site, West Roxbury, Boston, Massachusetts.* Report to the Massachusetts Department of Conservations and Recreation from The Public Archaeology Laboratory Inc. Pawtucket, RI.

Kerber, Jordan. 1988. "Where are the Woodland Villages? Preface." *Bulletin of the Massachusetts Archaeological Society* 49, no. 2: 44–45.

———., ed. 2006. *Cross-Cultural Collaboration: Native Peoples and Archaeology in the Northeastern United States.* Lincoln: University of Nebraska Press.

Kozakavich, Stacy C. 2017. *The Archaeology of Utopian and Intentional Communities.* Gainesville: University Press of Florida.

Kugler, Richard C. 1980. "The Whale Oil Trade, 1750–1775." *Old Dartmouth Historical Sketch Number 79.* New Bedford, MA: The Colonial Society of Massachusetts.

Kupperman, Karen. 2000. *Indians and English: Facing Off in Early America.* Ithaca, NY: Cornell University Press.

Landon, David B. 1996. "Feeding Colonial Boston: A Zooarchaeological Study." *Historical Archaeology* 30, no. 1: i–153.

———., ed. 2007. *Investigating the Heart of a Community: Archaeological Excavations at the African Meeting House Boston, Massachusetts.* Andrew Fiske Memorial Center for Archaeological Research Cultural Resource Management Study No. 22. https://www.fiskecenter.umb.edu/Pdfs/AHM_Final_Report.pdf

Landon, David, and Christa Beranek, eds. 2014. *2014 Plymouth County Archaeological Reconnaissance Survey.* Report on file, Massachusetts Historical Commission, Boston.

Landon, David B., and Teresa D. Bulger. 2013. "Constructing Community: Experiences of Identity, Economic Opportunity, and Institution Building at Boston's African Meeting House." *International Journal of Historical Archaeology* 17, no. 1: 119–142.

Laskowski, Amy. 2013. "Uncovering a Revered Utopia's History." *Boston University Today,* July 22. https://www.bu.edu/articles/2013/uncovering-brook-farm-utopia-history/

———. 2023. "Explore Cannonballs, Shipwrecks, and More at Boston's Newly Renamed Mary C. Beaudry Community Archaeology Center." *Boston University Today,* November 28. https://www.bu.edu/articles/2023/explore-the-mary-c-beaudry-community-archaeology-center/.

Law Pezzarossi, Heather. 2014. "Assembling Indigeneity: Rethinking Innovation, Tradition and Indigenous Materiality in a 19th-Century Native Toolkit." *Journal of Social Archaeology* 14, no. 3: 340–360.

———. 2019. "Brewed Time: Considering Anachronisms in the Study of Indigenous Persistence in New England." In *Indigenous Persistence in the Colonized Americas,* edited by Heather Law Pezzarossi and Russell Sheptak, 77–98. Albuquerque: University of New Mexico Press.

Lee, Nedra K. 2019. "Boarding: Black Women in Nantucket Generating Income and Building Community." *Transforming Anthropology* 27, no. 2: 91–104.

Lemire, Elise Virginia. 2009. *Black Walden: Slavery and its Aftermath in Concord, Massachusetts*. Philadelphia: University of Pennsylvania Press.

Levermore, Charles Herbert, ed. 1912. *Forerunners and Competitors of the Pilgrims and Puritans or Narratives of the Voyages Made by Persons Other Than the Pilgrims and Puritans of the Bay Colony to the Shores of New England During the First Quarter of the Seventeenth Century, 1601–1625 With Especial Reference to the Labors of Captain John Smith on Behalf of the Settlement of New England*. Two Volumes. New York: New England Society of Brooklyn.

Lewis, Quentin. 2016. *An Archaeology of Improvement in Rural Massachusetts: Landscapes of Profit and Betterment at the Dawn of the 19th Century*. New York: Springer.

Lindgren, James M. 1991. "A Constant Incentive to Patriotic Citizenship: Historic Preservation in Progressive-Era Massachusetts." *The New England Quarterly* 64, no. 4: 594–608.

———. 1995. *Preserving Historic New England*. New York: Oxford University Press.

Linebaugh, Donald Walter. 1996. "'The Road to Ruins and Restoration': Roland W Robbins and the Professionalization of Historical Archaeology." PhD diss., Department of American Studies, The College of William and Mary. University Microfilms International, Ann Arbor, MI.

———. 2000. "Forging a Career: Roland W. Robbins and Iron Industry Sites in the Northeastern US." *The Journal of the Society for Industrial Archeology* 26, no. 1: 5–36.

———. 2004. *The Man Who Found Thoreau: Roland W. Robbins and the Rise of Historical Archaeology in America*. Hanover, NH: University Press of New England.

———. 2011. "The Story of the Saugus Excavations." In *Saugus Iron Works: The Roland W. Robbins Excavations, 1948–1953*, edited by William A. Griswold and Donald W. Linebaugh, 57–98. Saugus, MA: US Department of the Interior, National Park Service, Saugus Iron Works National Historic Site.

Lipkin, Macy. 2024. "How Massachusetts Compares to the State of Black America Report." *WGBH.org*. https://www.wgbh.org/news/local/2024-03-05/how-massachusetts-compares-to-the-state-of-black-america-report.

Little, Barbara J. 2023. *Bending Archaeology toward Social Justice: Transformational Action for Positive Peace*. Tuscaloosa: University of Alabama Press.

Lombard, Percival Hall. 1927. "The First Trading Post of Plymouth Colony." *Old Time New England*, October: 70–86.

———. 1953. *The Aptucxet Trading Post*. Bourne, MA: Bourne Historical Society.

Loren, Diana DiPaolo. 2008. *In Contact: Bodies and Spaces in the Sixteenth- and Seventeenth-Century Eastern Woodlands*. Plymouth, UK: AltaMira Press.

Loren, Diana DiPaolo, and Patricia Capone. 2022. "The Harvard Yard Archaeology Project." *The SAA Archaeological Record*, 22, no. 2: 28–29; 48.

Luedtke, Barbara. 1975. *Final Report on the Archeological and Paleobotanical Resources on Twelve Islands in Boston Harbor*. Report on file, Massachusetts Historical Commission, Boston.

———. 1988. "Where Are the Late Woodland Villages in Eastern Massachusetts?" *Bulletin of the Massachusetts Archaeological Society* 49: 58–65.

Luiz, Jade W. 2018. "'A House Recommended': the Sensory Archaeology of Sexuality, Embodiment, and Creation of Space in a Mid-Nineteenth-Century Brothel in Boston, Massachusetts." PhD diss., Department of Archaeology, Boston University.

———. 2023. *Archaeology of a Brothel in Nineteenth-Century Boston, MA: Erotic Facades.* New York: Routledge.

Lutheran Works of Mercy. 1971. *A Century of Ministry and Mercy at Brook Farm, 1871–1971.* West Roxbury, MA: Lutheran Works of Mercy.

Lux, Thomas. 1991. "In Memoriam: Maurice Robbins 1899–1990." *Bulletin of the Massachusetts Archaeological Society* 52, no. 1: 31.

MacMahon, D. A. 1988. *Archaeological Collections Management at the Saugus Iron Works National Historic Site, Massachusetts.* ACMP Series No. 5. On file at the Northeast Region Archeology Program, Lowell, MA.

Main, Gloria L. 1987. "The Distribution of Consumer Goods in Colonial New England: A Subregional Approach." In *Early American Probate Inventories,* edited by Peter Benes, 153–168. The Dublin Seminar for New England Folklife Annual Proceedings 1987, Boston University, Boston, MA.

Malone, Patrick M. 1976. *The Lowell Canal System.* Lowell, MA: Lowell Museum.

———. 1983. *Canals and Industry: Engineering in Lowell, 1821–1880.* Lowell, MA: Lowell Museum.

Manning-Sterling, Elise H. 2012. *Samuel Harrison Homestead, Pittsfield, Massachusetts.* Report on file, Massachusetts Historical Commission, Boston.

Mansfield News. 1888. "Destructive Fire! Bailey's Bakery Burned." *Mansfield News,* November 23. On file, Mansfield Historical Society and Public Library Archives Room, Mansfield, MA.

Martin, Anthony F. 2017. *On the Landscape for a Very, Very Long Time: African American Resistance and Resilience in 19th and Early 20th Century Massachusetts.* Report on file, Massachusetts Historical Commission, Boston.

———. 2018. "Homeplace Is Also Workplace: Another Look at Lucy Foster in Andover, Massachusetts." *Historical Archaeology* 52: 100–112.

———. 2019. "Haven to the East, Haven to the North: Great Barrington and Pittsfield, Massachusetts." *Historical Archaeology* 53: 307–322.

Martin, Elizabeth. 2019. "Where Are the Outsiders?: A Discussion of Site Identity Formation through a Deconstruction of the Built Environment of Dogtown, Massachusetts." In *Archaeology of Identity and Dissonance: Contexts for a Brave New World,* edited by Diane F. George and Bernice Kurchin, 181–200. Gainesville: University Press of Florida.

Massachusetts, Commonwealth of. 2023. *Massachusetts Climate Report Card.* Office of Climate Innovation and Resilience. https://www.mass.gov/report/massachusetts-climate-report-card.

Massachusetts Historical Commission. 1981. *Reconnaissance Survey Report: Quincy.* Massachusetts Historical Commission, Office of the Secretary of State, Boston.

———. 2024. *MACRIS: Massachusetts Cultural Resource Information System*. https://mhc-macris.net/.

Masur, Laura E., and Aaron F. Miller. 2019. "Tempering Our Expectations: Drinking, Smoking, and the Economy of a Western Massachusetts Farmstead-Tavern." *Northeast Historical Archaeology* 48: 148–170.

Mastone, Victor T., Craig Brown, and Christopher Maio. 2011. *Chelsea Creek-First Naval Engagement of the American Revolution Chelsea, East Boston, Revere, and Winthrop, Suffolk County, Massachusetts*. Report for the National Park Service.

McBride, Kevin et al. 2016. *Battle of Great Falls/Wissatinnewag-Peskeompskut (May 19, 1676)*. Report to the National Park Service, American Battlefield Protection Program, Washington, DC, from the Mashantucket Pequot Museum and Research Center, Ledyard, CT.

McBride, Kevin A., and Suzanne G. Cherau. 1996. "Gay Head (Aquinnah) Wampanoag Community Structure and Land Use Patterns." *Northeast Anthropology* 51: 13–39.

McHargue, Georgess. 1998. "Great Expectations: The Public Interpretation Program for the Central Artery/Tunnel Project." *Historical Archaeology* 32, no 3: 19–23.

McManamon, F. P. 1978. *Archaeological Investigation of the Impact Area for Sewer Line Connections at Saugus Iron Works National Historic Site*. On file at Northeast Region Museum Services Center, Marine Barracks, Boston National Historical Park, Charlestown Navy Yard, Charlestown, MA.

McManis, Douglas R. 1975. *Colonial New England: A Historical Geography*. Oxford, UK: Oxford University Press.

Mead, Leslie. 1995. *Intensive Archaeological Survey at the Abiel Smith School House at Boston African American National Historic Site, Boston, Massachusetts*. Cultural Resources Center, National Park Service, Lowell, MA.

Meinig, D. W. 1986. *The Shaping of America: A Geographical Perspective on 500 Years of History, Volume 1: Atlantic America, 1492–1800*. New Haven, CT: Yale University Press.

Melish, Joanne Pope. 1998. *Disowning Slavery: Gradual Emancipation and "Race" in New England, 1780–1860*. Ithaca, NY: Cornell University Press.

Mercer, Henry C. 1960. *Ancient Carpenters' Tools, Illustrated and Explained, Together with the Implements of the Lumberman, Joiner, and Cabinet Maker in Use in the Eighteenth Century*, third edition. Doylestown, PA: Bucks County Historical Society.

Moran, G. P. 1976a. *Archaeological Survey in Vicinity of Carpenter's Shop: Saugus Ironworks National Historic Site*. On file at Northeast Region Museum Services Center, Marine Barracks, Boston National Historical Park, Charlestown Navy Yard, Charlestown, MA.

———. 1976b. *Preliminary Report of Test Excavations at the Saugus Ironworks National Historic Site*. Report prepared for National Park Service, US Department of the Interior, Denver Service Center. On file at Northeast Region Museum Services Center, Marine Barracks, Boston National Historical Park, Charlestown Navy Yard, Charlestown, MA.

Morison, Samuel Eliot. 1936. *Harvard College in the Seventeenth Century, Part 1.* Cambridge, MA: Harvard University Press.

Morse, Flo. 1980. *The Shakers and the World's People.* Hanover, NH: University Press of New England.

Mrozowski, Stephen A. 1994. "The Discovery of a Native American Cornfield." *Archaeology of Eastern North America* 22 (Fall): 47–62.

———. 2000. "The Growth of Managerial Capitalism and the Subtleties of Class Analysis in Historical Archaeology." In *Lines That Divide: Historical Archaeologies of Race, Gender, and Class,* edited by J. Delle, S. Mrozowski, and R. Paynter, 276–306. Knoxville: University of Tennessee Press.

———. 2009. "Creole Materialities: Archaeological Explorations of Hybridized Realities on a North American Plantation." *Journal of Historical Sociology* 23, no. 1: 462–485.

Mrozowski, Stephen, Katherine Howlett Hayes, and Anne P. Hancock. 2007. "The Archaeology of Sylvester Manor." *Northeast Historical Archaeology* 36 (Special Issue): 1–15.

Mrozowski, Stephen et al. 2015. *The Archaeology of Hassanamesit Woods: The Sarah Burnee/Sarah Boston Farmstead, Grafton, Massachusetts.* Report to the Massachusetts Historical Commission, Boston, from the Fiske Center for Archaeological Research at UMass Boston.

Mrozowski, Stephen A., and Stephen R. White. 1982. *An Intensive Survey of the North Andover Technical Park, North Andover, Massachusetts.* Report on file, Massachusetts Historical Commission, Boston.

Mrozowski, Stephen A., Grace H. Zeising, and Mary Beaudry. 1996. *Living on the Boott: Historical Archaeology at the Boott Mills Boardinghouses of Lowell, Massachusetts.* Amherst: University of Massachusetts Press.

Muehlbauer, Jared. 2021. *Creating Community: Examining Black Identity and Space in New Guinea, Nantucket.* Master's thesis, University of Massachusetts Boston.

Muller, Nancy Ladd. 1994. "The House of the Black Burghardts: An Investigation of Race, Gender, and Class at the W.E.B. DuBois Boyhood Homesite." In *Those of Little Note: Gender, Race, and Class in Historical Archaeology,* edited by Elizabeth M. Scott, 81–94. Tucson: University of Arizona Press.

Mullins, Paul. 2012. "Diversity and Anti-Racism in the Society for Historical Archaeology." Society for Historical Archaeology, August 1. https://sha.org/diversity-and-anti-racism-in-the-society-for-historical-archaeology/2012/08/.

Murphy, Darryl C., and Katelyn Harrop. 2023. "Climate Now: Erosion and the Boston Harbor Islands." *The Common, WBUR.* https://www.wbur.org/the-common/2023/04/18/boston-harbor-islands-erosion-climate-change-earth-week-environment

Nash, Gary B. 1979. *The Urban Crucible: Social Change, Political Consciousness and the Origins of the American Revolution.* Cambridge, MA: Harvard University Press.

Nassaney, Michael. 1994. "An Epistemological Enquiry into Some Archaeological and Historical Interpretations of 17th century Native American-European Relations." In *Archaeological Approaches to Cultural Identity,* edited by S. J. Shennan, 76–93. London: Routledge.

———. 2000. "Archaeology and Oral History in Tandem: Interpreting Native American Ritual, Ideology, and Gender Relations in Contact-Period Southeastern New England." In *Interpretations of Native North American Life: Material Contributions to Ethnohistory,* edited by Michael Nassaney and Eric Johnson, 412–431. Gainesville: University Press of Florida.

———. 2004. "Native American Gender Politics and Material Culture in Seventeenth-Century Southeastern New England." *Journal of Social Archaeology* 4, no. 3: 334–367.

Nassaney, Michael S., and Marjorie R. Abel. 1993. "The Political and Social Contexts of Cutlery Production in the Connecticut Valley." *Dialectical Anthropology* 18: 247–289.

———. 2000. "Urban Spaces, Labor Organization, and Social Control: Lessons from New England's Cutlery Industry." In *Lines That Divide: Historical Archaeologies of Race, Gender, and Class,* edited by J. Delle, S. Mrozowski, and R. Paynter, 239–275. Knoxville: University of Tennessee Press.

Nassaney, MichaelS., Uzi Baram, James C. Garman, and Michael Milewski. 1996. "Guns and Roses: Ritualism, Time Capsules, and the Massachusetts Agricultural College." *Old Time New England.* Boston, Mass.: Society for the Preservation of New England Antiquities.

National Park Service. 1992. *Lowell: The Story of an Industrial City.* A Guide to Lowell National Historical Park and Lowell Heritage State Park. Official National Park Handbook 140. Washington, DC: National Park Service.

———. 2011. *Blackstone River Valley, Special Resource Study.* Boston, MA: National Park Service, Northeast Region.

———. 2019. *Cultural Landscapes Inventory, Saugus Iron Works NHS Landscape, Saugus Iron Works National Historic Site.* http://npshistory.com/publications/sair/hist -sketch.pdf

———. 2021. *Aptucxet Trading Post Museum Historic District National Register for Historic Places Nomination Form. Prepared by The Public Archaeology Laboratory.* https://www.nps.gov/subjects/nationalregister/database-research.htm

NE Historical Services Inc. 1987. Lyman Pond Mill and Dam, STH.905, MHC Form F-Structure Form. On file, Massachusetts Historical Commission, Boston, MA.

Newell, Margaret Ellen. 2015. *Brethren by Nature: New England Indians, Colonists, and the Origins of American Slavery.* Ithaca, NY: Cornell University Press.

Nicholas, George, and Claire Smith. 2020. "Considering the Denigration and Destruction of Indigenous Heritage as Violence." In *Critical Perspectives on Cultural Memory and Heritage: Construction, Transformation and Destruction,* edited by Veysel Apaydin, 131–54. London: UCL Press.

O'Brien, Jean. 2010. *Firsting and Lasting: Writing Indians Out of Existence in New England.* Minneapolis: University of Minnesota Press.

———. 2019. *Monumental Mobility: The Memory Work of Massasoit.* Durham. University of North Carolina Press.

Old Dartmouth Historical Society. 1903. "Proceedings at the Dedication of the Gosnold Memorial at Cuttyhunk, September 1, 1903." *The Old Dartmouth Historical Sketches,* no. 4, New Bedford, MA.

Ordoñez, Margaret T., and Linda Welters. 2004. "Textiles and Leather in Southeastern New England Archaeological Sites." In *Perishable Material Culture in the Northeast*, edited by Penelope Ballard Drooker, 169–184. Albany: New York State Museum Bulletin 500, University of the State of New York State Education Department.

Orser, Charles E. Jr. 1996. *A Historical Archaeology of the Modern World*. New York: Plenum Press.

———. 2001. "The Anthropology in American Historical Archaeology." *American Anthropologist* 103, no. 3: 621–632.

———. 2007. *The Archaeology of Race in Historic America*. Gainesville: University Press of Florida.

Oswold, W. Wyatt et al. 2020. "Conservation Implications of Limited Native American Impacts in Pre-Contact New England." *Nature Sustainability* 3 (March): 241–246.

Ott, J. H. 1976. *Hancock Shaker Village: A Guide Book and History*. Hancock, MA: Shaker Community Inc.

Parmenter, Charles Oscar. 1898. *History of Pelham, Massachusetts, from 1738 to 1898, Including the Early History of Prescott*. Amherst, MA: Press of Carpenter and Morehouse.

Parno, Travis. 2013. *"With the Quiet Sturdy Strength of the Folk of an Older Time": an Archaeological Approach to Time, Place-Making, and Heritage Construction at the Fairbanks House, Dedham, Massachusetts*. PhD diss., Department of Archaeology, Boston University.

Parson, Kimberly, and Daniel Cassedy. 2007. *Phase III Archeological Investigations in Area 7 of the Saugus Iron Works National Historic Site, Saugus, Massachusetts*. Report prepared by URS Corporation for the National Park Service–Denver Service Center. On file at the Northeast Region Archeology Program, Lowell, MA.

Patton, Jonathan K. 2013. "Considering the Wet Homelands of Indigenous Massachusetts." *Journal of Social Archaeology* 14, no. 1: 1–25.

Paynter, Robert. 1990. "Afro-Americans in the Massachusetts Historical Landscape." In *The Politics of the Past*, edited by P. Gathercole and D. Lowenthal, 49–62. London: Unwin Hyman.

———. 2001. "The Cult of Whiteness in Western New England." In *Race and the Archaeology of Identity*, edited by C. E. Orser, 125–142. Salt Lake City: University of Utah Press.

Paynter, Robert et al. 2008. *Archeological Report of Fieldwork in 1983, 1984, and 2003 at the W.E.B. Du Bois Boyhood Homesite*. Report on file, Anthropology Department, University of Massachusetts Amherst. https://scholarworks.umass.edu/du_bois _boyhood_survey/

Paynter, Robert, Linda Ziegenbein, and Quentin Lewis. 2019. "Excavating the 'Garden of the North': Five Centuries of Materials and Social Change in Western Massachusetts." *Historical Archaeology* 53, no. 2: 236–250.

Paynter, Robert, Susan Hautaniemi, and Nancy Ladd Muller. 1994. "The Landscapes of the W.E.B. Du Bois Boyhood Homesite: An Agenda for an Archaeology of the Color Line." In *Race*, edited by Roger Sanjek and Steven Gregory, 285–318. New Brunswick, NJ: Rutgers University Press.

Paynter, Robert, and Whitney Battle-Baptiste. 2019. "Contexts of Resistance in African American Western Massachusetts: A view from the W.E.B. Du Bois Homesite in Great Barrington, Massachusetts." *Historical Archaeology* 53, no. 2: 323–340.

Peabody Museum of Archaeology and Ethnology. 2021. *Artifact Catalog*. Peabody Museum of Archaeology and Ethnology at Harvard University https://www.peabody .harvard.edu/collections

Pendery, Steven R. 1988. *Archaeological Survey of the Boston Common, Boston, Massachusetts*. Report on file, Massachusetts Historical Commission, Boston.

———. 1991. *Archaeological Testing at Brook Farm*. Report by the Boston City Archaeology Program. Submitted to the Massachusetts Historical Commission and the Metropolitan District Commission, Boston.

———. 1999. "Portuguese Tin-Glazed Earthenware in Seventeenth-Century New England: A Preliminary Study." *Historical Archaeology* 33: 58–77.

Pendery, Steven R., and William A. Griswold. 1995. *Management Summary: Archaeological Testing at Dorchester Heights National Historic Site South Boston, Massachusetts*. Cultural Resources Center National Park Service for the Easter Applied Archaeology Center, NPS. Report on file at the Massachusetts Historical Commission.

———. 1996. *Interim Report and Management Summary, Archeological Testing at Bunker Hill Monument, Boston National Historical Park, Charlestown, Massachusetts*. Archeology Branch, NCRC, NPS, Lowell, MA.

Pendery, Stephen R., and Leslie Mead. 1999. *Archaeological Investigations at the Boston African American National Historic Site, Boston, Massachusetts*. Northeast Cultural Resource Center, National Park Service, Lowell, MA.

Pendery, Steven R., and Robert W. Preucel. 1992. *The Archaeology of Social Reform: Report on the 1990 and 1991 Field Seasons of the Brook Farm Hive Archaeology Project*. Boston City Archaeology Program and Harvard University Department of Anthropology. Submitted to the Massachusetts Historical Commission and Metropolitan District Commission, Boston.

———. 2017. *The Archaeology of Social Reform: Report on the 1992 and 1993 Field Seasons of the Brook Farm Hive Archaeology Project*. On file, Massachusetts Historical Commission, Boston.

Perley, Logan. 2020. "350 Years of Searching: Wampanoag Still Looking for Historic Wampum Belt." Transcript of Canadian Broadcasting Corporation *Unreserved* radio program. https://www.cbc.ca/radio/unreserved/mayflower-400-a-deep-dive -into-american-thanksgiving-1.5807974/350-years-of-searching-wampanoag-still -looking-for-historic-wampum-belt-1.5807976

Pezzarossi, Guido. 2014. "Camouflaging Consumption and Colonial Mimicry: The Materiality of an Eighteenth and Nineteenth-Century Nipmuc Identity: Household." *International Journal of Historical Archaeology* 18: 146–174.

Philbrick, Nathaniel. 2014. *Bunker Hill: A City, A Siege, A Revolution*. New York: Penguin Books.

Piechota, D. V. 1973. *Report on Contract No. CX4220–3–002, the Recording and Preservation of the Archaeological Collection, Saugus Ironworks National Historic Site*.

On file at Northeast Region Museum Services Center, Marine Barracks, Boston National Historical Park, Charlestown Navy Yard, Charlestown, MA.

Pineo, Gretchen, et al. 2016. *National Register of Historic Places Nomination, Saugus Iron Works National Historic Site, Saugus Massachusetts.* US Department of the Interior, National Park Service, Washington, DC.

Plane, Ann Marie. 1991. "New England's Logboats: Four Centuries of Watercraft." *Bulletin of the Massachusetts Archaeological Society* 52, no. 1: 8–17.

Plane, Ann Marie, and Gregory Button. 1993. "The Massachusetts Indian Enfranchisement Act: Ethnic Contest in Historical Context, 1849–1869." *Ethnohistory* 40, no. 4: 587–618.

Plymouth 400 Inc. n.d. *"Our" Story: 400 Years of Wampanoag History.* Multimedia exhibit conceptualized, researched, and produced by SmokeSygnals Marketing and Communications and The Indian Spiritual and Cultural Training Council Inc. https://www.plymouth400inc.org/our-story-exhibit-wampanoag-history/

Presidential Committee on the Legacy of Slavery. 2022. *The Legacy of Slavery at Harvard: Report on the Recommendations of the Presidential Committee.* Cambridge, MA: Harvard University Press.

Preucel, Robert W., and Steven R. Pendery. 2006. "Envisioning Utopia: Transcendentalist and Fourierist Landscapes at Brook Farm, West Roxbury, Massachusetts." *Historical Archaeology* 40, no. 1: 6–19.

Pocumtuck Valley Memorial Association (PVMA). n.d. "Fort Massachusetts, North Adams, Mass." http://www.americancenturies.mass.edu/collection/itempage.jsp?itemid=15722

Poulsen, Jennifer. 2018. "'Training to Good Conduct, and Instructing in Household Labor': Sewing at the Industrial School for Girls, Dorchester, MA." Paper presented at the 2018 Annual Meeting of the Society for Historical Archaeology. New Orleans, LA.

Puckett, Newbell Niles. 1926. *Folk Beliefs of the Southern Negro.* New York: Negro Universities Press.

Puleo, Stephen. 2010. *A City So Grand: The Rise of an American Metropolis, Boston 1850–1900.* Boston, MA: Beacon Press.

Rahn, M. I. 1983. "Archaeology Labs Bite the Dust." *Harvard Crimson,* May 25.

Regan, Janet, and Curtis White. 2011a. "Hammersmith Through the Historical Texts." In *Saugus Iron Works: The Roland W. Robbins Excavations, 1948–1953,* edited by William A. Griswold and Donald W. Linebaugh, 27–54. Saugus, MA: National Park Service, Saugus Iron Works National Historic Site.

———. 2011b. "The Artifacts." In *Saugus Iron Works: The Roland W. Robbins Excavations, 1948–1953,* edited by William A. Griswold and Donald W. Linebaugh, 245–275. Saugus, MA: National Park Service, Saugus Iron Works National Historic Site.

Reinke, R., and Robert Paynter. 1984. *Archaeological Excavation of the Surroundings of the E. H. Williams House, Deerfield, Massachusetts.* Report to Water Resources Research Center, Amherst, MA, from the Anthropology Department, University of Massachusetts Amherst.

Richardson, James F. 1994. *In Service to God's Will: A Historical and Anthropological Reconstruction of the Martin Luther Orphan's Home at Brook Farm, West Roxbury, Massachusetts (1871–1945)*. Unpublished master's thesis, Department of Anthropology, Harvard University.

Ricketson, Walton. 1903. "The Gosnold Memorial Shaft and Something of the Geology of Cuttyhunk." *Old Dartmouth Historical Sketches*, no. 1. New Bedford, MA: Old Dartmouth Historical Society.

Riley, David. 2009. "A Sad Anniversary for Native Americans in Mass." *MetroWest Daily News*, September 21. https://www.metrowestdailynews.com/story/news/2009/09/21/a-sad-anniversary-for-native/41328482007/

Ritchie, Duncan, Joan Gallagher, and Barbara Luedtke. 1984. *An Intensive Level Archaeological Survey on Deer and Long Islands, Boston Harbor, Massachusetts*. Report to Massachusetts Water Resource Authority from The Public Archaeology Laboratory Inc., Pawtucket, RI.

Ritchie, Duncan, and Holly Herbster. 1997. *Archaeological Reconnaissance Survey of the Quarry Hills Recreation Complex, Quincy and Milton, Massachusetts*. Report to Sverdrup Civil Inc. from The Public Archaeology Laboratory Inc., Pawtucket, RI.

———. 1998. *Site Examination of the Buzzard, Quarry Lane, Quarry Hills Locus 2 and 19-NF-1061/North Section Sites Within The Quarry Hills Recreation Complex Project Area, Quincy and Milton, Massachusetts*. Report to Sverdrup Civil Inc. from The Public Archaeology Laboratory Inc., Pawtucket, RI.

Robbins, Maurice. 1949. "A Brief Review of the Progress of the Massachusetts Historical Society." *Bulletin of the Massachusetts Archaeological Society* 10, no. 3: 50–53.

Robinson, David S. 2002. "Recent Approaches to Assessing the Archaeological Potential for Submerged Ancient Native American Cultural Resources in the Northeastern U.S." Paper presented at the Conference of the New England Anthropological Association, Bridgewater, MA. Manuscript on file, Massachusetts Historical Commission.

Robinson, David S., and Cheryl Stedtler. 2011. "Project Mishoon: A Status Report." Paper presented at the 2011 Conference on New England Archaeology, University of Massachusetts Amherst. Manuscript on file, Massachusetts Historical Commission.

Robinson, Paul, Marc Kelley, and Patricia E. Rubertone. 1985. "Preliminary Biocultural Interpretations from a Seventeenth-Century Narragansett Indian Cemetery in Rhode Island." In *Cultures in Contact: The European Impact on Native Cultural Institutions in Eastern North America, A.D. 1000–1800*, edited by William Fitzhugh, 107–130. Washington, DC: Smithsonian Institution Press.

Rockman, Diana Diz., and Nan A. Rothschild. 1984. "City Tavern, Country Tavern: An Analysis of Four Colonial Sites." *Historical Archaeology* 18, no. 2: 112–121.

Rockman, Seth. 2024. *Plantation Goods: A Material History of American Slavery*. Chicago, IL: University of Chicago Press.

Romer, Robert H. 2005. "Higher Education and Slavery in Western Massachusetts." *The Journal of Blacks in Higher Education* 46 (Winter 2004–2005): 98–101.

Rose, Anne C. 1981. *Transcendentalism as a Social Movement, 1830–1850*. New Haven, CT: Yale University Press.

Roth, Rodris. 1961. *Tea Drinking in 18th-Century America: Its Etiquette and Equipage.* Washington, DC: Smithsonian Institution.

Rotenstein, David, S., Janet Friedman, and Kristen Heitert. 2000. *Phase II Archaeological Investigations of the Cato Freeman Site, North Andover, Essex County, Massachusetts.* Report on file, Massachusetts Historical Commission, Boston.

Rothstein, Robin. 2024. "Examine the Cost of Living by State in 2024." *Forbes.com.* https://www.forbes.com/advisor/mortgages/cost-of-living-by-state/

Russo, Paul A., and James C. Garman. 1998. *Results of an Archaeological Site Examination of a Portion of CON-HA-01 (The American Powder Mill Complex), Concord, Massachusetts.* Report on file at the Massachusetts Historical Commission.

Sanborn Fire Insurance Company. 1887. *Map of Mansfield, Massachusetts.* On file, Massachusetts State Library, Boston.

Savory, Samantha A. 2015. *Brook Farm: A Ceramic Analysis of a Short Lived Utopia.* Unpublished master's thesis, Indiana University of Pennsylvania.

Savulis, Ellen-Rose. 1998. *Vision and Practice: Resistance and Dissent in Shaker Communities.* Report on file, Massachusetts Historical Commission, Boston.

———. 2003. "Zion's Zeal: Negotiating Identity in Shaker Communities." In *Shared Spaces and Divided Places: Material Dimensions of Gender Relations and the American Historical Landscape,* edited by Deborah Rotman and Ellen-Rose Savulis, 160–90. Knoxville: University of Tennessee Press.

Sayers, Daniel O. 2023. *The Archaeology of the Homed and the Unhomed.* Gainesville: University Press of Florida.

Scarlett, Timothy James. 1994. "Pudding Pans and Broilers–Bread Pans and Pie: Redware, Consumption, and Economy in Eighteenth Century New England." Unpublished research paper at the Massachusetts Historical Commission, Boston.

Schmidt, Peter, and Stephen A. Mrozowski. 2014. *The Death of Prehistory.* Oxford, UK: Oxford University Press.

Schnitter, Nicholas J. 1994. *A History of Dams: The Useful Pyramids.* Brookfield, VT: A. A. Balkema.

Schultz, Kate Howland. 1988a. *Life at Brook Farm: A Framework for Interpretation.* Cultural Resource Management Study Series, Vol. 4a. Boston, MA: Metropolitan District Commission.

———. 1988b. *The Brook Farm Inventory of Images.* Cultural Resource Management Study Series, Vol. 4b. Boston, MA: Metropolitan District Commission.

Seasholes, Nancy S. et al. 2008. *Archeological Overview and Assessment of the Boston Harbor Islands National Park Area.* Report to National Park Service, Lowell MA, from Archaeological Services, University of Massachusetts Amherst.

Sebastian Dring, Katherine H. et al. 2019. "Authoring and Authority in Eastern Pequot Community Heritage and Archaeology." *Archaeologies* 15, no.3: 352–370.

Senier, Siobhan. 2014. *Dawnland Voices: An Anthology of Indigenous Writing from New England.* Lincoln: University of Nebraska Press.

Shackel, Paul. 2013. A Historical Archaeology of Labor and Social Justice. *American Anthropologist* 115, no. 2: 317–320.

Shurtleff, Nathaniel B., ed. (RMB)1853–4. *Records of the Governor and Company of the Massachusetts Bay in New England, 1629–1686*. Boston, MA: William White.

Silliman, Stephen W. 2018. *Engaging Archaeology: 25 Case Studies in Research Practice*. Hoboken, NJ: Wiley.

———. 2020. "Colonialism in Historical Archaeology." In *Routledge Handbook of Global Historical Archaeology*, edited by Charles Orser Jr., Andrés Zarankin, Pedro P. A. Funari, Susan Lawrence, and James Symonds, 41–60. London: Routledge.

Simmons, William S. 1970. *Cautantowwit's House: An Indian Burial Ground on the Island of Conanicut in Narragansett Bay*. Providence, RI: Brown University Press.

Smith, E. Ann. 1986. "The Beginnings of Modern Historical Archaeology in the Northeast and the Origins of the Conference on Northeast Historical Archaeology." *Northeast Historical Archaeology* 15: 1.

Smith, Joseph Edward Adams, and Thomas Cushing. 1885. *History of Berkshire County, Massachusetts, with Biographical Sketches of its Prominent Men*. New York: J. B. Beers & Co.

Smith, Merrit Roe. 1985. "Army Ordnance and the 'American System' of Manufacturing, 1815–1861." In *Military Enterprise and Technological Change: Perspectives on the American Experience*, edited by M. R. Smith, 39–86. Cambridge, MA: MIT Press, Cambridge/

Smith, Norman. 1972. *A History of Dams*. Secaucus, NJ: The Citadel Press.

Snow, Dean. 1980. *The Archaeology of New England*. New York: Academic Press.

Snow, D. R., and K. M. Lanphear. 1988. "European Contact and Indian Depopulation in the Northeast: The Timing of the First Epidemics." *Ethnohistory* 35: 15–33.

South, Stanley, ed. 1994. *Pioneers in Historical Archaeology: Breaking New Ground*. New York: Plenum Press.

Speiss, Arthur, Deborah Wilson, and James W. Bradley. 1998. "Paleoindian Occupation in the New England-Maritimes Region: Beyond Cultural Ecology." *Archaeology of Eastern North America* 26: 188–196.

Spencer-Wood, Suzanne M. 1987. "A Survey of Domestic Reform Movement Sites in Boston and Cambridge, Ca. 1865–1905." *Historical Archaeology* 21, no. 2: 7–36.

———. 2001. Phase I Non-Destructive Archaeological Survey of the Souther Tide Mill Site, Quincy, Massachusetts. Report on file, Massachusetts Historical Commission, Boston, MA.

———. 2006. "A Feminist Theoretical Approach to the Historical Archaeology of Utopian Communities." *Historical Archaeology* 40, no. 1: 152–185.

———. 2009. "A Feminist Approach to European Ideologies of Poverty and the Institutionalization of the Poor in Falmouth, Massachusetts." In *The Archaeology of Institutional Life*, edited by April Beisaw and James Gibbs, 117–136. Tuscaloosa: University of Alabama Press.

Spencer-Wood, Suzanne, and S. Baugher. 2001. "Introduction and Historical Context for the Archaeology of Institutions of Reform, Part 1: Asylums." *International Journal of Historical Archaeology* 5, no. 1: 3–17.

Spencer-Wood, Suzanne M., and Christopher N. Matthews. 2011. "Impoverishment, Criminalization, and the Culture of Poverty." *Historical Archaeology* 45, no. 3: 1–10.

Spiess, Arthur J., and Bruce D. Speiss. 1987. "The New England Pandemic of 1616–1622: Cause and Archaeological Implication." *Man in the Northeast* 34: 71–83.

St. George, Robert Blair. 1988. "Artifacts of Regional Consciousness in the Connecticut River Valley 1700–1780." In *Material Life in America,* edited by Robert Blair St. George, 335–337. Boston, MA: Northeastern University Press.

Stantec Consulting Services Inc. 2013. *Amethyst Brook Restoration Project/Bartlett Rod Shop Company Dam Removal: Post-Dam Removal Investigations.* Prepared for the Massachusetts Division of Ecological Restoration Boston, MA, by Stantec Consulting Services Inc., Northampton, MA.

Starbuck, Alexander. 1989 [1878]. *History of the American Whale Fishery from Its Earliest Inception to the Year 1876,* reprint ed. Secaucus, NJ: Castle Books.

Starbuck, D. R. 1998. "New Perspectives on Shaker Life: An Archaeologist Discovers 'Hog Heaven' at Canterbury Shaker Village." *Expedition* 40, no. 3: 3–16.

Strauss, Alan E., and Suzanne Spencer-Wood. 1999. *Phase II Archaeological Site Examination at the Artist's Guild/Old Poor House Building in Falmouth, Massachusetts.* Report to Town of Falmouth, Falmouth, MA, from Cultural Resource Specialists of New England, Providence, RI.

Steele, Ian K. 1989. "Origins of Boston's Revolutionary Declaration of 18 April 1689." *The New England Quarterly* 62, no. 1: 75–81.

Steinberg, John et al. 2021. *Final Report, Inventory and Monitoring Endangered Sites, Great Island, Cape Cod National Seashore, Wellfleet, Massachusetts.* Report to the National Park Service from the Andrew Fiske Memorial Center for Archaeological Research, University of Massachusetts Boston.

Stockbridge-Munsee Community. 2023. "Sacred Land: Local Cultural Heritage Projects." https://www.mohican.com/cultural-heritage-projects/.

Stockbridge-Munsee Mohican Tribal Historic Preservation Office. 2024. *Tribal Archaeology in Stockbridge, MA: Reporting Back on Fieldwork.* https://www.mohican.com/mt-content/uploads/2024/04/tribal-archaeology-in-stockbridge-ma.pdf.

Stokinger, William A., and Geoffrey P. Moran. 1978. *A Final Report of Archaeological Investigations at Fort Independence: 1976–1977, Volumes I and II.* Report to the Massachusetts Department of Conservation and Recreation, Boston, MA, from The Public Archaeology Laboratory Inc., Pawtucket, RI.

Stone, O. L. 1930. *History of Massachusetts Industries.* Boston, MA: S. L. Clark Publishing Company.

Stott, Peter. 1983. *A Guide to the Industrial Archaeology of Massachusetts: Middlesex, Norfolk, and Suffolk Counties.* Boston: Massachusetts Historical Commission.

———. 1988. Aldrich Mills Dam, MLB.932, MHC Form F- Structure Form. On file, Massachusetts Historical Commission, Boston, MA.

Stubbs, John. 1992. *Underground Harvard: The Archaeology of College Life.* PhD diss., Department of Anthropology, Harvard University.

Stubbs, J. D. et al. 2010. "Campus Archaeology/Public Archaeology at Harvard University, Cambridge, Massachusetts." In *Beneath the Ivory Tower: The Archaeology of Academia,* edited by R. K. Skowronek and K. E. Lewis, 99–120. Gainesville: University Press of Florida.

Taber, Martha Van Hoesen. 1955. "A History of the Cutlery Industry in the Connecticut Valley." *Smith College Studies in History,* vol. 41. Northampton, MA: Department of History, Smith College.

Tager, Jack, and Richard D. Brown. 2000. *Massachusetts: A Concise History.* Amherst: University of Massachusetts Press.

Tarlow, Sarah. 2002. "Excavating Utopia: Why Archaeologists Should Study 'Ideal' Communities of the Nineteenth Century." *International Journal of Historical Archaeology* 6, no. 4: 299–323.

Taylor, Robert J. 2010. *Massachusetts, Colony to Commonwealth: Documents on the Formation of Its Constitution, 1775–1780.* Chapel Hill: University of North Carolina Press.

Thee, Christopher J. 2006. "Massachusetts Nipmucs and the Long Shadow of John Milton Earle." *The New England Quarterly* 79, no. 4: 636–654.

Thomas, Peter. 1984. "Bridging the Gap: Indian/White Relations." In *Early Settlement in the Connecticut River Valley: A Colloquium at Historic Deerfield,* edited by John W. Ifkovic and Martin Kaufman, 5–21. Deerfield, MA: Historic Deerfield Inc.

Thomas, Suzie. 2017. "Community Archaeology." In *Key Concepts in Public Archaeology,* edited by Gabriel Moshenska, 14–30. London: UCL Press.

Tiernan, Erin. 2018. "Native American Tribes Join Fight Over Long Island." *The Patriot Ledger,* October 8. https://www.patriotledger.com/story/news/politics/county/2018/10/09/native-american-tribes-join-fight/9590331007/

Timms, Peter, Joyce Clements, and Hadley Kruczek-Aaron. 2006. *Archaeological Investigations of the Shaker Farm, Ashburnham, Massachusetts.* Report on file, Massachusetts Historical Commission, Boston.

Trigg, Heather, and David Landon. 2010. "Labor and Agricultural Production at Sylvester Manor Plantation, Shelter Island, New York." *Historical Archaeology* 44, no. 3: 36–53.

Trigger, Bruce G. 1990. *The Huron: Farmers of the North,* 2nd ed. New York: Harcourt Brace Jovanich College Publishers.

Turnbaugh, William A. 1974. *Archaeological Investigations at Fort Independence on Castle Island in Boston Harbor 1973–1974.* Archaeological Consultant for Massachusetts Department of Conservation. Report on file at the Massachusetts Historical Commission.

Tuttle, Michael C. 2017. *Marine Archaeological Inter- and Sub-Tidal Survey, Boston East Designated Port Area (DPA) Parcel, 102 Border Street, East Boston, Suffolk County, Massachusetts.* Report to The Public Archaeology Laboratory Inc., Pawtucket, RI, from Gray & Pape Inc., Providence, RI.

US Bureau of the Census (US Census). 1880. *Tenth Census, Report on the Water Power of the United States, Volume 16.* Washington, DC: Census Office.

US Environmental Protection Agency (US EPA). 1994. *The Massachusetts Ecological Regions Project.* Report prepared by the US Environmental Protection Agency, Environmental Research Laboratory, Corvallis, OR, for the Commonwealth of Massachusetts, Boston, MA.

Vaillancourt, Dana R. 1983. *Archaeological Excavations at the North Family Dwelling House Site, Hancock Shaker Village, Town of Hancock, Berkshire County, Massachusetts.* Master's thesis, Department of Science and Technology Studies, Rensselaer Polytechnic Institute.

Van Bueren, Thad M., and Sarah Tarlow. 2006. "The Interpretive Potential of Utopian Settlements." *Historical Archaeology* 40, no. 1: 1–5.

Voss, Barbara L. 2000. "Feminisms, Queer Theories, and the Archaeological Study of Past Sexualities." *World Archaeology* 32, no. 2: 180–92.

Ward, W.E.F. 1958. *A History of Ghana,* revised 2nd ed. London: George Allen and Unwin Ltd.

Warren, Wendy. 2017. *New England Bound: Slavery and Colonization in Early America.* New York: Liveright Publishing Corporation.

Waters, Thomas Franklin. 1905. *Ipswich in the Massachusetts Bay Colony, Volume I, A History of the Town From 1633 to 1700.* Ipswich, MA: The Ipswich Historical Society.

———. 1917. *Ipswich in the Massachusetts Bay Colony, Volume II, A History of the Town From 1700 to 1917.* Ipswich, MA: The Ipswich Historical Society.

Watters Wilkes, Margaret. 2016. *Parker's Revenge Archaeological Project Minute Man National Historical Park Lexington, Massachusetts.* Report for the Friends of the Minute Man National Park by Visual Environment Solutions, LLC.

Watkins, Lura Woodside. 1950. *Early New England Potters and Their Wares.* Cambridge, MA: Harvard University Press.

Wegmann, Edward. 1899. *The Design and Construction of Dams.* New York: John Wiley & Sons.

Weiss, Joanna M. 1992. "When Trash Becomes Treasure." *Harvard Crimson,* July 10.

Wesolowsky, Al B. 1991. "The Osteology of the Uxbridge Paupers." In *Archaeological Investigations at the Uxbridge Almshouse Burial Ground in Uxbridge, Massachusetts,* edited by Ricardo J. Elia and Al B. Wesolowsky, 230–253. British Archaeological Reports International Series No. 564. Oxford: Tempus Repartum.

WHDH. 2018. "Boston Ranks as One of the Hardest Working US Cities in New Study." *WHDH.com.* https://whdh.com/news/boston-ranks-as-one-of-the-hardest-working -us-cities-in-new-study/

Wheatley, Phyllis. 1778. Letter from Phillis Wheatley to Mary Wooster, July 15, 1778. Collections of the Massachusetts Historical Society, Boston. https://www.masshist .org/database/772.

Wilkie, Laurie. 1995. "Magic and Empowerment on the Plantation: An Archaeological Consideration of African-American World View." *Southeastern Archaeology* 14, no. 2: 136–148.

———. 1997. "Secret and Sacred: Contextualizing the Artifacts of African-American Magic and Religion." *Historical Archaeology* 31, no. 4: 81–106.

Wilson, Budd. 1986. "The Council for Northeast Historical Archaeology: The Early Years." *Northeast Historical Archaeology* 15: 16–18.

Wilson, John S., and Meredith Weiss Belding. 1979. *Cultural Resource Reconnaissance for a Streambank Erosion Control Evaluation and Demonstration Project, Northfield, Massachusetts.* Report on file, Massachusetts Historical Commission.

Winship, George Parker. 1905. *Sailors Narratives of Voyages along the New England Coast 1524–1624*. Boston, MA: Houghton, Mifflin & Co.

Winthrop, John. 1630. "A Modell of Christian Charity. Sermon given on the ship *Arbella*." *Collections of the Massachusetts Historical Society,* third series, vol. 7: 31–48. Boston: Massachusetts Historical Society.

———. 1908. *Winthrop's Journal "History of New England" 1630–1649*. Edited by James Kendall Hosmer. New York: Charles Scribner's Sons.

Winthrop, John, and James Savage. 1853. *The History of New England from 1630 to 1649: A New Edition*. Boston, MA: Little Brown.

Wisecup, Kelly. 2013, *"Good News from New England" by Edward Winslow: A Scholarly Edition*. Amherst: University of Massachusetts Press.

Wiseman, James. 2002. "An Appreciation of an Archaeological Life: Creighton Gabel, 1931–2004." *Journal of Field Archaeology* 29, no. 1–2: 1–5.

Yamin, Rebecca, and Donna J. Seifert. 2019. *The Archaeology of Prostitution and Clandestine Pursuits*. Gainesville: University Press of Florida.

Zoto, Daniel M. 2023. "New Insights from Old Collections: The PaleoIndian and Early Archaic Periods on Cape Cod and the Islands." *Bulletin of the Massachusetts Archaeological Society* 84, no. 1–2: 36–53.

Zumper. 2024. "Zumper National Rent Report." *Zumper.com* https://www.zumper .com/blog/rental-price-data/

INDEX

Abiel Smith School, 93–95

Africa, 46, 84, 88, 91, 97, 198; cultural heritage, 88; cultural practices, 91; descent, 96; diaspora studies, 88, 90; West, 78, 87; western, 4

African American, 15, 58, 82, 84, 87, 92–93, 97, 100; boys, enslaved, 79; children, 93; communities, 90, 100; history, 62, 81, 90, 100; Unity, 197. *See also* Black

African Meeting House, 92–94

Afro-Indigenous: identity, 101; individuals, 85

Agriculture, 37, 74, 184; fields, 75, 161, 181, 183; landholdings, 180; operation, 75; products, 37; structures, 74

Alcohol, 63, 94, 133, 164, 180, 192

Almshouses, 164, 166–67, 184, 186–87. *See also* Poor farms

American: ancient Native sites, 11, 89; archaeology, 10; colonies, 51, 55, 100, 106; colonists, 109; early seventeenth-century Native sites, 25; embargo, 130; factory industries, 120; frontiersmen, 136; history, 1, 13, 17, 32–34, 102, 116, 208–9; identity, 15, 158; independence, 100; industrial capitalism, 84; Industrial Revolution, 129; iron industry, 123, 125; mercantile class, 56; mythology, 30; Revolution, 1, 6, 9, 55, 82, 85, 96, 102, 104, 106, 108, 113; System of Manufacturing, 117, 135–36; whale fishery, 145

Amherst, Massachusetts, 74

Anderson, Virginia, 29–30, 34

Andrews, Edward, 179–80

Aptucxet Trading Post site, 9, 30

Aquinnah, Massachusetts, 5–6, 104, 161–62

Archer, Gabriel, 23–24

Atalay, Sonya, 9, 193, 197, 204

Bagley, Joseph, 13, 162, 172–77, 190, 197–203, 210

Bailey: Cracker Bakery, 139, 143; George, 139–44; ovens, 140, 142

Bain, Alison, 52–53

Baking, 11, 28, 31, 88–89, 139–44, 146, 157; commercial, 139; early twentieth-century, 141, 143; ovens, 140–43

Balicki, Joseph, 52, 79–80, 190

Banister, Jennifer, 107, 126–29, 149–51, 155–57, 181

Batchelder, John, 9, 30–31

Battle: of Breed's Hill, 114–15; of Bunker Hill, 61, 110, 114; of Chelsea Creek, 113–14; of Lexington, 106–7, 109–10

Battle-Baptiste, Whitney, 88–90, 96, 99–100, 190, 208

Beaudry, Mary, 8, 11, 70, 72–74, 95–96, 132–35, 183, 208

Belchertown, Massachusetts, 203–4

Bell, Edward, 166, 168, 171

Bellamy, Black Sam, 46

Beranek, Christa, 32–33, 68, 70–72, 93, 207, 209

Berkland, Ellen, 95–96

Bermuda, 101, 144

Black: Andover residents, 90; church building, 92; families, 88, 90, 92, 94–96, 99–100, 207; free, 88, 177, 208; free community, 92–96; histories, 82, 98, 100, 199; homesites, 15, 88, 95, 100; identity, 15, 82–101; institutions, 82; island community, 94; land ownership, 94–95; nationalism, 203; owned businesses, 94, 96; schoolchildren, 93; women, 10, 80, 89, 95–96, 98–99. *See also* African American

Joseph Bagley is the City Archaeologist and Director of Archaeology for the City of Boston. For over two decades, he has participated in CRM, municipal, and academic archaeological survey, research, and publications in Massachusetts. Bagley has earned a BA in Archaeology from Boston University and an MA in Historical Archaeology from the University of Massachusetts Boston. He is the author of *A History of Boston in 50 Artifacts* and *Boston's Oldest Buildings and Where to Find Them.*

Holly Herbster is a Senior Archaeologist/Principal Investigator at The Public Archaeology Laboratory Inc. She earned a BA in Anthropology from Kenyon College and received an MA in Historical Archaeology at the University of Massachusetts Boston. Over the past thirty years, Herbster has directed more than 300 cultural resource management archaeological projects in Massachusetts. She is a coauthor of *Historical Archaeology and Indigenous Collaboration: Discovering Histories That Have Futures,* which was the 2021 winner of the Society for American Archaeology's Scholarly Book Award.

The American Experience in Archaeological Perspective

Michael S. Nassaney, Founding Editor

Krysta Ryzewski, Co-editor

The American Experience in Archaeological Perspective series was established by the University Press of Florida and founding editor Michael S. Nassaney in 2004. This prestigious historical archaeology series focuses attention on a range of significant themes in the development of the modern world from an Americanist perspective. Each volume explores an event, process, setting, institution, or geographic region that played a formative role in the making of the United States of America as a political, social, and cultural entity. These comprehensive overviews underscore the theoretical, methodological, and substantive contributions that archaeology has made to the study of American history and culture. Rather than subscribing to American exceptionalism, the authors aim to illuminate the distinctive character of the American experience in time and space. While these studies focus on historical archaeology in the United States, they are also broadly applicable to historical and anthropological inquiries in other parts of the world. To date the series has produced more than two dozen titles. Prospective authors are encouraged to contact the Series Editors to learn more.

The Archaeology of Collective Action, by Dean J. Saitta (2007)
The Archaeology of Institutional Confinement, by Eleanor Conlin Casella (2007)
The Archaeology of Race and Racialization in Historic America, by Charles E. Orser Jr. (2007)
The Archaeology of North American Farmsteads, by Mark D. Groover (2008)
The Archaeology of Alcohol and Drinking, by Frederick H. Smith (2008)
The Archaeology of American Labor and Working-Class Life, by Paul A. Shackel (2009; first paperback edition, 2011)
The Archaeology of Clothing and Bodily Adornment in Colonial America, by Diana DiPaolo Loren (2010; first paperback edition, 2011)
The Archaeology of American Capitalism, by Christopher N. Matthews (2010; first paperback edition, 2012)
The Archaeology of Forts and Battlefields, by David R. Starbuck (2011; first paperback edition, 2012)
The Archaeology of Consumer Culture, by Paul R. Mullins (2011; first paperback edition, 2012)
The Archaeology of Antislavery Resistance, by Terrance M. Weik (2012; first paperback edition, 2013)
The Archaeology of Citizenship, by Stacey Lynn Camp (2013; first paperback edition, 2019)
The Archaeology of American Cities, by Nan A. Rothschild and Diana diZerega Wall (2014; first paperback edition, 2015)
The Archaeology of American Cemeteries and Gravemarkers, by Sherene Baugher and Richard F. Veit (2014; first paperback edition, 2015)

www.ingramcontent.com/pod-product-compliance
Lightning Source LLC
Chambersburg PA
CBHW031554060326
40783CB00026B/4073